# WHO AM I?
# HEPHZIBAH

PAMELA NICKSON

God bless
you always.
B. Nickson

# PREFACE

Bad memories from my past – they kept resurfacing and I couldn't understand why. I rebuked them over and over in the name of Jesus, telling who I thought was the enemy to get off my back and leave me alone: Jesus had forgiven me and put my past behind me.

Then, one day, something else popped into my head; something I hadn't even thought about.

I asked Jesus why I was remembering so much of my past, as He had forgiven me for it and put it to rest; I was healed from it all and had forgiven others, so why was it coming back to me and in such detail?

My Lord revealed to me that He wanted me to write about my life: traumas, divorce, grief and other things that many people experience. But also about some traumas that many people don't go through.

I was at the end of finalising my first book when the Lord revealed to me that He wanted me to write this second book about my life, to encourage and reach out to others who had lived through similar situations. He wanted them to know there is hope for them and that He can and will restore them to fullness. I'd been through a lot of difficulties in my life, but God wanted me to tell people that He is waiting to heal and restore them.

"Oh, dear Lord, that's a lot," I said. "There's so much to write. Where do I start?"

"From the beginning," He told me.

And that is how I began, from my earliest childhood memory.

Before I wrote this book, I told my husband Dave that God had put it on my heart to write about my life. There are many, many sensitive things in it where my loving Father protected my heart and guided me in the writing, as only He could. He healed and restored me from my past before I had to rake it up again. This is why I know He wants my words to reach out to others.

So, first and foremost, thank you, my Jesus, for all you have done and continue to do for me.

My dear husband Dave supported me in the writing of this book; in the going over of my past, time and time again. He encouraged and helped me in any way he could until it was finished. Thank you, my darling, for your love, patience and support.

And without the additional support and love of a dear friend, this book wouldn't yet have been published. She was prompted by the Holy Spirit to help get it out into the world, so God bless you, my friend, for all you have done.

Jane and Elaine, thank you, my lovely friends, for your help and encouraging me to get this book finished.

My dear brother and both my sons for your love and support.

Alexa, for all your time spent and guidance with editing.

Judah, your help and input with design work.

You are all amazing and I couldn't have done it without you. Thank you and God bless you all.

Just before this book went to print I was saddened to hear that Bob Gass had passed away. He was a great inspiration to me throughout my journey with God. I thank the Lord that Bob will now be in Glory with Him. I pray those who read my book will be encouraged by the contribution of his word which he and his wife Debby so kindly agreed I could include.

# INTRODUCTION

These are the words of someone who is neither a superstar nor well known. But by our Father's grace and love, I am well known to Him: the one who created heaven and earth; the one who knit me together in my mother's womb; the one who knew me before I was born. He is the famous one who knows me personally. And He knows you too.

Isn't that wonderfully exciting?

He chose us, He chose you and He chose me. I was fearfully made in His image.

I am far from perfect. "How could He love me?" I asked myself for much too long. I never realised those words were from the devil, the father of lies and deception himself. I thought I would only see Jesus when I died and went to heaven. I didn't know how real He is.

Although I'm not a famous person, known to man, I am to my Father who knows me even more than I know myself. I am unique and so are you. That's why I firmly believe that, as you read this book, our Father God will speak to you.

This is the unfolding of how I came to be the one God created me to be.

Here is my journey – the story of how my Father led me to know Jesus and how, by the power of His Holy Spirit, my mind is being constantly renewed.

So... who am I?

# CONTENTS

Preface

Introduction

# 1

# EARLY YEARS

*"Court?"* I cried over and over again. I was scared. I'd never been to court before.

I didn't go back to school for a few weeks but I knew I had to at some point. People were talking and things had got out but I didn't know what was being said.

Strange as it was, I discovered a lot about the group of girls who were supposed to have been my friends in school. Three of them were concerned and supportive but the other two sniggered. I told them without going into detail what had happened. They both grinned at each other and began laughing and said, "Is that it?" I couldn't believe what I was hearing from them.

It turned out that they'd been sleeping with their boyfriends since the age of thirteen and they belittled what had happened to me.

I hated my life. Why was I on this earth to be mocked and rejected by friends? To be hurt? Why was I different? Why all this pain and sadness? I would ask myself the same questions again and again.

"Why was I even born?" I remember asking my mum.

"Because we love you," Mum said, "and you have a great life ahead of you. And because you're part of God's plan. Growing up is hard but one day you will settle down and find someone who loves you."

"Is it part of God's plan for me to be made a fool of and hurt all the time? Why did He make me so big and so ugly and skinny? Even my uncle calls me a witch."

Mum did her best to comfort me. "One day, love, you'll see. It's not always going to be like this. And you're not ugly."

*"If God is for us, who can be against us?"*
*Romans 8:31*

*"So God created mankind in his own image"*
*Genesis 1:27*

*"Your eyes saw my unformed body; all the days*
*ordained for me were written in your book before*
*one of them came to be."*
*Psalm 139:16*

The day I dreaded finally arrived. There we were in the court waiting room, Mum, Dad and me.

"Pamela?" The court usher called from the waiting room, looked straight at me and said, "Stay calm now and remember, only answer what they ask you."

I nodded my head and walked in with my parents, and Jodie the policewoman who'd journeyed this horrible experience with me from the day she'd come to our house to interview me.

I answered the questions, but felt my voice quiver as I had to tell in detail what had happened, tears rolling down my face.

"Are you sure it happened exactly like that?" I was asked. "This seems to be very detailed and rehearsed."

Philip sniggered.

I couldn't believe the question. It sounded as if they didn't believe me.

"Yes, it's the truth," I answered. I was calm even though I was crying. I remembered being told this would be hard for me, but to stay very calm.

At that point, my dad jumped up from his seat. He shouted at Philip, who smirked at him.

Then, mockingly, Philip said, "What? I haven't done anything."

"Break, let's take a break!" the judge shouted, and he slammed his gavel down.

Philip was removed quickly from the courtroom. Things had got too much for Dad. What he really wanted was to hurt this lad for what he'd done to me.

Back in the courtroom, the judge adjourned my case to a later date.

The stress of all of this was becoming too much for me and my family. I didn't want to go through it all again but Jodie the policewoman told me it would be fine – it would be his turn to speak next time. She told me I'd given them enough evidence.

I asked her why the hearing was adjourned: "Didn't they believe me?"

Jodie explained that it was due to stress levels in court and because I was only just sixteen and Philip was fifteen.

I was so thankful that I had such loving and supportive parents who'd been with me through all of this. I remember looking at them both and wondering how they managed to keep it together.

Now, speaking of together...

My parents were beautiful. They met when Mum went to Bootle to cut her friend's brother's hair and Dad happened to walk in. Dad lived in Bootle and Mum lived in Norris Green, Liverpool. It wasn't long before they started dating – and the rest is history.

I was brought up in Bootle. I have three brothers who are all younger than I am: Jason, Richard and Sam.

Mum had to give up her full-time job as a sewing machinist to look after the family. Dad was a bus driver and worked long, hard hours to make ends meet. Then, in his later years, he worked as a taxi driver.

My first memory of church was when Anne, the lady with big glasses, turned up at our door one day to take me to Brownies.

"I don't want to go," I said to my mum.

There Anne was, chatting away to her. I looked up at this lady; she was a stranger to me.

Although I was a shy, serious, quiet child, Mum told me, "It'll do you good. Bring you out of your shell – you'll like it there. And Anne will look after you."

So, hesitantly, I took Anne's hand and off I went, leaving my mum behind.

The church was only three minutes' walk from where we lived. But Mum stayed home to look after my younger brothers until they were old enough to go to church groups themselves. It was too much of a struggle with all of us for her to take me when Dad was at work. So Anne started to pick me up every week to take me to St. John and St. James Church, where Brownies was held.

I soon discovered she was a lovely lady. She was fun, played lots of games and taught me how to make candles from broken crayons.

It was around this time when I started to understand a little bit about Jesus. I also went along to Sunday school, which is a very distant memory now. I just remember there being a Holy Ghost who no one was ever to be scared of. That's the only real recollection I have from Sunday school.

My parents had shown me my christening cards where angels looked over a baby in a cot. They told me that the baby in the cot was me and that Jesus always watched over me. This was their way of introducing me to the church and telling me stories of who Jesus was.

From Brownies, I joined Girl Guides and I loved it! One time I was asked to carry the Girl Guides' flag in a family service at church because I was tall, but I was a bit clumsy and I dropped it half way down the aisle. I laughed because I was so nervous. This was quite a serious thing, but no one shouted at me. Funny the things you remember.

When Girl Guides came to an end, I was really upset as I loved going there. Jan was a wonderful leader who encouraged me. She was a quiet lady with plenty of patience for us Girl Guides and she taught us lots of fun things like Anne did at Brownies. We learnt how to cook, sew and do many other activities, so it was a big shock and sad time for me when it all ended. I didn't know what to do next as I'd made many good friends there.

I can't remember the exact age when I gave my life to Jesus but I was only young. I didn't know He was real. I just thought that when I died I'd see Him in heaven.

"Why is everyone making such a fuss?" I thought, when people had heard what I'd done. I didn't feel any different. I'd just heard Bible stories and I wanted to know more.

I was encouraged to tell someone, so I told Anne. Anne was very excited and told me to tell other people too, which I did. But little did I know about this amazing God and the journey He would soon be taking me on.

*"Start children off on the way they should go, and
even when they are old they will not turn from it."*
*Proverbs 22:6*

*"For God so loved the world that he gave his one
and only Son, that whoever believes in him shall
not perish but have eternal life."*
*John 3:16*

A girl called Linda lived in the street behind me. She was eighteen months younger than I was and we soon became good friends. One evening, I asked her to come to Girl Guides but, because she was a Catholic, she wasn't allowed to go to our church, which was Church of England (or Protestant as they said in those days). I couldn't understand it.

The next thing I knew, she was to have her first communion. And she had to wear a beautiful little white dress that looked like a wedding dress.

It was my dream to dress up in something as beautiful as that. Linda looked lovely, but I couldn't work out why I would never have a dress like that. I didn't understand when people spoke of Catholics and Protestants.

*"Jesus answered, 'I am the way and the truth and
the life. No one comes to the Father except through
me."*
*John 14:6*

Linda's mum worked in the local sweetshop and when she wasn't working, the other lady there would give Linda free sweets, but not me.

One day, as I had no money, I boldly asked her, "Can I have one chocolate log finger, please, if it's two for half a penny?"

The lady just looked at me and said, "No, I'm sorry, you can't. If you haven't got half a penny then you can't have one."

I felt embarrassed after that as I wouldn't normally have been so cheeky.

Growing up, I also noticed that one of our neighbours wasn't very nice. She treated my brothers and me differently to the way she treated Linda. I didn't know if it was because Linda's mum was her next-door neighbour, but she would shout at us and often burst our ball if it went into her garden. Yet she always gave Linda and her Cousin Peter's ball back without shouting.

But one thing my brothers and I weren't and that was cheeky. We never answered back.

Many times, I'd cry to my parents and my grandma, who'd always tell me how loved I was and how beautiful I was. But I didn't believe them because they were my family.

**Emotions can be very difficult while you're growing up. When you're a child, it's awful when people bully or ignore you. Children are so sensitive in every area. They pick up on things that adults may not, and where adults can shrug something off, it can bother children and worry them immensely.**

**Little things to an adult can be huge things to a child and they can carry them throughout their lives. This can then damage both them and any future relationships they may have.**

> *"Before I formed you in the womb I knew you,*
> *before you were born I set you apart"*
> Jeremiah 1:5

Other friends filtered into our lives as we grew older, friends that Linda began to spend more time with. I always had to be home earlier than they did and they often made fun of me about that.

When I was around fourteen years old, I was with Linda and some friends in their parents' house. They were telling jokes and that somehow led into telling ghost stories. Because I felt socially awkward and was uncomfortable with who I was, I began to mess around and pretend that I had magic hands. I did an abracadabra-type of thing towards the electric light on the ceiling and, suddenly, it started to flash off and on. I thought it was hilarious – it was actually flashing in time with me raising my hands and putting them down.

My friends all became very scared. They told me to stop it and when I did, the light returned to normal. But when I messed around again, the flashing restarted.

After about ten minutes of this, all the lights in the house suddenly blew.

My friends were terrified but I wasn't and I didn't know why. Maybe because I felt I had some kind of power.

I'd had an earlier strange experience some years before when I was around eight years old. I was on holiday with my parents, my two younger brothers and my grandma. We stayed in a lovely farmhouse on the Isle of Man.

There was a strange smell in this farmhouse. My dad described it as a musty smell and it seemed to come from an old locked medicine box on the wall.

One evening, when my grandma had gone to bed early, she felt something under the bed, kicking the mattress from underneath her. She screamed in fright and my dad ran upstairs to see what was wrong. He looked all around but there was nothing in the room. No one was there. Yet my dad could see the mattress being jolted when Grandma tried to get back into bed.

My dad wouldn't let Grandma sleep in there again. He told her to sleep in bed with my mum whilst he used the couch.

Other strange things happened in that house that I only discovered years later. But it was when I asked my parents who the little old lady was who would come into my bedroom every night that they knew something was definitely wrong.

The little old lady had grey hair tied back in a tight bun and she wore black clothing and always smiled at me.

The last night that I saw her, she walked past me in my bed. She was carrying a large, old-fashioned ceramic water jug and bowl. Again, she smiled as she walked past me, and she said, "Ssh… Go back to sleep."

We later found out that the lady who let the farmhouse was the daughter of the old lady who'd died there.

# 2

# FEELING DIFFERENT

Growing up, I always had this overwhelming sense of being the odd one out; of feeling inadequate. I tried to push those feelings away but they kept resurfacing.

I must have been around thirteen or fourteen years old when I left my Pathfinders church group as I felt I didn't fit in. The youth there all seemed to hang out together and know more about the Bible than I did, which made me feel even more inadequate. I felt I was shrinking into myself with thoughts of, "You're not wanted here, you don't fit in… You don't even know what they're talking about – it's all above your head".

Even so, I didn't know what I'd do as church was the one place I felt safe other than at home. I loved the people there and I was upset because I didn't have any groups to attend anymore. I soon became bored and wanted to hang out with other people again. So Linda and I got together and began to spend time with a different bunch of friends after school.

School life had its ups and downs through the years. I was bullied early on but eventually I settled in and hung around with a group of girls who were fun to be with. We would dress up and try to get into school plays pretending to be parents, until I got caught by the teacher who couldn't stop laughing. He said I'd nearly pulled the wool over his eyes. I began to enjoy school a bit more after that as I realised I could make people laugh.

I'd play fun tricks on my friends, filling a Jiff lemon squeezy up with water and squirting them or the prefects on corridor duty. And I'd roll up bits of paper and throw them at my class mates. The teacher would tell them off and I'd feel guilty and own up to what I'd done. He'd accept my apology but would still tell my friends off.

I soon became full of mischief but at least I was being honest with it, and I liked this new life. I was having fun and I kind of felt accepted to a point – more than I'd done before. Yet I still felt different and I couldn't shrug it off.

As Halloween approached, I remember thinking it was all a good laugh. That's how it seemed for a while anyway. We did duck apple, or we'd tie and hang apples on string and try to bite them. Linda and her cousin Peter would come over and we'd celebrate it together.

But much later, I discovered that hanging and ducking for apples were symbolic signs. Many years ago, people were hung and drowned to find out if they were witches. Halloween is a night that pagans celebrate. It's like Christmas to the devil; like his birthday. As people take part in it, they don't realise what dark forces and powers they are activating.

Halloween is certainly not harmless fun or to be taken lightly.

*"Anyone who isn't with me opposes me, and anyone who isn't working with me is actually working against me."*
*Luke 11:23, NLT*

# 3

# TEENAGE YEARS

Although I began to enjoy being mischievous, I was a fairly naive teenager. After school, Linda and I would hang out with a group of lads who became our friends when we were in our early teens. The lads were a year or two older than we were. I recall the times we'd go to Bootle cemetery and sit in the little chapel doorway, before the chapel was knocked down, and tell ghost stories.

Rob, one of our friends, was a hippy. He was a heavy user of LSD and magic mushrooms and he would play his guitar while Linda and I and other friends would all sit there, singing.

To Linda and me, it meant nothing as the other lads smoked pot. She and I never used drugs, although we'd heard of them, of course, and we knew the dangers as our parents told us never to use them: they could kill you. But we also knew our friends took them and we saw the aftermath, when they would hallucinate and be paranoid, along with many other side effects.

Due to his heavy use of drugs, Rob began to have horrible experiences. At one time, his hallucinations became terrible nightmares. Even when he'd stopped using drugs altogether, he would still have hallucinations some weeks later.

Rob stabbed his mum when he was hallucinating. Tragically, he died through the effects drugs had on him. I think he was only in his mid-twenties or early thirties.

I was around fourteen years old when Linda and I became friends with Tony and Paul, who had motorbikes. We met them through Linda's friend Joan. Tony was her brother and Paul was his friend. We liked motorbikes although we'd never ridden them. We loved the freedom they seemed to give people. My dad had a motorbike when he was courting Mum so I knew a little about them.

Tony and Paul were a couple of years older than we were but that didn't matter. We were fascinated when Tony showed an interest in Linda and Paul in me. It was through hanging out with them that we got to ride on the backs of their motorbikes. We also met some of their biker friends.

Linda's mum didn't want her on any motorbike but my parents were all right with it, as long as I wore a crash helmet and the drivers had licences to ride on the road. Because Dad used to have one, they both knew the freedom of riding them.

Tony and Paul were fine except that they smoked pot. Although Linda and I never touched drugs, I liked the smell of burning wood, which is what pot smells like, but I was never interested in smoking it myself.

One day, we saw Paul looking back over his shoulder as if someone was chasing him. We soon discovered he thought he was being chased by Mars bars. Paul had been using LSD, which caused him to hallucinate. And this wasn't the only illegal drug our friends were using. They were taking pills, magic mushrooms and speed. I don't think their parents knew about it.

Often, we'd go to Tony and Paul's homes, where we'd listen to the likes of Pink Floyd, The Rolling Stones and other rock music.

Some of their other friends would also come over and, as we got to know them, that's how our own circle of friends grew. They used to ask us if we wanted to try a "joint", as it was known, but we always declined.

I think they were happy about us declining as they never pushed us. Besides, it meant more for them as they never had to share.

Tony became Linda's boyfriend and Paul was mine. We were happy to have a kiss and cuddle with them. But their real fun wasn't having girlfriends, as we soon discovered. It was getting stoned or high.

It was when Linda really fell for Tony that she started to spend a lot more time with him. Even though I was older than she was, my parents told me I had to be home earlier than she did. I resented this as I was always made fun of by our biker friends. So I rebelled against my parents. I often wound my watch back or made any excuse just to stay out the extra half hour or so.

After a while, both our parents found out the guys were taking drugs. They threatened us with the police if we went back to see them and they stopped contact between Linda and myself. My parents told me that our biker friends would be dead by the time they were thirty if they didn't stop using drugs. I didn't really understand what all the fuss was about as I wasn't taking them.

To be honest, though, I suppose I wasn't really bothered about not seeing them again because, throughout our relationships, I'd been hurt by them all. Things had come to a head when Paul, the guy who was supposed to be my boyfriend, had been putting me down in front of our friends behind my back. At one point he'd said, "I hope she comes off the bike and kills herself." The others laughed at the comment and didn't defend me. I was devastated.

I found myself beginning to reflect on my life again. I'd been protected by my parents who I know did their best for me and loved me deeply. I was their only daughter and they wanted to keep me safe.

But I still didn't understand what life was all about. I knew God was in heaven and when I died I thought I'd be going there too, but I didn't know Jesus. I knew I didn't do anything illegal – I didn't take drugs, I didn't set out to hurt anyone – but beyond that, why was I here, What was my purpose?

# 4

# ASSAULT

I was glad to be in my last year at school. Not that I hadn't had some fun. I was always joking about with the girls I hung around with.

During one French lesson, I realised I'd lost my pen. I asked my friends if they had a spare one but no one did.

It was Philip, the guy who sat in front of me, who turned round and said he had one I could borrow. I thanked him, but after the lesson finished, he'd left the classroom before I'd had time to give it back.

As I only lived five minutes away from school, I used to go home for lunch. I always walked out through the back alley because it was a quicker route and away from the crowds.

Walking down the alley, I noticed that Philip was in front of me. I went to give him his pen back but, before I knew what was happening, he'd turned into a monster.

He threw me to the ground and sexually assaulted me.

I remember thinking about the stupid hairstyle that got in my eyes so I couldn't see properly, as I'd recently had my hair cut. I felt clothing in my mouth and I bit his arm hard. He yelled and flung me round. I screamed as loud as I could to try to escape. He tried to stop me screaming.

In the end, he fled and I kept thinking, "I've still got his pen."

I couldn't cry. I was in shock.

I was numb.

My parents had a little shop at the time. They weren't due back until one o'clock.

When I got home, the first thing I did was put a record on to try to push the incident out of my mind. The song I played was "Diamond Smiles" by The Boomtown Rats.

Over the music, I heard a knock on the front door. It was my friend Billy.

"Are you all right, Pam?" he asked. "What's happened?"

I was frozen and couldn't speak. Tears started to roll down my cheeks.

Billy knew this was something bad.

"Speak to me, Pam, what's happened?" he asked again.

With difficulty, I started to tell him.

I watched his face change. He said he was going to tell my mum and dad and that he was going to kill Philip. Then he turned to leave.

I begged him not to tell anyone. I felt dirty and didn't want any trouble. He promised me he wouldn't do anything although he would tell my parents. I didn't want him to but within minutes, they were home.

Mum was very gentle and sensitive with me. Dad paced up and down in the kitchen. His face looked wrought with sadness and anger at the same time. I kept looking at him.

Then Mum told me the police were on their way and I was so scared.

I tried to smile at the policewoman who arrived at the house. I always tried to smile in every situation, no matter what I was feeling. Even when I broke down and cried while the policewoman logged everything down in detail, I still tried to smile through my tears.

She told me it wasn't my fault and I wasn't to worry. Then she asked if I'd be prepared to give evidence in court as this boy might do it again to someone else if he got away with it with me.

So I was glad I was in my final year at school and could leave all this horror behind me. I'd already been to court to give my evidence and feared having to go a second time as the hearing had been adjourned. The words kept rising up in my mind: "Didn't they believe me? Is that why it was adjourned?"

During the interim months before the next court hearing, school was hard for me. Philip's girlfriend was in the year below me and known to be a school bully. She would shout things to me in the schoolyard in front of everybody, humiliating me and making a mockery out of me about going to court. She'd say I lied about her boyfriend and he didn't touch me.

One of my friends, Shirley, told me to stand up for myself, as the abuse was growing worse over the weeks and this girl wouldn't leave me alone. Other pupils began taunting me over what they'd heard, too, and things got exaggerated. It was all getting out of hand.

Then, one day, I'd finally had enough and something snapped inside me.

I grabbed Philip's girlfriend and, shoving her up against the wall in the corridor, I shouted at her to leave me alone and get off my back. My face was red with rage and so was hers. I remember how her legs dangled down as I lifted her up off the floor by grabbing the top of her jumper. I'd been pushed to a point where I had to stand up for myself. I didn't want to use fighting and violence but I couldn't help it. I'd been pushed too far.

Philip's girlfriend didn't say anything to me after that – but neither did my so-called friends.

Soon after this incident, the police told me Philip had raped his girlfriend and she'd become pregnant and it was important for me to attend court.

A couple of months later, it was time to go back there. Philip was called to give his evidence about what had happened to me. His statement didn't make any sense. He tripped himself up with lie upon lie.

It came out in court that Philip had always wanted to join the Navy or the Armed Forces. But when he was charged and found guilty of sexual assault, he was told that would never happen now. This punishment was the only thing throughout the whole trial that had any effect on him.

Philip no longer looked so smug and he broke down.

He was ordered to pay court costs plus a fine for all he'd put me through, but this was never paid and my parents didn't want anything from him anyway. I think perhaps he had to do some community work for a while. All I remember is wanting to leave that awful place and being scared as I saw him getting angry again.

As we left the courtroom to come home, the whole thing fast became a blur. I just kept thinking to myself: "What am I supposed to do now?"

Twelve months passed.

I was walking to the New Strand Shopping Centre with a friend when a house brick came flying out of an upstairs window from one of the flats.

A man shouted: "There's the bitch that got Philip done for rape!"

I looked up and briefly saw two men as the brick smashed to the ground at my feet.

I felt sick as we hurried on past.

That was the last horrid experience I had relating to him.

# 5

# COLLEGE YEARS AND
# DABBLING WITH DARKNESS

As my time at school was coming to an end, I had to make a decision about my future.

I loved working with people. I did my work experience with young children and the elderly. I also loved art.

Art was my favourite subject at school and I did well in my art exam, gaining the equivalent to an O-level result. This was the only high grade I achieved. Although I passed my exams, I only came out with average results.

I was told by the careers officer at school that my passions of art and working with people were worlds apart. They advised me to focus on art as, one day, I'd probably have my own family and then I'd be looking after children all the time. This made some sense to me, so I looked into going to college to study art.

After discussing things with my parents, I went to Hugh Baird College to do a two-year Design Exhibition and Display and Graphics course (D.E.D.).

I enjoyed college. It was so different from school. However, there were two subjects I didn't like – photography and window dressing. These weren't my strong points so I'd mess around a lot in these lessons.

But something I discovered I did enjoy was woodwork and I learned how to use power tools. I actually made my son's first toy – a little wooden pull-along cart with wooden blocks. On each side of the blocks I painted the alphabet and numbers in bright colours. I was proud of my work and told myself I'd keep it for when I had my first child – and I did!

Graphics was a subject I enjoyed too. But when I was asked to do a topic on zodiac signs, things didn't work out well.

We were asked to design a shop fascia board and a sign for the side of a van.

"Great," I said to myself. "I'll enjoy this one, I've got loads of ideas."

I went to the college library to choose a book to help me with the project and, as it was getting late, I picked one up quickly. The title, I think, was *Signs and Symbols*. I took it home, put it under my bed and forgot all about it.

Not long after that, I began to have weird dreams. In them, I saw a shape like an upside-down triangle with curved corners. Every night I'd have the same dream but more features began to form inside the shape. The dreams eventually started to become nightmares and I was scared.

When I was woken up one night feeling frightened, I ran into my parents' room and woke Mum up to tell her.

She told me it was just a bad dream and to go back to bed and say my prayers.

The only prayer I really knew at the time was the Lord's Prayer. So I said it and the dream ceased.

During Graphics lessons, my lecturer told me my work was very untidy and asked why. I couldn't tell him. I had no idea. I tried to paint but every time I put the brush to the paper, it smudged. He told me it was the worst piece of work I'd done.

As the days passed, I got on with my other work, which was coming along fine, but I really struggled to put the zodiac signs project together.

The dreams continued for a while. Night after night, the shape formed into something scary; something evil. It was beginning to look like a goat with huge horns. There were now eye sockets. The eyes were missing and the rest of it looked horrible.

Another night, I woke up feeling terrified. It was as if I was being watched; as if there was something in my bedroom. Again, I said the Lord's Prayer after waking my parents up. I didn't even want to sleep in my bedroom anymore.

When I returned home from college one evening, I found my mum really angry. She shoved the book I'd got from the library under my nose and shouted, "Is this what you've seen in your dreams?"

I'd forgotten all about it. I hadn't even looked through it, just glanced at the index. If I had, I certainly wouldn't have borrowed it.

I gazed at the book and I saw the awful figure I'd been dreaming about nearly every night. The book showed a picture of the devil but in my dreams it didn't have eyes. They were the only thing missing as it began to take shape bit by bit every night.

I was told to take the book back immediately. I said I couldn't as the college library would be closed – it was after 5pm. Mum didn't care. She said she'd throw it out if I didn't take it back right there and then. So I did, but obviously I couldn't get into the library so I had to leave it outside.

Another subject I liked was sociology. We were taught by a man called Neil and we certainly had some laughs with him.

When you're young, I suppose when someone tells you not to do something, that's exactly what makes you go and do it. And I did!

Neil told us about out-of-body experiences but he warned us that we weren't ever to attempt them on our own. I didn't believe any of it so, of course, when I got home from college, I decided to sit in the quiet of my bedroom, think of nothing and stare at myself in the mirror, just to prove to myself that it was all nonsense.

But as I sat there, all of a sudden, I found I was looking down on the top of my own head. I could see myself looking at myself in the mirror!

Then I heard my mum shouting at me angrily.

Somehow, I'd put myself into some kind of trance, which I should never have done on my own. We'd all been warned in class that we mustn't try it on our own as, if we did get into a trance, we may not be able to get ourselves out of it again.

I didn't understand what had happened, but my mum said she'd been shouting at me for fifteen minutes to come down for my tea and I hadn't heard her.

Some of the strange experiences I had at college made me reflect on the other odd occurrences that had happened when I was younger. I hadn't understood them and I certainly didn't realise the dangers.

Because of the negativity I'd created in myself, I suppose I messed around a lot to cover up my true emotions – to disguise who I really was – so no one could hurt me.

# 6

# REBELLING

After two years of full-time education at college, I was devastated to discover that I hadn't passed the course. And I felt such a failure all over again.

"Just when I thought things were going right for me for once," I kept thinking.

Apart from my family and a few college friends, I didn't want anyone to know that I'd failed, so I kept it to myself. I began to think I'd never be good at anything in my life.

I lived with this negative feeling casting a shadow over me for many, many years and because of it, there was a knock-on effect on my views and my relationships. I felt second-best with friends and boyfriends.

I was eighteen years old now and, although in my heart I was still a young girl, my dad would often tell me I was a young lady and it was time to start dressing like one.

I didn't know what to make of that remark. What did my dad mean by it? Did I want to be treated like an adult or a teenager? I knew I didn't want to be serious all the time, I wanted to enjoy life. I certainly didn't want to be boring old Pam again.

As I never followed fashion and didn't enjoy the same type of music all my friends seemed to listen to, I found my own style in clothing and continued to listen to the same music I'd liked for years. It hadn't really mattered what I wore when I attended college as it was full of punk rockers with different coloured, pointy hairstyles and many piercings, bikers, men with long hair, hippies. I felt comfortable there.

It was at college where I suppose I felt I did fit in – especially as the people who loved the same kind of music as I did were bikers and rockers.

As time passed, I began to think I'd found my identity. I started to recognise that this was my path. I had a lot of good friends and enjoyed going out to rock concerts and music festivals with them. But Dad still wanted me to be home by a certain hour.

I thought that because I was now eighteen I could come and go at whatever time I wished, and wear whatever I wanted to wear, but no!

Dad was a taxi driver and he told me he'd be looking out for me to bring me home if I didn't get in by midnight.

I knew my parents were only concerned for my safety and I was their only daughter. But my thoughts were, "I'm an adult now and I don't need protecting!"

I didn't like it when I was just about ready to go out for the evening and Dad would tell me I couldn't leave the house in what I was wearing, so I'd have to change my clothes. But then, I'd run out with a carrier bag behind my back so he couldn't see it. And when I got to my friend's house, I'd change into my "Cinderella skirt" that looked as if it had been shredded and just about exposed the tops of my stockings.

Lee was my boyfriend then. I think I fell for him because he had lovely long golden-brown hair that fell into ringlets. He wore a headband around his forehead and, at the time, I remember telling my parents I thought he looked like Jesus because he had green-coloured eyes. He also had a motorbike.

When I took him to meet Mum and Dad, they couldn't believe it when they saw he'd sewn beer mats onto the seat of his jeans.

"Oh, my word, Pamela!" My parents were alarmed. "Where did you find him?"

"And you think he looks like Jesus?" my mum added.

My parents weren't keen on Lee and I knew it, but they realised I was young and growing up, so they let me be.

There were no mobile phones in those days and I knew Dad couldn't ring Mum from his taxi, so I often stayed out until after The Cave in Mathew Street had closed, which was around 2am. I loved dancing until I could dance no more.

It was when we couldn't get a taxi in the early hours of one morning that a group of us began to walk home.

We'd been walking a while and still no taxi had come when, suddenly, a group of lads who were walking on the other side of the road shouted over to us. Lee was slightly ahead of us with some friends. The lads casually strolled over and split off into two groups. Some made their way towards my friends and me.

The next thing I remember was seeing my friends and Lee fighting, and there was blood on their faces.

One lad said something to me. I didn't catch it, but he smiled and I thought he'd tapped me on my back. Then he ran back across the road into the night with the rest of them.

"What's happened?" we all shouted.

Lee's and our friends' faces were red with blood and it dripped down onto their clothes.

Then one of them shouted: "You've been slashed!"

It had all happened so fast, they didn't realise. They didn't even feel any pain.

I don't remember how we got to the hospital but I do know that Lee had to have several stitches in his face. Another friend had broken ribs and stitches to his face too.

I was asked by police at the hospital if I was hurt. When I told them someone had just tapped me on the back, I couldn't understand why the policeman seemed so interested – until he pointed out the deep slash right across the back of my leather jacket. He couldn't understand why my thin, Indian-cotton blouse wasn't ripped and I wasn't cut. He said I was very lucky!

Much more than lucky. I know now someone was watching over me.

*"Though I walk in the midst of trouble, you*
*preserve my life. You stretch out your hand against*
*the anger of my foes; with your right hand you*
*save me."*
*Psalm 138:7*

My parents didn't know what had happened that night. I somehow managed to cover it up. But I avoided going out into the town centre again for a long time, although I missed going dancing. It was all right going to our local pub but there was nowhere to dance there, and my energy was building up inside me.

Whilst I was discovering the new Pam and what I could get away with (trying to be cool and giving a good impression of being a grown up), I found myself a little hampered by my naturally scatty behaviour.

One day I was late for work as I'd missed my bus, so I got the next one. I recognised a girl who must have been running late too as she was on the same bus as me. It was snowing and I never liked the twenty-minute walk to work from the bus stop in the snow as I found it so hard not to slip over.

As we got off the bus, the lights were on red. I heard a car horn beep and said to the girl, "Oh, great! It's Terry from my work. Come on, we'll drop you off."

The girl just looked at me and crossed the road.

I proceeded to jump into the back seat of the car, only to see a stranger's face staring at me in his rear-view mirror.

The lights had changed to green as I blurted out, "Just drive, just drive!"

I couldn't believe it. There I was in a complete stranger's car, telling him to drive.

He didn't say a word apart from: "Where to?"

I made sure I didn't get the same bus as the girl again. I didn't want her to know what I'd done.

Months later, we did end up on the same bus. She looked at me and began to laugh.

It turned out that the man I thought was Terry was her boss. He'd beeped the horn to offer to give her a lift. Then a complete stranger had jumped into the back of his car and demanded that he drive.

He'd told everyone at work what had happened and it had got around the industrial estate.

I was so embarrassed – but at least it gave everyone a good laugh!


I was around nineteen years old when I decided to go on my first holiday on my own with my boyfriend Lee. We settled on Majorca.

"Great!" I thought to myself. "I'm all grown up and can afford to go abroad."

So, we paid our deposits and started saving for our holiday.

But things began to change in our relationship. Lee started to drop me off home earlier than normal, saying he had to be up early for work.

Next thing I knew, we'd split up.

I found out he'd been cheating on me with his ex-girlfriend. He was meeting up with her after he'd taken me home.

What were we supposed to do now? We were only weeks away from our holiday, and there was no way I was missing out on going to Majorca.

How foolishly focused I was on getting there. And I couldn't see any other way of doing it than making up with Lee. So I forgave him. He said he really did want to go away with me – it was me he wanted not his ex – and off we flew to the sun.

What a mistake that was! We were soon arguing again; he went his way and I went mine.

I don't remember much about the holiday, apart from one night. We were both walking along the beach having a civil conversation, probably trying to give our relationship another try, when a gang of lads appeared out of nowhere.

They spoke in Spanish and split Lee and me up somehow. One of the gang members talked to Lee, while another guy, who moved quickly over to me, started chatting and smiling.

Then, all of a sudden, he pulled a flick knife out on me.

Smiling down at it, he spoke to me in Spanish, and guided me, using the knife, towards the sun loungers. They were left out overnight under the palm huts. All the while, he kept pushing up against me and grabbing at me, glancing down at the knife with a threatening smile.

I don't know where I got the mind to do what I did next. I began to laugh and said, "Come on, then. Why don't we go and get some drinks first?"

He seemed to understand me and shouted in Spanish to the others.

As we edged our way towards the pub that we frequented most nights of our holiday, the gang thought they were getting what they wanted.

But the minute we were close enough, I suddenly legged it into the bar and told one of the barmen what was happening. Lee wasn't far behind me.

The barman instantly jumped over the bar with a baseball bat and, along with a few other men, chased the gang off.

We later learned that the same gang had been into other bars, smashing them up with baseball bats and attacking people. I was told I was very lucky as I could have been raped that night – that was their intention. Fortunately, the police had told bar staff to be on the look-out for these guys as the rapes had been reported.

*"The* LORD *will keep you from all harm – he will watch over your life; the* LORD *will watch over your coming and going both now and for evermore."*
Psalm 121:7–8

As I said, apart from that terrifying incident, I don't remember much of that holiday. But I was glad to get back home, where Lee and I ended our relationship for good.

**The lesson here is, don't just stay in a relationship because you want a holiday! This could so easily have turned out really badly. Worst of all, I might not be writing this book now.**

Although I had a lot of fun during my late teenage years, there was always a nagging at the back of my mind and I never really knew what it meant. I just felt incomplete and sensed that something wasn't right.

But as I didn't understand my emotions at the time, I just carried on regardless.

# 7

# TRAUMAS AND TRAGEDIES

I was in my early twenties when I heard that Linda had become sick. I hadn't had any contact with her for a couple of years and I was so upset when my mum told me she'd been diagnosed with Hodgkinson's disease. This was someone I'd grown up with, who was only eighteen years old.

"How can she have this?" I questioned. "She isn't old enough."

Then I started to pray for her. I hadn't prayed for a long time but now I poured out my heart to God.

But how could I visit Linda in hospital when I hadn't seen her for so long? I wondered what reception I'd get. Then I pulled myself together. There I was worrying if she'd tell me to get out or not, when she was very ill and I just needed to go and see her.

I decided to go to the hospital with my friend. We went on the motorbike as this was something I knew Linda loved to talk about.

The silence was awkward at first as she had family and other friends there who knew we hadn't seen each other for a while. But as we began to chat, the atmosphere warmed, and I gave her a hug on leaving. I was happy that this was a breakthrough in our relationship.

Linda was still sick, though, and hadn't yet finished her chemotherapy. She was in Clatterbridge hospital for quite a while. She went through a lot, including losing her beautiful hair and having to undergo different types of treatment. Then she was told she'd never be able to have children.

It was heart-breaking to hear this and I continued to pray for her.

As the years passed, Linda did become well again and she got married. She now has two beautiful grown-up daughters. The hospital and consultants all said this was a miracle. And we Christians believe in miracles.

In the early eighties, my family were invited to my Cousin Eric's eighteenth birthday party. For some reason, I had an uneasy feeling that I shouldn't go. I thought it might be because I didn't feel one hundred per cent well. I was on antibiotics so I wouldn't be able to drink. But I loved dancing and my friend Helena was also invited, so I threw the uneasy feelings off.

My parents and my extended family were all at the party enjoying themselves and the night seemed to pass by quickly.

I was dancing with my friend and had taken off my shoes. I'd put them on the floor and we danced around them. But then, an older man came over and started to kick my shoes towards other people. I ran to pick them up and moved away from him. He just kept kicking them.

Then he said, "You've had it, you're dead. Wait 'til my daughter sees you. What do you think you're doing?" And he made some very racist comments to me about black people.

I didn't know who this man was or what he was talking about. He was only small in height but he was quite scary and I had a very bad feeling about him.

"What have I done? Who are you?" I asked. But he kept staring at me and repeating the same horrible words.

Eventually, I left the dance floor and went to find my dad.

"Get your coat on," Dad said. "We're leaving – now."

I paid a quick visit to the ladies and was on the toilet when, to my horror, the door of my cubicle was kicked in.

A small, muscly, strong woman who looked like a man, with very short, shaved, cropped hair, dragged me to the floor by my hair and tried to push my head down the toilet.

Next thing I remember, the ladies' toilets seemed to be full of people – men and women.

Someone pulled my attacker off me and two doormen took hold of this violent, aggressive woman, who proceeded to shout threats at me.

The doormen told me to hurry up and leave and they'd hold her back.

I ran, confused and in a state of shock, back to my parents. They were getting their things together to leave when, without warning, a woman from the other side of the table shouted something at me and punched my mum in the face.

I was horrified! My parents were the most beautiful people you could ever meet. They'd never hurt anyone. I was so angry that, before I could stop myself, I'd hit out across the table at this wicked woman.

It was like a film in slow motion. The force of my punch seemed to lift her up from the floor and she landed on the tables two rows behind her.

*What on earth was that?* I didn't do that, I couldn't have done. It was some supernatural thing that had happened, wasn't it? I certainly didn't have the strength to do something like that. That kind of thing only happened in movies.

There was worse to come. My head was grabbed and banged on the table and I remember clumps of my hair being pulled out. But the worst thing was seeing broken glass right next to my eye as a bottle broke over my head. People shouted. They were everywhere and I was being pushed and pulled.

I don't know how I ended up by the entrance doors with my dad's protective arm round my shoulder, holding me close to him to get me out safely. The one thing that stuck in my mind were the words I heard: "Get her out of here quickly – we can only hold them back for a while. They're a bad family, they're known for this. Take a different route home. Travel separately if you can."

My dad didn't let me out of his sight. Then a taxi appeared to take us home. All the way back I was scared. Nobody was following us, we were certain of that. But why didn't the feelings of unease and fear leave me? What on earth did all this mean?

I had no idea. Until a few days later.

Over the next few days, I was badly bruised on my face and my body ached. I went to work as usual but I still felt afraid and couldn't rid myself of the uneasiness that hung over me.

> *"My God is my rock, in whom I take refuge, my shield and the horn of my salvation. He is my stronghold, my refuge and my saviour – from violent people you save me. I called to the* LORD, *who is worthy of praise, and have been saved from my enemies."*
> *2 Samuel 22:3–4*

What happened after this was a tragic event.

I was at a St. John's Ambulance class that I went to every week when I had a horrible feeling something wasn't right and I should head back home. I left early after contacting my friend who came to pick me up on his motorbike, and we ended up chatting outside my home for a short while.

I told him what had happened a few nights earlier at Eric's eighteenth birthday party and thanked him for dropping me home. He left me at my front door and rode off as I went indoors.

I sat down to watch TV with two of my brothers, Jason and Richard. My parents were out. They'd taken my aunty home and Sam, my youngest brother, had gone with them.

Our house looked bare as my dad had been decorating. The only pieces of furniture left downstairs were the three-piece suite, TV and a large onyx coffee table in the living room. There was also a huge mug, half-full of tea that Dad hadn't finished.

It was 10.53pm when a programme called *St. Elsewhere*, a hospital drama, was on its last few minutes on TV. In the episode, a man in a black balaclava was hiding behind the door with a knife, ready to attack one of the nurses on the show.

All at once, I thought I was seeing things. To my horror and disbelief, a similar figure stood in the doorway between the kitchen and lounge – *our* kitchen and lounge.

In fact, there wasn't just one. Two figures dressed in black stood there. They clutched baseball bats and wore black ski masks. It looked as though their clothing was padded. My brothers, who were only fifteen and eighteen years old at the time, had not long had a bath, so only wore shorts and had towels draped round them.

Another figure then appeared dressed the same as the other two, all in black. I'm not sure if there were three or four of them in the end as everything happened so quickly.

Within moments, my brothers were flung over the shoulders of these horrific figures and there was blood everywhere. Our home had literally become a bloodbath.

There was no time to feel fear. My body was in overdrive as I ran to the front door to scream for help. As I did so, I was being hit repeatedly across my shoulders and head with a baseball bat. It knocked me down but I kept getting back up like a spring when the figure ran back into the kitchen to join the attack on my brothers.

One of my brothers and I managed to grab one of the ski masks. We tried to drag it off but the figure pulled away. The bodies of all of them were padded up so we couldn't get hold of them properly. Our hands just slid off their jackets.

My brothers fought back as best they could whilst these evil figures continued to slash at their main tendons and arteries.

Richard and I managed to jam one of them in the kitchen door as he tried to flee out into our small yard, but he got away and Richard collapsed in a pool of blood by the back gate.

Then, as suddenly as they'd arrived, they were gone. They escaped out into the darkness through the narrow entry at the back of our house.

I helped Richard indoors and sat him down on a chair. Every time he spoke the blood shot out of his neck. I got a clean tea towel and held it firmly to his wound. I told him to keep it pressed down and not to talk whilst I dealt with his chest wound.

"Shall I throw this away?" I asked him, and I lifted up a huge, bloody mess that lay on his lap.

"I don't think so, Pam," he muttered. "I think it's from inside of me somewhere."

That's when I realised. It was muscle hanging from his chest. As gently as I could, I laid it back down and continued to clean both my brothers up.

There was a ridiculous thought rolling round my head. I needed to clean the mess up before my parents got home. All I could think was that Mum and Dad would be back in a minute and there was a flood of blood on the kitchen floor, spattered on the ceiling and up the walls.

Frantically, I began to mop it up. I didn't want them to see it. How would they cope?

By now, our next-door neighbour was there in just his socks and trousers. He'd heard our screams for help and had shot out of bed to see what was going on. He'd chased after the intruders but couldn't catch them. They'd escaped into the night.

Another friend and neighbour arrived too, and tried to assist with the clean-up before my parents arrived.

At 11.05pm, two ambulances were outside our house. The whole hideous event had happened within twelve minutes.

I don't remember much in detail from then on. Both my brothers were taken away to hospital and I clutched at my shoulder. The ambulance crew asked if I was hurt. I didn't know. I was running on adrenalin and shock, I suppose, but they took me to hospital too.

This was a horrific attack that was treated as attempted murder on my dear brothers. Their attackers had used Stanley knives and knew exactly what they were doing, the police told us. They'd gone for their main arteries, Achilles tendons, wrists, heart, neck, face and head.

Richard was wrapped in foil and put in intensive care for a while. The doctors didn't know if he would live.

But, praise God, both my brothers did come through this.

I don't know how long we were in hospital and I can't remember the extent my own injuries as they were nothing like my brothers. I think I was told my shoulder was dislocated but I still don't know to this day. I don't remember the pain. My only pain was in my heart and mind, and I was terribly afraid.

The police and hospital staff told me I'd saved my brothers lives. But now I realise it was because of other people's prayers that God saved us.

Mrs. Hagan, an elderly lady who lived opposite to us, told us she saw a huge bright light over our home after this happened. "I know God is watching over and guarding you all," she said. "He won't let anything happen to you."

I couldn't understand how Mrs. Hagan could say this. How could God be watching over us and guarding us if He'd let something like this happen?

The inner fear I had and the sense of heaviness that there was something evil lurking in the shadows to my mind were totally founded. That horrendous attack on my brothers was a reality.

When the police visited us in hospital, I told them repeatedly about my bad feelings from the events that had happened at Eric's eighteenth party a few days earlier. But, at first, they didn't think what had happened there was anything to do with it.

At least they didn't until they investigated further.

Eventually we were told it was a case of mistaken identity.

The whole terrible event was reported on the news and in the newspapers. We were overwhelmed with people's cards, good wishes and prayers from all over the world.

When the perpetrators were at last identified, sadly there was never enough evidence against them as it was destroyed before the police got to them.

The police told us they'd help us to find another place to live if we wanted. They treated it as attempted murder on our family and said it was an open file that wouldn't be closed. I often wondered why the CID came to see us on such a regular basis. Maybe it was their way of protecting us.

Those people have never been caught. After further investigations, it was clear that the attack did have something to do with the violence that had broken out at Eric's party. The attackers at the party had mistaken me for my cousin Noreen, who was in a relationship with someone who was up to no good. That was why that awful man had made such horrible, racist comments to me that night.

We later heard that my aunty had been pressed for our address, which she gave through fear, I imagine, and she didn't tell our attackers they were hunting the wrong people or give any details of my cousin, who was the one they actually wanted.

We've not seen my aunty and her family since all this happened. Sadly, she was friends with the people who'd done this to us and they lived close to her. Although I've been able to forgive her, it was best left that we never had any contact again. The people responsible were never caught, even though the family were well known to the police, and we didn't want any further repercussions.

It took a long time for the physical wounds from the attack to heal. One of my brothers had to have skin grafts. And mentally, it took me about twenty years before I could talk about it without shaking and crying.

Sam was only around 12 years of age when he and my parents walked into that horrific bloodbath. He still has the mental scars and nightmares to this day. The impact it had on us as a family was devastating. My parents even thought of moving us out of the country, but after some long, hard thinking decided against it.

I can't remember how long we stayed in hospital but when we were discharged to go home, I remember being afraid. Walking into the house felt strange. There was no blood but I was shaking and upset as the memories came back to me.

My brothers didn't go out much after this. Even now, Richard doesn't remember much of what happened, even though he carries the scars. Jason talked about it a lot, and every year afterwards, he remembered the horrific events that took place on that date.

My parents worried and felt helpless as they didn't want to let us out of their sight. Dad constantly blamed himself for leaving us alone whilst he, Mum and Sam took our aunty home that evening. As the weeks went by and my brothers were recovering from their physical scars, humour became our only coping mechanism.

The local radio had been in touch with my parents to ask if we'd do an interview, but we never did. Mentally, it was too much for us to cope with.

The CID and police became regular visitors to our home and this did make us feel a bit safer. In a way, I felt like they were our bodyguards.

We also had lots of visitors from the church. Someone asked if we had forgiven the people who'd attacked us. I can't remember what any of our answers were to this question. I was only twenty then and my thoughts were not as they are now. Back then, I didn't see why they should be forgiven. As far as I was concerned, they were pure evil.

"Why would God want to forgive evil?" I thought, and part of me wanted revenge for what they'd done to my brothers and my parents. I hated to see the sorrow and sadness and the fear in their faces. And then I thought, "What revenge can I take that will match what those evil people have done to us?" But I didn't know what revenge would do, so the thought disappeared as quickly as it came into my head.

For months, even years, the word "forgiveness" kept rising up from deep within my soul and I didn't understand why. It just played over and over in my mind.

But how could I forgive them when they'd tried to kill my brothers? What was I supposed to do?

God's Word says: *"For if you forgive other people when they sin against you, your heavenly Father will also forgive you"* (Matthew 6:14).

So, does this mean that if I don't forgive then God won't forgive me?"

That's exactly what it means!

Don't ask me how long it took me to understand this. It's an area I will return to as my walk with my dear Father God deepens, but one thing I did realise was that I had to forgive them. That's not to say it happened immediately – it didn't. It was many years later.

I know my God is faithful and true to His promises because I have written this book and God's protection has been upon me. He is my healer and the restorer of my mind.

And He has never left me.

*"So do not fear, for I am with you; do not be dismayed, for I am your God. I will strengthen you and help you; I will uphold you with my righteous right hand."*
*Isaiah 41:10*

*"Dear friends, never take revenge. Leave that to the righteous anger of God. For the Scriptures say, 'I will take revenge; I will pay them back,' says the* LORD*."*
*Romans 12:19, NLT*

# 8

# MISSING THE BRIGHT LIGHTS

A few months later, to help me cope, I decided I wanted some normality back in my life. I was trying hard to put the attacks to the back of my mind and get on with things. I was at work again and hearing stories of fun nights out from my friends.

I hadn't had a night out in months. My parents were worried that something else would happen to me and had become even more protective. I understood that they were worried but I was young and when my thoughts began to return to the bright lights, I realised how much I missed it all.

Josh was in the CID and played a part in the investigations until he retired. He became a good friend to the family for many years.

"What if Pam comes out with me and I look after her?" Josh suggested to my parents.

Josh was great. It was as if he was my own personal bodyguard, even though he wasn't. He was a lot older than I was and he'd take my friend and me wherever we wanted to go to avoid us going into Liverpool town centre.

There were a few nightclubs in Bootle and surrounding areas, but they weren't rock clubs and the scene was totally different to what I enjoyed.

That funny feeling crept back again. This time I recognised it: "You're not good enough to go here. You need money and you can't afford these places.

Only people who have money go here. Look at you – you don't even dress the way they do..."

I tried to ignore the feelings and went along anyway, but I didn't enjoy it. I loved rock music and the leather-and-jeans look, not all this trendy stuff.

For years I'd told myself I didn't have enough money. It's only now I realise that I did have enough money to get into those places. I just refused to pay the ridiculous amounts demanded to get into a nightclub and what they charged for drinks.

Josh told my friend and me that we couldn't take alcohol into the place we were going. But me being cheeky, I roped him into smuggling some in. I shoved a half bottle of spirit into his pocket as people were being searched going into the night club. Josh didn't get searched. The doormen knew who he was when he showed his ID.

I was so cheeky back then and he knew I always got away with things.

One evening, my friend and I were really bored. We wanted to go to The Cave in Matthew Street in Liverpool. But Josh had promised my parents he'd look after me and he was trying so hard to deter me from going out into the city. So, he introduced us to a few colleagues from the police club and we did become friends with some of them.

Most of the policemen were all right. They knew what had happened to my brothers and to me and they really looked after us when we were out. There were the odd ones who thought they might try their luck, only to realise we weren't interested in anything like that.

On one particular night, before Bootle New Strand Shopping Centre became a covered mall, the police had a call out. Josh had to go off on an emergency somewhere and left us with his friends who were on duty. We asked them if we could sit in the police car as we wanted to know what it was like. So they let us sit in the back until they got a call out too.

But Helena and I were up for a bit of excitement. We wanted to know what it would be like to go out with the blue flashing lights on – and we wouldn't get out.

Off they had to go with us in the back as they didn't have time to argue! As it turned out, they were pulled off that job as other police had got there first – which was a good job really.

But we ended up being driven round the shopping centre at night in the back of their car. It was great!

When Josh eventually came back, he dropped us off home. I know we'd never get away with things like that now, but they were real highlights of my mischievous life back then after all that had happened.

# 9

# AND BABY MAKES THREE

The years passed and one day I met Sean. He was a few years older than I was.

I met him in the rock club I used to go to. He asked me out three times and each time I refused – until his friend told me he only ever asked a woman out twice at the most.

I pondered this over in my mind and wondered why I'd refused. I wish I'd listened to those first thoughts.

Our first date was at the movies to watch a horror film I didn't like. Still, Sean treated me well and we often went out to the pub.

But for some reason, I felt uncomfortable when he told me he was going out with his friends for a drink. Something inside me didn't feel happy about it and I couldn't shake this feeling off whenever I had it.

When I was twenty-two, I fell pregnant. I was terrified to tell my parents. Mum guessed when I told her the toothpaste tasted different, so she took me to Liverpool to have a pregnancy test done. Sure enough the test showed positive.

Mum was very supportive when I asked her how I'd manage. She told me not to worry. She knew I was concerned about my dad's reaction.

"God doesn't send a little mouth without something to put in it," she said. "If God feeds the birds of the sky, how much more will he provide for you both? And don't worry about your dad. He'll be fine. He already had an idea anyway."

I didn't really understand all this God stuff then. He was real, I knew that, and I still thought that if I always believed, I'd have a place in heaven with Him when I died. I was more worried what my dad was going to say.

We arrived home and I waited for Dad to shout. But he was so loving and kind, and he told me the same thing Mum had said about God providing for us. I started to cry. He put his loving arms around me and said it would be all right. He was looking forward to his little grandchild and he told me we wouldn't go without.

> *"Look at the birds of the air; they do not sow or*
> *reap or store away in barns, and yet your heavenly*
> *Father feeds them. Are you not much more*
> *valuable than they?"*
> *Matthew 6:26*

It was a strange experience being pregnant and I felt very insecure. When Sean asked me to marry him, I was overjoyed and immediately said yes. At last, someone loved me for me. I was the first choice this time, not second best.

I was excited to tell my parents but was surprised to hear my dad say: "You don't have to marry him just because you're pregnant, you know."

I immediately sensed Dad didn't want me to marry Sean and I rebelled against his words. "I know," I said, "but I want to marry him." Even as I said it, though, I had that niggling, doubtful, insecure feeling again.

I put it down to being insecure because I was pregnant and told myself that the feelings would go once I was Sean's wife.

But during my pregnancy, our relationship became quite difficult. I wanted Sean to spend time with me rather than him going out clubbing with his friends. He just told me I was nagging him and we wouldn't be getting married if I didn't stop. He said he was only having a couple of pints after work and he deserved it after a hard day's graft.

It wouldn't have been so bad if it was only a couple of pints, but it never was.

When I was six months pregnant with Joe, Sean told me he'd been to the hospital and may have passed something on to me, so I needed to go and get checked out. I was horrified. He wouldn't come with me as he said he had to go to work, so I went on my own.

I was examined and the nurse told me I'd have to receive treatment over a couple of weeks. I was so naive I didn't even know I'd contracted anything. I certainly didn't think Sean had been with another woman as he told me he must have caught it before we met and I believed him.

Eventually, I was given the all-clear and I didn't think any more of it.

Time passed – and so did my baby's due date. He was late. Very late. I was four weeks overdue, which I knew would be dangerous for him.

My waters finally broke at home and Sean took me to the hospital. But then he went back to work (he was a self-employed mechanic in the family business) and I felt scared. Scared and alone.

The midwife told me I had a long way to go before my baby would be born. Mum came and stayed with me, then left again when Sean was supposed to be coming back in.

After a while, I felt the urge to push but was told I was only four centimetres dilated and had another six centimetres to go. I had no pain relief and was left in the room on my own. Then, when I shouted for help, the nurse wasn't very happy. She repeated that I had a long way to go, then banged the door shut behind her, leaving me alone again.

Suddenly, I felt as if my baby was really coming and again I shouted. This time they rushed me up in a lift to the delivery suite: I was still only four centimetres, but my baby was definitely on the way.

Sean finally arrived as I was giving birth to Joe. He was overjoyed at being a dad and, despite all my insecurities, I hoped this would be the happy ending I'd been longing for.

At long last he was here, my gorgeous son Joe, born in October, four weeks later than the due date. Big, beautiful, blue eyes stared into mine. He didn't cry. He only wanted to stare at me.

It was the most astonishing feeling in the world, as any mum will know. Just like that, my fears were gone and all I wanted was to protect and love him.

Joe was jaundiced and had to be taken from me overnight to have a special lamp treatment in the nursery. I couldn't stop crying. Even after the little time we'd been together, I missed my baby.

We left hospital three days later. My parents were delighted when both Joe and I arrived home. We lived with them, and Sean continued to live with his parents too.

As the weeks went by, Sean didn't mention marriage much. He just said he was still thinking about it and I didn't want to push him. But my feelings of insecurity didn't go away and I didn't feel loved the way I thought love should feel. I had so much love to give but didn't seem to get the same in return.

Joe was two months old when Sean's mum rang my mum one day, out the blue, and asked what we were going to do about the wedding.

I spoke to Sean and he said, "Well, do you want to get married?"

"Of course I do!" I replied. I wanted to feel secure and loved and I hoped things would settle down. And I didn't want to be an unmarried mum.

We set a date towards the end of January, which only gave us a couple of months, but Sean convinced me there wasn't much to do as his mum would organise the buffet and make the wedding cake.

Then, as I began to make plans, I started to get excited.

Sean didn't seem to want to have much involvement. He said it was a "woman's thing", so I carried on planning our wedding on my own.

# 10

# DOMESTIC VIOLENCE

I was twenty-three years old when Sean and I married. Sean was twenty-seven and Joe was only three months.

We got married in St. John and St. James Church in Bootle, the same church where I'd given my life to Jesus as a child.

We didn't have a honeymoon as Joe was only a baby, so I moved straight in with Sean, his parents and his sister in Huyton. It was a long way out for me, just over eleven miles away and, as I didn't drive, I soon began to feel isolated.

The house where we lived was big. Everyone was out at work during the day and I was left alone with Joe and no money. They told me never to answer the door to anyone.

And I didn't have any friends apart from Joanna, Sean's sister. We got on well at first but after a while our friendship deteriorated.

Sean worked with his dad in the family business and his mum worked too. The family accepted Joe and myself into their home and gave us one of the front rooms in their house but, although it was good of them, I didn't feel comfortable. Before long, I began to feel the pressure of living with them. I wanted my own things around me and I was worried in case Joe broke any of the family ornaments, which he did once he started crawling around.

I didn't want to sound ungrateful, but I felt like I was living on a knife edge. I was young and wanted family time with Sean at weekends. The trouble was, he worked and only took time off to go out with his friends to the pub or a football match and then on to night clubs.

His dad often said that Sean worked hard and deserved a few pints with the lads and that he was a man of the world, which I didn't understand. His mum said the same. I felt like I had no support from them.

I wasn't used to this kind of environment. My family had always been loving and affectionate but this family seemed the complete opposite and I couldn't settle.

When I began to complain, Sean told me he was working hard to save up so we could have our own home. He didn't understand that I just wanted to have family time with him and Joe. Anyway, was he drinking the money away? I certainly didn't see any signs of him saving up.

One evening, Sean's mum said she would babysit for us while we had a night out together. We'd been invited to a house party as a friend of Sean's was emigrating. It was a huge house with many rooms and bathrooms.

As soon as we arrived, a group of women immediately came over to talk to Sean and totally ignored me. I tried to make conversation with them but they blanked me. Sean lapped up all the attention and the more he drank, the more friendly he and the other women became.

Throughout the night I was left on my own, then made to feel like a pest when I went to speak to him. There was a point during the party when I couldn't even find him. I just wanted to leave – I felt so uncomfortable. That's when I got upset and ran to the bathroom to cry. I was in there a while when someone heard me sobbing and asked to come in. I opened the door and a young man stood there. He said he wanted to see if I was all right.

The next minute, Sean shouted at me to get ready as we were leaving.

We walked out of the house but, without any warning, Sean suddenly turned really nasty. He pushed me over onto the road and stood on my foot, which was still on the high pavement. The pain was horrible and I screamed to him to please let me go. He grabbed my hair then and used it to drag me along the ground.

A man came out from the party and told Sean to stop it. He even threatened to call the police. Sean just threatened him back, and told him what he'd do to him if he did. Then he yelled at him to get back inside.

I'd never seen Sean like this before. His face was twisted and looked demonic. He accused me of being with this man when I hadn't. I hadn't done anything.

That was the first time he assaulted me.

"Am I really this bad?" I asked myself. "Maybe I deserved it for talking to another man. Maybe I wound him up and it was my fault." And I believed what I was saying to myself.

An ambulance arrived shortly afterwards, then the police. I was relieved but I was still convinced it was all my fault because I'd also been drinking. As I got into the ambulance, I couldn't put any weight on my foot and I was sure it was broken because of the swelling.

The policewoman was lovely. But, over her shoulder, I could see Sean threatening me. She told me he'd do it again and again if I didn't press charges now. When she turned to look at him, he seemed his normal self – but I could see something evil and wicked when he looked at me.

"What is it?" I kept asking myself. "What is that horrible, twisted, evil expression that's there when he has his eyes on me?" I was scared.

Sean's dad was embarrassed by his behaviour. When he saw my black, swollen eye and cheek, and bandaged, sprained foot the next day, he said he was disgusted his son could do this.

I never did press charges. I was scared but I didn't think it would ever happen again, not after he'd apologised. I felt crushed and didn't know where to turn. I wondered how it had come to this. Joanna was shocked when she saw me and said he'd never done anything like that to anyone before and his mum said the same.

As time went on, I began to feel that Sean would never adapt to married life. He drank every night after work, then every spare moment at weekends if he wasn't working. When he came home from work, if Joe was crying, I had to take my little boy upstairs out of the way. Sean would be agitated, saying he'd had a hard day and didn't need to come home to this.

Another time, his Alsatian dog turned on him because he started to argue with me when he came home from work. Sean wasn't at all happy about this and it made him angrier. He said I'd even turned his dog against him.

I began to cry out for help to his parents and sister, expecting some support or advice, but it was always the same: he worked hard and he deserved a few pints.

The only money I had coming in was a small family allowance. Sean didn't give me any money as he said the family allowance I received was enough for nappies and food and I didn't need any more. He told me he gave his parents keep for us all but I soon discovered he didn't. I felt extremely uncomfortable when I realised they were keeping us.

Things carried on as normal but I became very subdued. On Sean's drunken nights out with his friends and in between or when his parents babysat, I would drink a lot too, just so I could be on the same wavelength as him. It was Sean's favourite saying: so we wouldn't clash, he said. It wasn't true as we always ended up arguing, even though it may have been a good start to the night.

I daren't tell my parents what was going on. I knew my dad would go mad. I remembered his wise words: "You don't have to marry him just because you're pregnant, you know."

I wondered, was this my life now? Would he ever settle down?

I did question the beatings of that night at his friend's house party and the threats and aggression that followed. I thought maybe I deserved it. But then I'd think, "Hang on a minute, sometimes you only ask him a question. You don't deserve for him to scream and shout or threaten you like that. And Joe only cried or put toast in the video – did I deserve to be punished for those things too?"

I did have many questions in my head and things were difficult because I felt I didn't have anyone to turn to apart from his family. It became so tricky that they even sided with him at times, and I began to think I was old-fashioned in my own thinking.

Married at twenty-three, I'd suddenly had to grow up because we had a new baby. Sometimes I blamed myself and felt I'd put a strain on our marriage. But then I'd question this and blame Sean for the way he treated me. I did also think, though, that if we had our own home, things might be different, as I wanted our marriage to work. Yet when I mentioned to Sean's mum, full of excitement, that we could move into a council house, she laughed mockingly in my face and said, "What? You'll starve! You won't be able to afford it. You're best buying your own place."

I was so crushed by her remark that I felt myself sinking down. I couldn't see a way out or forward. I just felt trapped.

I'd confided in Sean's mum on another occasion too. I'd been so upset when Sean had told me that he'd thought about visiting a prostitute when I was pregnant with Joe. His mum wasn't phased when I told her, though. She simply said, "A lot of men do."

I had no support and it seemed that everyone's morals were different to mine. I wouldn't have been surprised if Sean had visited a prostitute when I was pregnant.

Sean's wayward lifestyle continued. He still went to see every Liverpool football game and continued with the lads' nights out. I never went out on my own as I'd lost contact with my friends when I married and I didn't know anyone where I lived. I didn't want my parents to know what was happening either. Mum always said she could tell something wasn't right by the sound of my voice on the phone. So I didn't ring her as much as I used to either. The only bit of excitement I had was when I went to the shops in Huyton village with Joanna on a few occasions, but even that soon changed.

I found I was afraid of her and I didn't want to get on the wrong side of her. She was quite a big lady and wouldn't think twice about fighting with a man so she could handle herself. She'd become very angry with me one day and had kicked me in the stomach. She said she'd had enough of seeing me so low and hearing about our marital problems.

"One minute you're arguing," she exclaimed in frustration, "the next you're back together again!"

At the time I couldn't understand her response. I was married and it wasn't something I could just walk away from.

What neither of us knew was that I was pregnant. Not until I started bleeding.

My GP told me I was having a miscarriage and would have to go into hospital for a DNC. Apparently I was around nine weeks pregnant.

At this point, my emotions were in shreds. I didn't even really want to go on living but at least it was a relief to be in hospital for a rest. A break away from the situation.

I didn't get any support from Sean or his family. Sean's dad told me to get it in black and white from the hospital that Joanna's kick had caused my miscarriage. I felt so alone.

Just before Joe's first birthday, with our marital problems ongoing, Sean's mum phoned mine and told her to come and pick me up and take me back home. She said she'd had enough of me and wanted someone to come and get me immediately.

I was crying. I still felt like I didn't want to live anymore. "My parents are better than me," I told myself. "They'll be able to bring Joe up better than I can."

I loved my little boy more than myself. He was everything to me, but I felt I wasn't a good enough parent as he didn't deserve all this.

When my mum and brother came to pick me up, I was devastated. Sean had packed Joe's cot and all our belongings as quick as a flash and, before I knew it, I was on my way back to Bootle.

Sean just stared at us as we drove out of the driveway of his family home.

I don't remember much about coming home. I know I expected my family to ask me all kinds of questions, but they didn't. They were lovely and sensitive and they let me be me and find my own way back into life.

I found myself back in my little box bedroom with Joe. There was no space but we managed, and we stayed there until I finally got a little two-bedroomed council house a couple of months later on Monfa Road. It was the same road my parents lived on and right opposite the church I went to as a child.

I was overjoyed as I decorated it myself, and I cashed in a small policy I had so that I could furnish it.

A couple of months later, Sean and I started to speak to each other again. We were civil this time. He wanted to give our marriage another try, he told me. I agreed but he didn't want to move into a council house and I wasn't going to move out of my new home in a hurry unless things changed between us.

Little by little, Sean gradually did begin to move in. But he hadn't changed. The same pattern as before continued. If he wasn't out drinking, he was bringing cans home from work every night. Then he'd bring me a bottle of cider at weekends to enjoy with him as we didn't go out.

One evening, I was waiting for him to come home after a football match. He'd promised to be back right after the game. In the end, I got fed up and went to see my parents up the road.

Sean came knocking about three hours later. He was very drunk and slurring. He told me he'd smashed the glass in our front door. I tried not to show any emotion as my fear flooded back and I told him I'd make my way home. But I saw that his face was twisted and antagonising again, although when he spoke to my parents in the kitchen, he seemed fine. As if nothing was wrong.

Mum told me to walk back home with Sean and she'd get Joe ready and follow me. That's when the threats started.

Back at the house, I could see that the front door glass was smashed where Sean had punched it in because I wasn't home when he got there.

I went upstairs to use the bathroom and avoid any confrontation but he followed me up. He dragged me off the toilet, smashed the bathroom door window and pushed my face next to a large shard of jagged glass, right close to my eye. I wrestled with him and punched him in the face to escape. He told me I'd broken his nose.

Mum arrived about twenty minutes later with Joe and walked straight into our domestic. Sean told her I was off my head because I was sober – unlike him, who had a reason for his behaviour because he was drunk. Then he left and I didn't see him for a while. Until, scared of being alone, I took him back a couple of months later.

Nothing changed, however. I never knew if he was going to come home or not, and if I questioned him, there would always be another argument.

When we did go out together, Sean would blatantly eye other women up in front of me, so the cycle of feeling worthless continued. On one occasion, I was so upset with his flirting that I walked into the toilets and punched the mirror in despair. Then I went back into the bar and sat down alone, only to see him laughing and joking with two girls and touching them up. In frustration and turmoil, I crushed the bottle I was holding and it broke in my hand. It severed the tendon on my wedding finger.

Sean told me to go to the hospital. He didn't leave with me but he was hiding, watching me crying on the street. I saw him but was afraid of what he'd do if I approached him.

It was a police riot van that picked me up and took me to hospital. Sean stopped the van and told them he was my husband. When he got in, he threatened me, telling me not to say anything to the police about what had happened.

My injury turned out to be bad. I had to have an operation and wore a cast for about six weeks. It made it difficult to bathe Joe but my mum came and helped me a lot.

Thankfully, since I'd got my own place and put the past behind me, things with Joanna had settled down. But I still wasn't one hundred per cent comfortable with her as I knew what she was capable of.

One night we went out with her and a friend of Sean's, who was a nice man. Joanna was a taxi driver and she drove us that night. At the end of the evening, I was outside ready to leave but Sean was still in the club, so Joanna asked me to go in to get him.

When I found him, he was chatting to a few women and wasn't happy to be told we were waiting for him.

It was when we got into the car that he started digging me in the ribs with his elbows, telling me I'd made a show of him. I ignored him and Joanna told me to sit in the front, which I did.

Suddenly, Sean grabbed me from behind and started punching me in the face. Joanna was shocked and stopped the car. She screamed at him to get out. Thankfully, he did. His friend said he'd never seen him so violent before – he couldn't believe it. He chased after Sean to calm him down and eventually they both got back in with us.

When I arrived home, my brother Sam, who was babysitting, was furious. Sean said he was sorry when he saw my split eye. Then he smashed a mug over his own head and cut himself – to hurt himself the way he'd hurt me.

He seemed to calm down after that, but when I was changing Joe on my knee, out of the blue he became angry again. Because I wouldn't retaliate, he threw a can of opened lager at me, just missing Joe. He really was like a Jekyll and Hyde as his moods switched. And there was no reason for him to behave in this way, only that he was drunk.

I began to feel very, very angry with my situation. I just didn't know what to do about it. I wanted to tie Sean up and gag him, just so that I had a chance to speak and make him listen to me.

I cried myself to sleep many a night and felt afraid when he came home. What mood would he would be in? He'd poke me with wire coat hangers to wake me up, and threaten me, but would then act differently the following morning.

My emotions were so up and down. One minute I thought I was in love, the next I knew wasn't. Neighbours started to notice things. They told me the twinkle had gone out of my eyes. I was told many times I looked unhappy and was often asked what was going on.

One neighbour told me to get out while I was young and still had the chance to start a new life. Otherwise I could end up like her. She smiled and said, "Look, you don't want to lose your teeth like I have." She'd had a terrible life, she told me.

My brothers would help us out in any way they could. When Sean was convicted of drinking and driving and given a ban, they would take it in turns to drive him to Liverpool every day to his place of work.

Sean had a big influence on my youngest brother, Sam, who went to football games with him. Sean would drink enormous amounts of spirits and cause trouble. On a number of occasions, he would start a fight and then run off like a coward, leaving Sam to deal with it.

Many nights after Sean's drinking binges, I'd be woken up suddenly with him choking on his vomit. His face would be pale and his lips had turned a bluey-purple colour. I would roll him onto his side and slap him between his shoulder blades. The vomit would project out of his mouth, up the walls, on the curtains and all over the floor. He was none the wiser as I'd be the one cleaning it all up in the early hours of the morning. He wouldn't believe it when I told him what had happened the next day.

It wasn't just alcohol that fuelled our relationship. Sean also enjoyed smoking pot. This seemed to mellow him but he acted very silly with it too. It became a problem when I asked him to stop. He told me that, ultimately, it was either drink or pot – one or the other – but he wouldn't give up both.

His compromise was to cut the alcohol down to a few cans a night, but he started smoking pot in between. This led to other drug use.

Sean started pestering me to take magic mushrooms. I hated drugs. I'd seen the damage they did to people and how they messed with their minds.

Sean had been telling me for a long time that I couldn't say anything about him using drugs. He said I didn't know what I was talking about because I hadn't tried them. He told me not to tell him what to do.

One of my brothers went through a phase with drugs at the same time as Sean. Then, one evening, they finally talked me into it. They said I wouldn't notice any difference if I had them in a glass of coke.

Joe was in bed and, foolishly, I had half a glass of Coke with the juice of the mushrooms.

Very soon I began to hallucinate. I was violently sick and the rooms and furniture were moving around me. I more or less passed out on the couch but I could hear Sean and my brother talking. It was clear my brother was afraid. He said he thought I needed to go to hospital, but Sean said, no, I'd be all right.

They then seemed to decide that, if I wasn't up in two hours, I'd need medical help and they contemplated what to tell the hospital. I couldn't respond at all. It was terrifying.

I don't remember coming round from this but the next day, Sean threatened what he would do to me if I ever took any kind of drugs. He was scared.

I thought then he genuinely cared about me and, once again, I felt very loving towards him.

**Alcohol and drugs don't fix your problems. They exaggerate the underlying problems and can damage families and relationships. This is not what God wants for you.**

**If you have been affected by or can relate to any of this, please don't be fooled like I was. Remember, drugs can kill and what happened to me could have gone drastically wrong. God created you to be unique. You don't need drugs or alcohol to change you, as this is all they do. They mess up the chemicals in your system. They go against all that God created you to be.**

**If you're going through anything like this yourself, please see the list of organisations at the back of this book that you can contact for help.**

# 11

## UNFAITHFUL

There came a time, at long last, when I finally began to understand that my marriage wasn't healthy. If we stayed together, I knew one of us would end up dead and I started to have very dark thoughts. They weren't loving thoughts. I began to hate Sean and I made minor attempts to hurt myself.

But it wasn't just the domestic violence that was poisoning our marriage. I now strongly suspected that Sean was being unfaithful with other women.

Sean had a great way of playing mind games. He would turn things back on me, confusing me so I began to blame myself. I fell into this trap. It was the mind games that were more painful than the physical violence; the physical pain would pass but the mental pain – that was always there.

My brother told me he had found Sean with another woman. When I confronted him on the phone and he confessed, I lost all control. I smashed and scratched over five hundred of his LP records – his prize possessions. Then I didn't see him again for another couple of months.

It was during this time I found out that he had visited prostitutes; that he'd carried on with other women on a regular basis, even though he denied some of it and confessed the others to me on the phone.

I felt such a failure in my marriage that I didn't know what to do. I hated him, I loved him. I didn't know what I felt. I wanted to do the right thing and forgive him because he had now confessed to all my suspicions; I wasn't going mad after all. Maybe now, I thought, we'd be able to move forward and put it all behind us. Joe was only three and I didn't want to be a single mum. So, as I was feeling so low and vulnerable, yet again I took him back. It was approaching Christmas and I couldn't bear the thought of being alone then.

In the midst of our relationship problems, Joe kept having kidney and urine infections that were getting worse. I was expecting our second child when Joe eventually had to go into Alder Hey Children's Hospital for a big operation when he was just three and a half years old.

Eight months pregnant, I spent most nights sleeping in the hospital chair next to Joe's bed. Sean said he had work to do. I know he worked hard but we never saw any benefit from his hard work as he played hard too.

On many occasions I had contacted my solicitor about a divorce. But, because I was pregnant, my solicitor told me it was best to wait until I had given birth due to hormones affecting how I felt. This made sense somehow and I stuck things out longer.

One day, I was taken into hospital while I was pregnant with an infection and bleeding and I was kept in overnight. Sean was nowhere to be found. He wasn't answering his mobile or work phone. No one had seen him.

Then, after visiting hours were over, he stormed into the hospital ward, drunk and shouting at me, blaming my parents as he thought they hadn't contacted him. He was very angry and, again, I was afraid.

I returned home next day to find that he and his mum had been to our home and emptied it of half the contents. I was devastated. My life was an absolute mess. I was in turmoil. I hated it!

Once more, that feeling of being a failure returned: *you can't even keep a marriage together, you're hopeless* etc. Those painful feelings of insecurity – like I was bottom of the heap, not good enough for anything – they all came back. My baby was due in June – how much longer could I last?

I didn't know how to escape as I knew Sean would always find me. He even seemed to know what I talked about with my family; things that were nothing to do with our relationship. It was scary. It was like he knew everything. He told me he'd bugged the house but he also knew things I didn't ever speak about to anyone.

I lived in fear and I wanted out. But there didn't seem to be a way.

*"For the Spirit God gave us does not make us timid,*
*but gives us power, love and self-discipline." 2*
*Timothy 1:7*

At last, along came baby Mick. He was beautiful and he certainly had a good set of lungs on him. He was born in the afternoon with the sun shining down into the hospital room where I gave birth to him.

Not long after Mick was born, my doctor advised me to be sterilised due to my gynaecological problems. He told me if I became pregnant again, I could die or lose my baby at childbirth. So I took his advice. Even so, my symptoms still persisted.

Despite the new addition to our family, nothing changed. Times had been very hard for me and I began to question things. Did I really love Sean? Dad had often said that my marriage wasn't a loving one. He asked if I enjoyed being treated that way.

"Of course I don't enjoy being treated like that!" I yelled at him.

I began to realise very quickly then that I didn't love Sean. Mick was seven months old and now was the time to get out. Fast. This could be my one and only chance of escape.

My parents didn't know exactly what was happening in my marriage. I used to hide the black eyes with as much cover-up makeup as I could and, if I couldn't hide them, I'd lie and say I was playing with the boys and they'd hit me with their toys or I'd banged myself on the corner of a cabinet. I always lied when I was bruised.

Mum told me that, if Sean was hitting me, my dad and brothers would do something about it and he wouldn't do it again. So I was always living in fear that more trouble would escalate if they did find out what was going on.

As I'd never been out without Sean in all the four years of our marriage, I finally plucked up the courage to ask my friend Linda if she wanted to meet me for a drink in our local pub. I'd lost contact with my friends when I moved to Huyton after I got married. I just never kept in touch with them. Not being able to drive didn't help and I didn't want them knowing about my marriage problems as I felt such a failure.

I rang Sean at work and told him I was going to the local pub, which was walking distance from our home. I told him I was going out at 7.30pm and would be home by 10pm. I said the baby's bottles were ready made up in the fridge in case Mick woke up.

"Who's babysitting?" he asked.

I was shocked. "Well – you are, aren't you?"

"Nah, get your mother or your brother to do it. I'm no baby sitter," Sean said.

That did it for me. I had to make my escape. No turning back now, I thought to myself, and off I went to get ready to go out. I knew Sean wouldn't come home so there was no point in begging him. I was done with that.

My mum babysat in the end and told me to be in by midnight. I had a great night out, dancing with my friend, something I hadn't done in years. I'd missed it. I was never going back to my husband.

Just as I thought he would, Sean rang me the next day to ask what was for tea.

"I don't know," I said. "You'd better ask your mum."

He thought I was joking as he hung up on me. He rang me back a few times and asked the same question, only to receive same response.

I'd done it. I was free. *Free!*

But there was still something telling me to be careful. I knew we'd separated and this time it would be for good, but I couldn't shake off this feeling of fear and unease. I didn't know if I was afraid of being alone – bringing my boys up on my own – or whether it was because I was still scared of him. I soon discovered it was both.

Sean moved back to his parents. But his sister Joanna began to interfere when he realised our marriage was over. She'd spit at the windows of my home and intimidate me by staring in while I was getting the boys ready to go with Sean at weekends. She often came with him to pick them up. Many times I had to call the police. I was just so afraid.

# 12

# FREEDOM AND DECEPTION

I t sounds like an extreme thing to say, but I didn't really know who I was anymore. I had no identity. Sean's abusive words kept flooding my mind. Why did I still feel like this? I didn't know what was happening to me.

*"The* LORD *will call you back as if you were a wife deserted and distressed in spirit – a wife who married young, only to be rejected,' says your God."*
*Isaiah 54:6*

*"...'but with everlasting kindness I will have compassion on you,' says the* LORD *your Redeemer."*
*Isaiah 54:8*

Sean would pick the boys up at weekends and keep them overnight. That was when I would let my hair down. Off to the Bootle pubs and clubs I'd go and dance the night away, trying to block out the thoughts in my head, drinking until I was confident – confident enough to dance. But it wasn't just confidence that the alcohol gave me. I drank myself into oblivion many times.

My confidence was boosted when men paid me attention too. I was noticed, and it felt good to be noticed and spoken to nicely.

Little did I know I was in a downward spiral, only to be used again.

I thought I could start afresh. I was finally free from Sean. But whilst the physical wounds healed, the mental abuse wouldn't go away.

I loved my boys. They were the ones who kept me going. I loved to hear and see them waking up in the morning, smiling at me. I loved holding and cuddling them. I just wanted them to be safe and secure; not corrupted by this big bad world. I often thought I could bring them up alone without society hurting them. But I'm sure plenty of parents must have had those thoughts.

My parents and my three brothers had a big influence in my son's lives and my sons loved them. We were a very close family and supported each other whenever we could.

As my parents only lived a couple of blocks of houses away, I would visit them most days. And the boys loved it when they were old enough to run down to their grandparents' house on their own without me. My mum would wait at her gate and watch them tear up the street, whilst I kept an eye on them from mine. She would wave to me when they jumped into her arms. This was their little bit of independence.

Life went on and I got a part-time job delivering car magazines. But what I really looked forward to was my night out at weekends.

A night out would cost me around ten pounds. My friend and I would go halves to buy a half bottle of Bacardi or vodka. We'd buy one or two drinks from the bar, then top up with our bottle of spirit.

I had no confidence and felt myself slipping further down, lacking more and more confidence until I topped up with more alcohol. It was never long before its effects on me showed. Oh, yes, I could dance now and not care if anyone was looking at me. Not care about anything. This new confidence made me come alive, I thought.

Alcohol can have a devious effect on you. One minute you can be withdrawn and quiet. Then, before you know it, you're a different person. And not always a nice person. Alcohol can change you like the wind, and I know because there were many stories on my wild nights out. I was shocked when I saw women grabbing men and taking them into the ladies' toilets where I could hear them having sex.

I started to ponder on my nights out on the things I'd seen. Were my eyes being opened and was I so naive that I didn't know things like this happened? Was I old-fashioned in my views and thoughts? Were my parents over-protective?

I began to dwell on the things my ex-husband had told me about his nights out with his friends; the things that made me feel insecure; the women, the drinking and his flirting.

"Well, we're living in different times now," I began to tell myself. "This is the twentieth century. The way I was brought up by my parents doesn't exist anymore. They were old-fashioned times. This is how it is now – this is normal life and this is what everybody does." Gradually, I convinced myself.

No wonder I felt different. "It's me who's the odd one out. I've been living in the past," I told myself and I believed it.

This was a turning point. All my life I'd felt insecure, second-best, different, rejected. Now it was time to catch up on the fun that everyone else seemed to be having. Time to let go of the past and enjoy my life. After all, this was what life was all about, wasn't it? That's what the little voice inside me would remind me every time I got ready to go out on the town. Out would come the bottle of vodka or Bacardi as I began to get ready at home, and I made sure there was plenty left to give me that extra boost when I needed it. It's strange when you've been in a violent relationship and subject to mental abuse. You begin to believe every negative thing that person has said to you. Mind games are not good.

*"Do not conform to the pattern of this world, but
be transformed by the renewing of your mind.
Then you will be able to test and approve what
God's will is – his good, pleasing and perfect will."*
*Romans 12:2*

I enjoyed most of my nights out, until the following day when reality crept in.

"Oh, no! I hope I didn't say or do anything stupid," I'd wonder to myself, and my mind and heart would fill with dread.

My friend would come round or ring me, and we'd talk about the evening before and have a laugh about it.

Somewhere in the midst of my wild times, a lady from the church came over to give me a small hamper – a gift from the congregation. This really touched my heart and soul, as she told me she and other people in the church were praying for me. After she'd gone, I remember staring at the food hamper and crying over such kindness.

At the time, I didn't know what was going on inside me. I cried as I didn't feel I deserved them being kind to me. Now I can see that God was in the centre of all of this. God was working in me and for me.

Alongside the alcohol-fuelled nights out were men. I wanted to be loved. But although I searched and searched, I couldn't find what I was looking for. I just didn't know what was missing in my life.

I had a few on-and-off relationships as I was always on the lookout for that emptiness to be filled. I thought that, if only I had a partner, someone who could love me and my boys, I'd be all right. That was very far from the truth.

**Don't deceive yourself by thinking that a person can fill that gap inside you. They can't. That space that's in all our hearts – only God can fill it. He is the missing link.**

# 13

# OPEN EYES

My parents knew I was broken and yearning to be loved and they asked me to go to church. I was adamant it wasn't for me anymore. I didn't want to sit in a cold, hard pew. I liked live, loud music, so a church organ and choir weren't what I wanted now. They were all right when I was younger but not these days.

"Oh, no, Pam, it's great!" Mum would say. "You'll love it. It's what you like – drums, guitars, singing. I suppose it is live music."

"What?" I asked in disbelief. I thought she was making it up to get me back there.

But when I did go, I found she was right. So I began to attend church, although only now and then. I was still lost and lonely. I never felt good enough.

And there I was, broken, inadequate, in a church where everyone seemed to be happy and to have it all. I felt I stuck out like a sore thumb. I always cried at the worship songs but I didn't know why. I enjoyed being in the services but I felt bad in myself; unclean somehow – dirty.

What I didn't know at that time was that God was doing something new in me. He was creating a new heart in me.

Before I attended the church, when I was at home I was sometimes vaguely aware of the people singing there. But suddenly, that awareness seemed to increase in a way it hadn't in all the time I'd lived there. Something in my spirit stirred and I began to cry more and more each time I heard the music.

I didn't know then that it was the Holy Spirit moving inside me, bringing me back to Jesus. But a very strange thing happened one evening, not long after I'd begun attending the church.

I'd gone to bed and was woken up a little before midnight. I don't remember what woke me but as I opened my eyes, I saw a huge hand, from the elbow down to the finger, pointing in the direction of my bedroom door. I wasn't afraid. I just stared at it.

My bedroom was opposite the church. I began to pray, asking God what this meant. I thought it should be pointing towards the church, not in the opposite direction.

Then I thought maybe I was seeing things. I rubbed my eyes but the image didn't go away. It was real: a huge hand with a finger pointing towards my bedroom door, the arm dressed in a long, white, draping sleeve.

I got out of bed and watched it as it slowly began to move along between the wall and ceiling towards my bedroom door. I rubbed my eyes again and looked out of the bedroom window towards the church to make sure I wasn't imagining it. I wasn't. This wasn't a figment of my imagination.

Every time I took my eyes off the hand, it stopped moving. Each time I looked at it, it began to drift slowly towards the door again. All this time, I felt very peaceful and I wasn't at all afraid.

I went to church the following morning and told Jen, the vicar's wife, what had happened. She asked if I'd been asking God for some sort of sign, and I had.

My mum laughed when she heard. She said it was a sign to show Sean the door of our marriage, even though we'd already broken up!

I knew my relationship with Sean had come to an end and I knew Jesus was calling me back to Him, but I didn't know exactly why I'd seen this image. Obviously I was very emotional going through the break-up, yet something different was also happening to me and I couldn't control it.

Looking for a way to fill the hole in my heart, I began to date lots of men over the following two years. I had a lot of love to give and wanted the same back, but it never happened in the way that I hoped it would.

During one of these passing relationships, Stanley, a beautiful man of God, approached me after church one Sunday. He became one of my future mentors.

"Pam," he said, "God has put on my heart that you should get out of this relationship you're currently struggling in. It's certainly not good for you and it's dishonouring to God."

Wow! What had made him say that and how did he know? I hadn't told anyone.

Stanley then went on to talk about David and Bathsheba. I didn't know that story then, but I did know God wasn't happy with me and I had to do something about it and quickly.

I'd been dating a man who was unhappy in his open marriage. His wife was fine with our relationship, but I'd begun to feel uncomfortable in it as it wasn't going anywhere. So when Stanley spoke to me like that, I knew I had to get out of it.

It was extraordinary because nobody knew about it. And all of a sudden, I wanted to know more about this amazing God, who Stanley seemed to be so close to.

Unfortunately, the emptiness and the loneliness seemed to grow deeper and deeper as each relationship ended. What was I even looking for? It was something it seemed no one could give me. No one!

I prayed lots of prayers, too many to count, for a sign from God that He was real. That He was with us. I suppose I didn't really know what to ask for – just for Him to prove Himself.

One cold, bleak, windy day, I was busy doing the usual housework when something caught my eye through the front window. In my tiny front garden, there was a blue balloon. The wind was blowing dust and papers around in the street like mini tornados, yet this balloon seemed to stay put.

I carried on with my housework but, every time I looked towards the window, I got a glimpse of this blue balloon.

"Why hasn't it blown away?" I asked myself.

My sons spotted it and shouted, "Mummy, there's a balloon in the garden! Can we have it?"

I told them it would be gone by the time I went outside to retrieve it, but they kept pestering me to go out and get it.

As I was nearly blown away by the wind myself, I picked up the balloon – only to find scripture printed in bold letters on it that was very relevant to my situation at the time.

I don't remember the exact scripture now, but the big, bold word "Jesus" jumped out at me.

And that's when I knew: God was real!

I cried and cried. This was God answering my prayer – giving me the sign I'd asked Him for. Even in the strong winds, He made sure that I had that balloon in my hands.

I gave it to the boys to play with, but they knew not to burst it. I told them God wanted us to have it and I was going to keep it.

I did keep it too. It slowly went down, of course, so then I put it in my Bible as a reminder of God's reality. After a few years, though, the pages began to stick to it and eventually I had to throw it away.

But it was a reminder to me that God was speaking to me in other ways; ways I could never have imagined. The balloon was just one sign of many.

I began to join in with other activities in the church.

I asked questions about Jesus too and started to read my Bible more, even though I didn't understand it much.

I loved making craft things to sell at church fairs to raise funds. I made little plaques with scripture on, and painted glass bowls and vases to sell. It made me so happy to see my stall quickly sell out.

Whilst I was involved in this, I realised that my hands had stopped shaking for the first time since I'd split up from my ex-husband. It had got so bad, I didn't think I'd ever be able to draw or do craftwork like this again.

God had healed me!

So, I began to settle down in my life. I enjoyed discovering God and I wanted to know more of His love and His power. I wanted to learn more about Jesus too.

That's when I started to find out about something else: the enemy and his tactics.

**The battle belongs to the Lord! Jesus conquered death and defeated Satan at the cross. Thank You, Jesus!**

# 14

# DON'T DABBLE WITH THE OCCULT

*"Many people seem to be interested in what the future holds and often look to others for guidance. But God warns us about looking to the occult for advice. Mediums and psychics were outlawed because God was not the source of their information. At best occult practitioners are fakes whose predictions can't be trusted. At worst they are in contact with evil spirits and are thus extremely dangerous. We don't need to look to the occult for information about the future. God has given us the Bible so that we may obtain all the information we need – and the Bible's teaching is trustworthy."* (Leviticus 20: 6 Study Notes, NLT)

*"Satan is behind the occult. Today people are still fascinated by horoscopes, fortune telling, witchcraft and bizarre cults. Often their interest comes from a desire to know and control the future. But Satan is no less dangerous today than he was in Moses' time. In the Bible God tells us all we need to know about what is going to happen. The information Satan offers is likely to be distorted or be completely false. With the trustworthy guidance from the Holy Spirit through the Bible and the church we don't need to turn to occult sources for faulty information."* (Deuteronomy 18:10–13 Study Notes, NLT)

I was now a single mum who had a lot of support from my family, but I still longed to be loved in a relationship. Joe was in infant school and Mick still a baby, and all the while I was now discovering more about this incredible God who never failed to amaze me as I absorbed myself into Him. I couldn't get enough.

A lady had recently moved into a new house in the road opposite to me. She also lived opposite the church. She was new in her faith, a young Christian, and held a housewarming party. But she'd invited a fortune teller too. Many people went to the party because the fortune teller was there, and this lady actually had her fortune read. The fortune teller told her that the police would be coming to her door. A few days later, they did.

The lady's young son was out on his pushbike going round a roundabout when he was hit by a car. It was a hit-and-run. He was in intensive care and his mum was told he wouldn't survive as he had severe brain damage and would never recover.

Due to the accident, one side of his head was deformed and misshapen, and one side of his body was in constant spasm, his arm and leg lashing out.

The church got a prayer chain going. I didn't know what this was so I asked about it.

The prayer chain was a twenty-four-hour commitment broken into fifteen-minute intervals. This meant that someone would pray for fifteen minutes; then another person would be signed up to continue for the next fifteen minutes, and so on. I put my name down on the prayer chain to pray for this young boy's healing.

The chain continued for a few weeks as we believed God would heal the boy and give him back to his broken-hearted mum.

And God did the miraculous.

He healed him completely.

The surgeons and those who looked after him said he was a miracle.

Someone from the church was in regular contact with his mum and spoke to her about the fortune teller. The boy's mum, who'd invited the fortune teller to her housewarming party, thought it was just a bit of fun having her there. She wasn't aware that she'd invited in the wrong kind of spirit. But she also knew our sovereign God had healed her son.

*"For we are God's handiwork, created in Christ Jesus to do good works, which God prepared in advance for us to do."*
*Ephesians 2:10*

It was during my first year of becoming a Christian that I developed a friendship with Ray. And it wasn't long before our relationship developed further. Again, I was trying to find love in the wrong places. What I didn't know was that he was a white witch who was already in a relationship.

Ray was one of the workmen who was contracted to work on the gardens where I lived. Making cups of teas for the men was something all the neighbours did, especially when it was cold and raining. Through that, we built up good friendships with them.

The church needed some rubbish taking away (a lot of rubble and broken slate tiles that had fallen off this once beautiful, old building) and my vicar asked if I'd see if Ray and a few of his work friends could remove it.

Ray was more than happy to offer his services and was very interested in the church. He asked me a lot of questions about God that I didn't have all the answers to, but it made me study my Bible more and look for those answers.

He later told me he was a white witch and had a friend called Nadine, who was a high priestess.

This didn't mean anything to me, but I knew my God knew all things even the devil didn't know.

**Never mess around with powers of darkness.**

> *"...do not let your people practice fortune-telling,*
> *or use sorcery, or interpret omens, or engage in*
> *witchcraft, or cast spells, or function as mediums or*
> *psychics, or call forth the spirits of the dead.*
> *Anyone who does these things is detestable to the*
> LORD.*"*
> *Deuteronomy 18:10–12*

As our friendship deepened, Ray and I discussed his faith and mine. He told me his relationship with Nadine was strong. When they did rituals, he would wear a long gown and sit inside a circle of salt on the floor while she recited scriptures from the Bible. She would then call on other powers. They would see their guardian angels in the forms of lions, tigers etc. The circle of salt was supposed to protect Ray from other forces.

I explained to him that this was not our God, as he thought there were many paths to the same God. I found the verse in the Bible and showed him there was only one God and no other – and only one way to that God:

> *"Jesus [said], 'I am the way and the truth and the*
> *life. No one comes to the Father except through*
> *me."*
> *John 14:6*

Ray and I would have deep debates about the things he thought were the truth of his faith. He told me that Nadine wanted to marry him in the occult. This meant he would marry her but he could still have a relationship with his girlfriend. Only in the occult would he be Nadine's husband.

This didn't make any sense to me whatsoever.

Ray told me the high priestess would also take his measure, which meant he would have his measurements taken so that, when he died, he'd be buried through the occult and not have an ordinary funeral in a church.

Ray always said it would be great to have me in the occult due to the experiences I'd had in life in my younger years. He said I was very susceptible to things. I knew what he meant as he said I could use my gifts to help others. I told him I would only be used by God, and certainly not by anything like the evil forces that were using him. He didn't believe that evil forces *were* using him as he thought he was a good man.

Discussion after discussion, Bible verse after Bible verse, I kept talking to him and showing him scriptures, until things started to slowly sink in.

**White witches, pagans, black witches, witchcraft – the occult is altogether evil, although white witches say they use their powers to help others whereas black magic is used for self-gain. Do not be deceived by this lie. White witches call on powers that are not of Jesus. Whether white or black, both call on demonic influences. These powers are not from our God, even though practitioners may quote scripture. Witches play with dark forces in the unseen world. Don't be drawn in by them.**

**Another thing that witches and pagans say is that you come to them – they don't go looking for you. To draw you in, they say you found them because you have an interest in them. Don't fall for it!**

**John 14 verse 6 says that Jesus is the ONLY way, the ONLY truth and the ONLY life.**

I was woken up one night by a very strange noise outside my home. It woke my sons too. It was windy and it sounded like the high-pitched whirring of a milk float coming from the roof. I looked up as I told my young sons to get in my bed and not to be afraid. I couldn't see anything unusual. But we could all hear this strange, loud sound.

I prayed for God's protection on our home and got back into bed too.

A couple of days later, Ray called in and I told him what had happened. He replied that he'd called to see me that night on his way home from Nadine's, but there were no lights on in my house so he left as he thought I'd gone to bed.

He later told me that Nadine had been playing about with powers and had sent them to him as a gift. This was the sound we'd heard – the wind, the weird whirring noise that sounded like a milk float.

When Ray next saw Nadine and told her that I'd heard the noises, she was angry. She was also angry that I hadn't been afraid, so she hexed me. That meant she put a curse on me.

Ray went on to say, "I'm realising your God must be much stronger than ours. Nadine has hexed you many times and nothing has touched you. I think she's jealous of what you have."

I asked what he meant by "what I have".

He said, "Your power."

I explained to him, "I don't have any power! It's the power of God, of the Holy Spirit who lives in me. It's Jesus who's alive in me, nothing else!"

Ray told me how he was discovering more about my God through our conversations, and how he was in bed one night when he was suddenly aware he couldn't move. He felt a heavy weight crushing his chest. He tried and tried to move and to shout, but he discovered he couldn't even speak, so he prayed the Lord's prayer. Immediately, whatever it was released him. He said he was gasping for breath as he was so afraid. He didn't know what it was. He'd never experienced anything like that before.

I told him he couldn't walk two paths: there is only one God and our God is stronger. It was our God who'd rescued him from that experience.

Ray believed what I told him and began to follow the Christian path – although at that point he hadn't asked Jesus into his life.

One evening, Ray loaned me a book. I couldn't believe the contents. It was as though I was reading about my own relationship with him.

As I continued reading, however, I felt a tight band begin to form around my head. The story was beginning to unfold, but I knew I didn't want to read anymore.

When I told my mum, she told me to burn the book or bin it. I thought at the time that was a bit harsh as it wasn't mine, so I put it in a carrier bag, tied it up and hung it on the fence in my back garden in the pouring rain until Ray collected it.

*"A number who had practiced sorcery brought
their scrolls together and burned them publicly.
When they calculated the value of the scrolls, the
total came to fifty thousand drachmas."*
*Acts 19:19*

During my friendship with Ray, I prayed continually. He was in darkness, being deceived, and I prayed for God's armour of protection upon us.

I had many dark experiences during this time. Although we were very close friends, Ray's partner wanted him to be married to Nadine in the occult. He called it "the craft". His partner liked Nadine too and was friends with both her and me.

However, being friends with darkness invites darkness into your home. And darkness and light can't walk together, as I soon discovered. During my first year of finding Jesus, my past would come back to haunt me.

Ray was supposed to come to see me one evening but he didn't turn up, which just wasn't like him. Suddenly there was a knock at my front door. I was hesitant to answer it as I had a strong feeling that I shouldn't. However, in the end I did, to find someone I'd had a brief fling with about twelve months earlier standing on my doorstep.

Before I could speak, this man wedged his foot in the door and pushed himself in. He was very big, and he filled the height and width of the door frame.

"Hello," he said. "I bet you didn't expect to see me again, did you? I've missed you." Then he grabbed my head in his hands and forced a kiss on me. I couldn't breathe, he was so strong.

Eventually, he let me go and told me to sit down next to him. He asked what I'd been doing and I told him about my faith and new walk with Jesus. But I wasn't comfortable. I didn't want him in my home. He blocked me from answering the phone when I tried to get up so I knew this could be a dangerous situation if I wasn't wise, and my sons were in bed.

When he told me he was going to the shop to buy wine, I saw my chance to lock him out.

"Oh, Jesus, please help me," I remember praying silently.

Suddenly, the man grabbed my neck. He squeezed it and sneered, "Let's see if your God can save you now..."

I felt lightheaded and faint when he let go of me, but I acted calmly.

As he left, immediately I locked the door behind him and went to bed. I broke down crying in fear and shock, but then I felt an inner peace rise up inside me like I'd never experienced before. I knew I was safe.

I never saw that man again. I knew God was there protecting me.

*"The eyes of the* LORD *are on the righteous, and his ears are attentive to their cry"*
*Psalm 34:15*

Many weird things began to happen in my home through my involvement with Ray. On a few occasions, I'd be cleaning up when I'd hear whispering in the lounge. I'd turn to look in but the whispers would stop. These voices and whispers continued on and off for many months. There were times I thought they'd gone for good, but they'd return. My phone would ring too, but when I picked it up, there'd be nobody there. I thought it was my ex-husband playing tricks as this is what he used to do. So I'd disconnect the phone completely from the wall – only to find it would begin ringing again in my hand.

I started to feel a heavy presence in my home, and Mick would cry when I carried him up to bed or brought him down the stairs. He would point to the top of the stairs and scream as though he could see something that scared him.

I also had bad dreams and I wouldn't always remember them. One dream I had was that I was in a very large mansion with a beautiful view outside. Through some huge patio doors, there was a swimming pool. It was beautiful. There seemed to be a party going on inside where I was a guest, and there were lots of very attractive men and women all dressed up in suits. One man asked me if I'd like to live there. I smiled and said, "It's lovely." He told me it could all be mine if I followed him.

As he said that, I began to feel pain in my back and kidney area. The man was smiling, telling me it was all mine if I'd just say yes. The pain in my back grew worse and I fell to the floor on my knees.

"JESUS!" I shouted.

As I did so, I looked up, and I saw that every person had turned into dark shadows and they disappeared out of the patio doors.

Then I woke up. But I had a dull ache in my back where I'd had the pain in my dream. This pain went immediately as soon as I prayed.

Another night I was dreaming and was woken by the Holy Spirit as I was rebuking some dark shape that crept up beside me in my bed. The shape was like a dim mist unfolding itself as it came in through my window. Again, my God who is sovereign over all, protected me, waking me up as I rebuked it in my sleep.

When I woke the following morning, I vomited violently. I was supposed to help out at the church that day but couldn't make it as I didn't feel too good after my experience in the night.

I rang Jen, my vicar's wife, to ask her if we could have a chat, and I told her about everything that had happened since my relationship with Ray. She was amazed and said not everyone had these kinds of experiences. She also told me that every time Ray came into my home, I must command any unclean spirit that came in with him to leave. I was to do the same thing when Ray left.

Jen told me that not all Christians believe in the devil but that I was having experiences of both the Holy Spirit's power and also of the demonic side of things.

Ray loved talking about our experiences of God's holy power and his faith, as he was discovering more and more about Jesus. Sadly, though, this still didn't seem to be enough for him.

One evening, he'd been to visit Nadine because he hadn't seen her for a while and he didn't visit her as much as he used to. When he went home, during the night, he had another spiritual attack. He was suffocating in his sleep.

He woke and, as in a previous experience, he couldn't move. He felt paralysed. He tried to shout to his partner who was sound asleep beside him but the crushing on his chest was too much. He began to pray the Lord's prayer, but nothing happened. He tried again but this entity just wouldn't get off him. So he prayed his old pagan prayer, and that's when he said it left him. He was more terrified this time than with the first attack.

Again, I told him that only Jesus could save him as He was the only one who could release him from this darkness. Ray was walking two paths, which was dangerous.

Sadly, there was always that pull for him – the pull back to the occult.

*"When people reject Jesus and His authority, they put themselves on the side of the demons and are heading in the same direction. Every person must ask, 'Will I choose authority and self-will leading to destruction, or will I choose Christ's loving leadership over my life, giving me forgiveness, healing from sin, cleansing and true freedom?' The answer has eternal implications."* (Mark 5:1–2, Study Notes NLT)

My nephew was getting christened and Ray and his partner were invited. He didn't sit with us. Nadine had told him he must sit on a different side of the Christian church as this was the only place where witches could sit in a church building. It was something else to do with the dark side of their belief that he was still naive to.

Suddenly, I saw him get up and run out.

I didn't see him for a few days after that. When I did see him again, he told me he felt very angry with me, something he'd never felt before. But the reason he'd left the church so suddenly was because he felt sick. When he got outside, he'd actually vomited.

I know my Father God gave His only Son Jesus to die for us and, in rising from the dead, He put all these things under His feet. By faith and trust and belief in this, He can and will set us free. But we can't walk both paths. The demons will always fight against us. It's their job to do so.

However, the battle is already won. Jesus has defeated them. He is stronger than Satan, and we have Jesus living in us when we make Him Lord and Saviour over our lives.

Earlier on in my friendship with Ray, I would visit his home and see the pagan masks Nadine had made of Medusa and others. He'd hung them on the walls.

His partner also liked them. They were very ugly and were made from leaves and branches – "Things of nature," Ray told me. This was the pagan belief.

But somehow, I always felt as if I was being watched when I stayed there. Some weekends, when my sons stayed over at their dad's, I'd sleep on the couch in Ray's house and I'd feel very strange. I was aware there was a presence but I always prayed God's protection over myself.

Ray told me one day when I mentioned the feeling of being watched that Nadine breathed life into her masks. I knew this was demonic and I never stayed there again.

It was when I suddenly woke up spiritually that I realised I couldn't do much more to help Ray. I was feeling in my spirit that I had to move on. I was also afraid that I was becoming attached to him, but I knew this was wrong and it could never work.

Ray was going back to see Nadine occasionally, not as much as he did before but the connection was still there. We discussed our beliefs again. He knew Jesus was stronger than his pagan belief but he admitted that it was always going to draw him back.

Eventually, I had to tell him our relationship was only friendship and that I had to move on as light and darkness couldn't work or walk together. He struggled with this and I suppose I did too as I really wanted to see him saved. And I really liked him.

As Ray went to leave my house and we gave each other a hug, without warning I was thrown off him to the other side of my kitchen. I didn't know what had happened. We always gave one another hugs, but this was a powerful force. I felt sick, lethargic, weak and very tired. I could hardly speak.

Ray felt guilty. He couldn't apologise enough. He gave me his ring, which he never took off. It was a gold ring with a star inside a circle.

He told me there were two ways to wear it. One was with the point of the star facing down. That way it looked like the devil's head and that's how people who are into black magic wear it. The other way was like the star of David, which was how he wore it. That was how they distinguished one another.

The ring would protect me, he told me, and he slipped it onto my finger as I began to drift off to sleep on the couch.

I didn't want the ring and tried to pull it off my finger. I told him I didn't need that kind of protection. Jesus was my protector and had always protected me from all this.

I prayed over the ring as I drifted in and out of sleep. Although I knew there was no power in objects, I was aware that things can attach themselves to objects. That was why I prayed over it.

The next day, I felt so much better, as I knew my Saviour Jesus was watching over me.

The whispering and phone ringing still went on, and the feeling at the top of the stairs as if something was there that hadn't left.

I spoke to my home group leader who said that I should think about asking my vicar to come in and cleanse and bless my home now that Ray wasn't visiting anymore.

Sue came with other elders of the church to do this. She also said she had felt some kind of unclean presence at the top of the stairs.

Both my sons and I had prayers and communion in our home after the vicar and elders had been through it, praying and cleansing it in Jesus' holy name. All the demonic influences and forces were wiped away, and there were no further incidents after this.

# 15

# BE CAREFUL WHAT YOU ASK
# GOD FOR IN PRAYER

A few years after my divorce, I was settling down. I attended church on a regular basis and was involved in a little home group. God was revealing so much to me about Himself and I loved the relationship I had with Him. I was discovering more and more about Jesus and how real He is. I'd come to realise that Jesus is for now – not just for when we die and go to heaven.

I discovered a lot about relationships too; all the messy things I could have avoided if only I'd been walking in step with God.

But although I was learning, I was still a baby in my faith and had much more to discover. And I was aware of that old, familiar feeling sneaking back: I didn't have a partner and it bothered me.

I knew I had a lot to give and I had a lot of love in me. My dad always said I wore my heart on my sleeve like my mum. Sadly, this also meant that I could easily be taken advantage of.

I didn't go out on the town as much as I used to and I'd previously asked God to help me reduce my intake of alcohol when I did go out, as I didn't want to slip back into my old ways of getting drunk. I'd also been asking God to give me a sign if He wanted me to give up drinking alcohol completely.

The signs came and I didn't immediately recognise them.

I'd suffered throughout my life since a young teenager with period problems, which eventually led to me having a hysterectomy at thirty-three years old. One of the signs came with the medication I had to take. A warning on the packaging read: "AVOID ALCOHOL".

It was when I was on a night out in Bootle that I saw one of the local lads, John. He was very quiet and didn't bother much with anyone when he was young. He had long hair and was passionate about motorbikes, which I still liked too.

Because of the bad choices I'd made in past relationships, I'd been praying for someone to come into my life, and John seemed to fit.

John knew I was a Christian. He accepted me as I was and even came to church and church events with me on some occasions. He believed in Jesus but didn't want to take it any further.

Things went well for the first twelve months of our relationship. But then he was involved in a car accident. He was a passenger and his friend was driving. John suffered with whiplash and was off work for a long time and soon he lost his job. He smoked pot and so did his friends, who he started to hang out with more frequently. This eventually caused a huge rift in our relationship.

My old insecurities came back with a vengeance. John never showed up when he said he would and became very unreliable and paranoid. I wanted him to change as I was convinced he was the man for me. But God had other plans.

This in itself took a toll on us. I loved Jesus and I wanted John to love Him as I did. To know Him as I did. I thought God would change him as He was changing me.

It was around this time that I was taken into hospital to have the hysterectomy due to my ongoing gynaecological problems. I'd also been diagnosed with endometriosis so was kept in for five days.

After the hysterectomy, I'd never felt so ill. I was in a lot of pain and couldn't understand why I wasn't feeling any better.

While I was in hospital, I found myself discussing Jesus with other patients on the ward and praying for them. They thanked me for my prayers and for sharing my faith.

I remember being in the ladies' toilet in so much pain and thinking about the pain Jesus went through for me. I talked to Him and said, "I know You made me, Lord, and You know my body better than I do – better than any surgeon does – and I pray myself into Your caring hands. Please take this terrible pain away. I don't know what it is."

I sat there, unable to cry because the pain was even worse than childbirth. Many of the other ladies on my ward who'd had the same operation were up and walking about after a few days.

Before I could be discharged, I was asked if there would be anyone at home to look after me on my first night. The staff at the hospital knew I had two young sons and my parents were looking after them.

John had said he would stay with me that night, so I was able to go home even though I wasn't walking unaided as I couldn't stand up on my own.

But as soon as I got back from hospital, John left me and told me he'd be back to cook my tea at five o'clock. My mum was going to send some food down to me with my brother, but I thanked her and declined it as John had said he was coming back. My parents weren't happy about the situation. They knew how unwell I was.

Five o'clock came and went, and there was no sign of John. I couldn't stand up so I couldn't get anything to eat for myself.

When my friend came round and let herself in, she rang my mum straight away. Mum came immediately and left my sons with my dad. It was early evening and she was furious that I was still on my own. She told me I should get out of the relationship with John as he was no good for me – especially leaving me in this situation.

I just didn't want to hear it. I kept telling myself he wasn't that bad and my parents didn't know him. But they could see things more clearly than I could. And although I made every excuse to protect him, deep down in my heart I knew they were right.

The doctor came out to see me and said I needed to go straight back to hospital. He said I should never have been discharged in the state I was in. He wanted to phone for an ambulance but my brother had just arrived and he said he'd take me.

On arrival at the hospital, I was taken for a scan. It turned out that I had a massive blood clot but, because I'd only just had major surgery, the surgeon didn't want to operate on me so soon afterwards. Instead, I was put on a high-dose antibiotic drip, which fortunately seemed to clear whatever the problem was. But I was kept in hospital for seventeen days.

This was a tough time as I was on morphine for my pain. My parents and brothers brought my sons in to see me. I was unconscious most of the time and very ill. But I praise God, who brought me through it all.

John visited too. He knew my parents weren't happy with him. He asked why I hadn't rung him the night I was taken into hospital and he blamed me. He had a good way of turning things back on me when he wanted to. Things were starting to sound all too familiar; unpleasant echoes of my relationship with Sean.

On one of John's visits, I became very distressed. He was angry with me because my family weren't happy with him. I remember him walking out on me, shouting and then mumbling things as he left, whilst I tried to follow him, pleading with him to come back.

As my good health began to return, another relationship was falling apart.

My brother Richard had just got engaged and had bought his fiancée a beautiful engagement ring. I was happy for him but, inside, I still craved to be loved the way he seemed to love his fiancée. I knew my brother had a good job and was doing well for himself, so he was in a position to get married and do it all properly. I just longed for someone to love me enough too. The familiar feelings of inadequacy rose up inside me again, and I thought and believed I was second best.

When I told John of my brother's engagement, he was happy for him and said we could get engaged too if that's what I wanted. But a voice inside me cried out: "DON'T!" After all, I already felt second best in the relationship so what would being engaged mean? Nothing.

I could see how our relationship had become heavier in the time we'd been together. The oppression had set in as John became more paranoid. He'd got involved with another crowd and ended up taking a drug called speed along with the pot, and I don't know if other drugs were being used too. I'd watched his personality change and seen him become verbally abusive.

I was so upset one day that I went to visit the friends who were supplying him with drugs and spoke to one of the wives. John went mad when I told him what I'd done. He said I didn't know what I was doing and it was dangerous for me to go there. I hadn't given a second thought to the possible consequences of my visit.

Eventually, John did stop using the harder drugs, but he continued to smoke pot.

I began to struggle with forgiveness and my past, as John constantly brought this up. When I talked to Sue, our Bible study leader, she told me, "It's up to you. You can believe what man says or you can believe what God says about sins being forgiven."

I told John that his problems with unforgiveness were his, not mine to carry anymore. God had forgiven me and I wasn't going to put up with his abuse of my faith. He tried to turn the Word of God against me and use it to hurt me, but I had to trust what I believed; what I knew God was saying to me in His Word.

So, here I was, in another relationship that was not where God wanted me to be. And I'd been in it for six years. It was abusive and eventually became violent as John grew more paranoid. He pushed and pushed me mentally, asking over and over, "How can God forgive you? Don't you feel any guilt?"

> *"No longer will they call you Deserted... But you will be called Hephzibah... for the* LORD *will take delight in you"*
> *Isaiah 62:4.*

> *"He has sent me to... comfort all who mourn... to bestow on them a crown of beauty instead of ashes, the oil of joy instead of mourning, and a garment of praise instead of a spirit of despair. They will be called oaks of righteousness, a planting of the* LORD *for the display of His splendour."*
> *Isaiah 61:1–3*

God laid firmly on my heart that this relationship wasn't good and it wasn't right to remain in it. I thought I really loved John but, the more he hung out with his friends, the more he changed. It was smoking pot that seemed to give him the most pleasure in life – not being with me.

What I didn't realise at the time was that I was also changing. God was changing me. The more I sought after His heart and the more I read my Bible, the more I began to notice and see things differently. It was as if the mysteries of God's Word were waking me up. I know now that the Bible is the Living Word and this Living Word was coming *alive* in me. I was seeing things in a new light.

Recently out of hospital and slowly on the road to recovery, I remember sitting on the couch, listening to worship music and wrapping up presents. I'd sent a present to a close friend at the time and it had been returned to me unopened as she'd fallen out with me. I was very upset and became tearful. But I prayed that God would forgive her, and that He'd forgive me too in any areas where I'd hurt her.

Suddenly, as I was singing along to the worship, out of my mouth came this strange sound. Through tears of joy I carried on singing and singing – I didn't want to stop!

This continued for a long time and eventually I rang my friend Sue to tell her. We were both full of joy. We knew what this was. Sue also knew I had been eagerly seeking this gift: the gift of speaking in tongues.

Sue and Alan, who were leaders in the church, had prayed over me in the past for the gift of tongues, and now I'd received it just at the right time – as I was worshipping God in my own sadness over the fallout with my friend.

*"All of them were filled with the Holy Spirit and began to speak in other tongues as the Spirit enabled them."*
*Acts 2:4*

*"When Paul placed his hands on them, the Holy Spirit came on them, and they spoke in tongues and prophesied."*
*Acts 19:6*

The Word of God is powerful and alive and can transform our mind-set when we seek Him with all our hearts. He is the only one who can renew, transform and change our lives. We can't do this in our own strength.

I'd been chasing a relationship that was no good for me or for my boys. John did have some good points, but he wasn't what I needed in a relationship and he certainly wasn't what God had in mind for me.

I was angry with myself that I'd put my trust in someone who'd constantly let us down. The truth was, God wanted me to put my trust in Him completely and not in man.

God wanted all of me – not a piece of me.

John now lived on his own in the family home as his father had passed away. One evening, I turned up on his doorstep and he wasn't there. He'd gone out and left his friends in the house. For some reason, when his friends saw me standing there, they started laughing.

Now, these friends of John's thought I was the quiet one; the one who never said a word. The quiet Christian girl who'd put up with anything. They sniggered as they lied to me about his whereabouts.

Eventually, I snapped. I marched in and upstairs to destroy the photographs he had of the last six years of our relationship.

When John got back, he lied to me when I asked where he'd been and who he'd been with. Through my tears and frustration, I knew I couldn't just walk away. Six years of pain and anger rose up within me. This time, I was the violent one. I lashed out at him with my car keys in my hand. I was shaking, shouting and crying: "Stop lying to me! Tell me the truth!"

Eventually he did. He'd been out with a woman to buy pot.

He'd promised me he wouldn't let me down as he was supposed to be coming with me to take my son Joe to Alder Hey hospital for his check-up.

Memories flooded my head of how he'd hurt me in the past – mentally as well as physically when he didn't realise what he was doing because of the drug abuse that made him paranoid.

And now, here I was, hurting him. Who was this horrid beast rising up inside me? I didn't recognise myself. What else was I capable of doing?

I arrived at my parents' house, horrified at what I'd done. My dad didn't seem angry when I told him I'd attacked John. He seemed to understand what my life with him had been like. He just told me to pull myself together and move on.

I still felt disgusted with myself when I saw my friends from church, Stanley and Jean. They didn't look surprised when I gave them the details. I told them again, but still there was no sign of disgust.

Stanley told me there was only one way if I wanted to move on from this. If I really wanted God to take my love for John away, God would do so but there was a price to pay.

Stanley pondered and thought carefully about the words he was about to say to me: "You would have to mean it and not go back into the relationship," he said. "God could fill your heart with a love for John in a way that God would want you to love him. But not with a relationship type of love."

Yes, yes, I really wanted this. I was tired of making all the same mistakes, searching over and over again for love in the wrong relationships. I was tired of having my heart broken. I didn't want to become violent or hurt anyone just because they had hurt me. I didn't like the person I'd become on that day. That wasn't me. I wanted to be free from all my hurt and to begin to live a life that was pleasing to God. A life that He'd tried to give me while I was still trying to walk two paths – attempting to bring John into that same life that God had given me.

But I couldn't change John. John had made his own choices. He enjoyed getting stoned with his friends as opposed to walking with God.

"Yes, please, Stanley!" I cried, as Jean toddled off into the kitchen to make drinks. We talked more and both Stanley and Jean prayed for me.

It was the first beautiful moment that I can remember.

I saw a gold heart in the sky. There was a large gold hoop through the heart, and flames in the sky reaching down to my hands as they were lifted in praise.

I didn't realise that, as I was sitting on the couch, I had passed out in the Spirit.

*"Create in me a pure heart, O God, and renew a steadfast spirit within me."*
*Psalm 51:10*

I had heard of things like this happening and had seen it, but it didn't trouble me or concern me when it happened to me.

When I eventually came round, Stanley told me to go home to bed and let God minister to and restore me. I said, "I'll read my Bible."

"No," they both said at the same time. "Just go to sleep."

I had the most beautiful night's sleep that I could remember. I woke feeling so refreshed, so different. Things had been broken off me, I knew they had. I felt happy.

I saw John a few days later but I didn't have the feelings that I used to have for him. I loved him like a friend. It was different. Something had changed in me. "Did I ever love him?" I asked myself.

After a few more weeks, I saw him with the same woman who'd taken him to buy his drugs. I cried a little, but nothing like I would have done only a short while before.

I praised and thanked God that He'd given me a new heart and a new, different love for John; that I now loved him as God wanted me to.

My tears stopped immediately when I prayed. I smiled and looked heavenwards. There was one place I had to keep my eyes fixed as well as on my children – Jesus.

God had healed and restored me.

This was the wonderful God I was falling back in love with. Had I ever stopped loving Him? No. I had just tried to find the same joy and happiness in man, when my relationship with God is irreplaceable.

# 16

# TRANSFORMING

I was a new person. I saw John a few times and talked to him on the street, but I had a fresh joy in my heart.

I felt proud to be this new person that God loved. He'd always loved me – not just because I had changed, but because He wanted to protect me from all the hurt I'd gone through. I felt special because He was talking to me and transforming me; because He'd shown me that lovely picture of the gold heart when His Holy Spirit had come upon me.

Stanley asked me what I thought it meant. I just felt it was God's unfailing, never-ending love. Stanley told me the flames were the Holy Spirit. As for my hands raised up in praise, well, that was something I'd never done and couldn't see myself doing. At least, that's what I thought!

When my sons stayed with their dad at weekends, I would look forward to spending time with my parents. I loved sharing with them about my new relationship with Jesus.

The nights I didn't go to my parents, I went to see Stanley and Jean. Stan would tell me lots of stories about prisoners' lives that had been touched by God. Stanley was a Gideon who took Bibles into prisons and did pastoral visits. I asked him to take me with him but he smiled and said, "You wouldn't like it there."

He did eventually take me a couple of times on prison visits with him, when I'd matured in my faith. Little did I know that this was preparing me for future visits to people I'd be looking after who were homeless.

My nights out now consisted of visiting Stanley and Jean or my parents, instead of going to nightclubs and pubs. During the daytime after school, I always took my sons up to my parents' home, where we had lots of lovely times.

People who'd known me for years were beginning to see changes in me. On one occasion, one friend commented, "You look like you're in another world, Pam. You're either singing or you look as if you're praying."

My initial reaction was to feel embarrassed and to worry about what I looked like. However, then I received a prompt from God in a soft whisper: "Why are you embarrassed about me? Why don't you tell him what I've done for you?"

So I told my friend about my faith and invited him to come to church. He started to go with me, became a Christian and got confirmed.

> *"I tell you, whoever publicly acknowledges me*
> *before others, the Son of Man will also*
> *acknowledge before the angels of God. But*
> *whoever disowns me before others will be*
> *disowned before the angels of God."*
> *Luke 12:8–9*

Around this time, I had a vision. I can't remember exactly how it transpired except that, during my prayer time, I saw myself in what looked like a derelict house or other building, where the walls seemed to be cracked and the doors were hanging off. It appeared to be a dark place but I had to help people there. They didn't have much and seemed to be homeless.

I prayed about this and spoke with my home group leader.

It was many months later that one of my older friends, Marg, became involved with a project for homeless people and asked me to pray about getting involved too. Joe and Mick were still very young, and I'd heard that a lot of the homeless were involved with drugs and alcohol. Sadly, my defences came up. I was not in any way going to be involved in anything like this. It was too close to things that I'd gone through in my own life.

"Don't worry, Pam," Marg said. "If this is something God wants you involved with in the future, He'll bring it back to you."

"What?" I shook my head. "Drug and alcohol issues? No, thank you. I've seen enough to last me a lifetime."

It soon became apparent that the people Marg worked with had drug and alcohol issues because they were homeless.

Unfortunately, I didn't understand it all at the time and thought nothing more about getting involved. It would be years before I'd finally listen to God, who kept steering me in this direction.

I found that, the closer my relationship with God became, the more difficulties life would throw my way. I began to feel I was in a never-ending spiritual battle, one that would try to crush and break me.

There was a Christian event on in the park where I saw healings and worship like I'd never experienced before. The speaker invited people up for prayer and I asked for prayers for my dad's healing from obstructive airways disease. I was given a piece of cloth that the speaker had anointed with oil. He told me to put it on my dad's head and pray for him.

Within an hour of arriving home, I received a call from the school to say that Joe had hurt his foot in P.E. and needed hospital treatment. An x-ray revealed that his foot was fractured.

Bible study took place in my home a lot of the time, which I really looked forward to, but often the school would ring me regarding Joe. It was always

Joe – something had happened to him or he'd had an accident. It was as if something was trying to prevent me from focusing on God so that I focused instead on the problems.

In between this happening, I was having ongoing issues with my ex-husband. For a short time he'd be nice, then, all of a sudden, he'd turn nasty on me. I could never understand why as he had regular access to the boys. But he continued with his pranks of ringing me up and staying silent, or winding me up on the phone to break my peace.

Things came to a head when I discovered that, during one of Sean's access times, he was out with our boys in a taxi. His friend was with him – carrying a gun. Not only that, but the taxi they were in was being followed by a gang who were out to get Sean's friend. To make matters worse, Sean wanted this friend to be my son's godfather.

Because of the ongoing battles with Sean, I had to take him back to court to organise proper access. If I didn't allow access when he wanted it, he would intimidate both me and my family. We were all under attack from him. The abusive phone calls to my parents' home made it impossible to have any peace there. And if it wasn't him, it was his sister, who revelled in making trouble and intimidating us.

It didn't stop me from visiting my family, but a lot of the conversation would come back to the same old thing: Sean and what he was up to. There were occasions when I had to ring the police, or he would ring them because the boys weren't ready on time or because I'd stopped access when I felt they were in danger.

The intimidation and threats were constant while I waited for the court date to arrive. It was a horrible time.

Although I hated what was happening, I'd forgiven my ex-husband on many occasions over and over again, but each time I forgave him, I was subject to another attack of verbal abuse. Each attack seemed to be worse than the one before, and I didn't know how much longer I could take it all, physically, mentally, as well as spiritually.

Thankfully, home group was a safe place of rest and fun. I seemed to switch off when I was there and looked forward to hearing what God wanted to say to us.

A very strange incident happened one time, just before my friend Jackie was due to lead our home group, and she was preparing her notes. She'd been cleaning in her home and had forgotten that she'd left a bowl of water at the top of the stairs. As she sat down to prepare her home group study, suddenly, the bowl was tipped over and the water spilled out over the open plan staircase.

Jackie had previously said a few times that she felt there was something in her home. She'd had experiences of things going missing or being moved, and a feeling of being watched. Her husband was a Christian but had backslid, and they both read horror books by authors such as Stephen King.

I felt this was something Jackie had to get rid of and I told her this. She agreed and began to have a clear out. I went round too, to help and to pray, as she'd asked me if I would.

As we were clearing out, we prayed for God's guidance, listened to worship music and sang along to it. And we prayed as the Holy Spirit led us.

It was at the top of the stairs that I felt a presence; something that was unwelcoming.

I continued to pray, moving down to the middle of the stairs where the Holy Spirit was leading me. I could feel the hairs on my neck stand up and my back felt this strong presence.

Jackie suddenly shouted: "Pam! It's there behind you – look!"

I just told her to carry on praying. We were praying in tongues and she prayed even louder.

Then, in Jesus' name, I commanded this thing out and I asked Jackie to do the same.

Jackie's dog was sitting on the floor, looking up to us. She seemed to follow this thing down the stairs with her eyes.

I felt it move past me and Jackie said, "It's gone through the front door."

We prayed in every room of her home, cleansing each one of any unclean spirit and inviting Jesus back in. And we invited the Holy Spirit to dwell amongst those who lived there.

We did feel a difference in the atmosphere and, after that, no more strange events happened.

Our God is all-powerful and, as Christians, we have the authority to rebuke and cast out demons. That's what Jesus said:

*"And these signs will accompany those who believe: in my name they will drive out demons"*
*Mark 16:17.*

God was taking me to another level. He tells us to use the authority He has given to us as believers and that's what I was beginning to do.

As I looked back over my life, it was exciting to see how God had rescued me from all sorts of darkness, physically, spiritually and mentally, and now, here I was, casting out evil in Jesus' name.

Don't get me wrong, it wasn't fun. But God did not give us a spirit of fear or intimidation, but one of power, love and of sound mind. It is only in His Word that we find these things. They are useful weapons God has given us for life in general and to fight against the enemy, Satan.

*"For our struggle is not against flesh and blood, but against the rulers, against the authorities, against the powers of this dark world and against the spiritual forces of evil in the heavenly realms. Therefore put on the full armour of God, so that*

*when the day of evil comes, you may be able to
stand your ground, and after you have done
everything, to stand. Stand firm then, with the belt
of truth buckled round your waist, with the
breastplate of righteousness in place, and with
your feet fitted with the readiness that comes from
the gospel of peace. In addition to all this, take up
the shield of faith, with which you can extinguish
all the flaming arrows of the evil one. Take the
helmet of salvation and the sword of the Spirit,
which is the word of God. And pray in the Spirit on
all occasions with all kinds of prayers and requests.
With this in mind, be alert and always keep on
praying for all the Lord's people."*
*Ephesians 6:12-18*

Above all, we must always remember that Jesus loves us. He has already won the battle and has given us spiritual weapons but they are not to be used like a magic wand. The full armour of God is there for us to put on so that we'll be able to resist the enemy.

Little do we realise, as we go through life that these things are around us every day. There are demons and unseen forces constantly at war in the heavenly realms. That doesn't mean just in heaven but here on this earth and in the air around us; things that our eyes don't see. I only began to realise this more as my journey went on.

From the age of three, Mick would wake up during the night, screaming from pains in his legs. This continued throughout his infant years. The doctor said they were growing pains and to give him Calpol to settle him. As I was learning more through Bible study home group, I started to place my hands on his legs and pray for the pain to go away. Mick always settled down and went back to sleep after prayer.

One night when he woke up, crying in pain, I was in a deep sleep and so tired I told him I would give him some Calpol.

"No, Mummy!" he cried, and grabbed my hands, placing them on his little legs. "Prayers, no Calpol, prayers!"

Wow! Well, that certainly moved me. My baby son was asking me to pray for him, not give him medicine.

I did pray and, again, he went off to sleep and settled for the rest of the night. I couldn't wait to tell my family and friends about this.


I can recall my own mixed emotions as I was slowly growing in my Christian faith. There were times when I'd be with some of my friends who cursed and swore. Although I didn't swear generally, if I became frustrated or upset, I'd become so wound up that I'd swear then.

I'd cry in anger at how this horrible venom could pour from my lips. Then, not long after that, I'd be speaking about Jesus. The two didn't tie up. They just didn't go together.

I remember feeling horrible inside myself, so I prayed to God, "Lord, every time I go to swear or speak out in anger, I pray that You will take my voice away, or that I'll lose it until I stop behaving in this way. Put a sock in my mouth or something to stop me."

I'm not saying this is something you should pray but it was what I did at the time.

I forgot the prayer I'd prayed, but my voice would just disappear sometimes. I never had a sore throat and I wasn't unwell. I'd just lose my voice.

It was when someone pointed out that this seemed to happen when I was in very stressful circumstances, that I recognised it. Then I remembered what I'd asked God for in my prayer time!

*"...but no human being can tame the tongue. It is a restless evil, full of deadly poison. With the tongue we praise our Lord and Father, and with it we curse human beings, who have been made in God's likeness."*
*James 3:8–9*

This was certainly God speaking to me. I began to read in James what this was all about and I knew the Holy Spirit was changing me.

I needed to be very careful what came from my mouth.

# 17

# GETTING INVOLVED

Our church was very good at reaching out to the community and had a number of groups running. I found myself involved in a single parent group that Jen ran. She told me God was using me in many ways but I certainly didn't expect to be used in the following way!

One Christmas time, the designated Father Christmas didn't turn up as he was ill, so I was nominated to stand in. Off to the ladies' bathroom I went to get changed into the Father Christmas outfit. I put on the deepest voice I could as the various children sat on my knee.

My son Mick was one of my visitors. He stared at me the whole time as he sat there and eventually asked, "Are you my mummy?"

"Oh, no!" I replied quickly, trying to make my voice even deeper. "Your mummy has gone to the shops!"

Every so often, the vision of the derelict building and me helping people – homeless people – would appear in my thoughts or during my prayer time. I didn't understand what it was about.

I mentioned it to friends and family. They all told me the same thing each time: if God wanted me to be involved, it would manifest in God's timing and not mine. I was also reminded that my children were still only young and they needed me around to bring them up.

"But I don't want to be involved with people who have drug and alcohol issues," I moaned. "I've been through it all before. Anyway, what can I offer them?"

"Pam, you'll be surprised how God can use you," my friends and parents all told me. "You've been through it so God will use you to help other people going through similar troubles."

I listened, but I still couldn't understand why I kept getting this vision.

As well as being our Bible study leader, Sue was also a good friend. She'd been through a lot herself and she always told me I should write a book as she knew my story.

I'd been attending church regularly for a long time now and my faith was growing deeper. I got involved with anything I could to help in the church, even painting the walls of the new extension that joined the building to the new church hall.

The boys loved the little church groups, and there was a beautiful lady called Barbara who had no children of her own but was like a mum to them all. She always kept them entertained so their parents could spend time with God, and would bring them gifts when she came back from a holiday or even a day out. God really used Barbara in this ministry.

I loved my church family. So many of them had amazing stories to tell. God had transformed their lives and I wanted to be like them. But God had other plans for me, as you'll discover.

*"Blessed is she who has believed that the Lord*
*would fulfil his promises to her!"*
*Luke 1:45*

The first big project I got involved with at church was Operation Christmas Child, run through Samaritan's Purse. Stanley asked me if I would help with making up shoe boxes for children in other countries like Serbia and Romania. I said I would and I got both my children involved too. They were very excited and encouraged their school friends to join in.

I loved collecting the filled shoeboxes from schools and churches with my brother Sam, who also threw himself into this wonderful project. His van would be crammed from floor to ceiling with the boxes filled with gifts. We did many trips in a day back and forth to the warehouse to drop them off for checking.

This project took up a lot of our time and it was good for Joe and Mick as they could help make the shoeboxes up at home. We'd pack them high up the walls in our house before taking them to the warehouse and helping out there.

When everything was complete, we'd go to see the Russian Antinov aeroplane take off from Speke Airport, Liverpool. It would tip its wings to say thank you and goodbye. This was a very emotional time for everyone involved.

The project brought many people together, and new friendships were made as thousands of shoeboxes filled with donated books and toys and treats were gathered together, then sent off to children for whom these were their only Christmas presents.

After that, we would all then concentrate on preparing for Christmas with our own families.

# 18

# CHANGES

As my journey with God continued, I found myself very susceptible spiritually. He was giving me dreams and visions that were becoming more frequent.

Our vicar, Dave and Jen, his wife had left our church to continue their ministry elsewhere, and we now had a new vicar – Rich.

Before Rich came, I had sensed a lot of things going on within the congregation and that God was saddened by it all. I didn't know exactly what was happening but I just felt called to pray into the things that God had put on my heart. I loved my church and church family, but I felt God's sadness about some division within it. There were things that were not pleasing to Him; areas where the church wasn't listening to Him. He put on my heart that there was gossiping, relationship breakdown, slander and general division amongst the church family.

Satan doesn't want the church to get along. He loves division.

*"The thief comes only to steal and kill and destroy"*
*John 10:10*

"What's happening, Lord?" I asked. "What are you telling me to do?"

As this was new to me, I didn't really know what to do about it all except pray. It was during one of my prayer times that I got a picture: I was standing at the front of the church with the vicar and God wanted me to speak to the congregation.

This was totally out of my comfort zone. I wasn't used to public speaking and laughed at the very idea.

However, God kept giving me nudges the following day during house group Bible study, through the house group leader and our little group itself. That evening, I couldn't shake off this message and I prayed, asking God to guide me. During my prayers, I felt overwhelmed by the Holy Spirit as I spoke in tongues. Things were constantly being confirmed to me.

I'd also had a dream a few weeks earlier. I dreamt that Satan was in the vestry of our church. He was on a tall speaker stand, breathing and laughing. I told him to shut up in my dream and to get back where he belonged. He breathed and laughed louder and, as the sound was all around me, I felt my head and my sides being pressed in.

"I'm going to have you all," came Satan's voice. "I've got most of you already but I'll have you soon too, just wait!"

"Jesus is in control of me," I replied, "so just shut up and get back to where you belong!"

But the noise of him became louder and louder as he repeated, "I'm here now. I've got most of you and will have you too!"

I knew I needed to tell Rich, although it was a few weeks before I spoke to him about it.

As I went over everything with him, I felt as though Satan was stirring people up in the church, with more gossiping and backbiting. It was awful but real. I also felt there was a part of the church building that was unclean and needed prayer. It was in the vestry.

The vicar listened carefully and told me to continue to pray for further confirmation. When I asked if I would have to speak and when would it be, he told me, "During my sermon." Just like my dream.

One night before church, I dreamt again. In my dream, I was praying and Satan was there, looming large, but he had a frightened look on his face this time and he was falling. When I turned to him, God said, "Don't look at him. Concentrate on praying, not on him." Then I woke up saying the same prayer.

I went to church that morning and met with the vicar and other church leaders and we prayed in the vestry.

I felt sick as we prayed, commanding Satan out of the church. Then, I had a sensation as if something had hit me and passed right through me and out of me. I felt I was in a spiritual battlefield and I was so tired. Again, we were not fighting against flesh and blood but against rulers, authorities and spiritual forces of evil in the heavenly places (Ephesians 6:12).

But God's power is stronger. His love and protection were again upon us, as always.

After we'd prayed in the vestry, we went straight into the church service.

The service was good as it led to things being said that God wanted us all to hear. Then the vicar called me out to speak.

I told of what God had put on my heart about the gossiping, backbiting, hurting and falling out with each other; of how sad He was when He saw this in His church. He wanted us all to move forward in the things He had for us. But we couldn't unless we turned away and repented from what we were doing.

This is what God wants us all to hear:

- God isn't happy with the backstabbing and bickering going on. This has taken us away from God's truth.
- How can He bless us when we aren't listening to His Word?

- He wants us to turn away from the darkness and look to the light.
- If we want to know anything, He wants us to ask Him!
- I did ask Him for us all and this is what He said: "My plans are to prosper you not to harm you" (Jeremiah 29:11).
- "I have my plans for you all, but be patient."
- "Are you listening?"
- Our God came in peace, love and truth and He wants that peace and love to continue throughout our lives with Him and each other. Then He can do His work and bless us when we look to Him.

People later said that those were things that should have been said long ago to the church. Long before now.

Around this same time, I had another dream.

I dreamt I was with my friend Jackie. We were walking through the streets, which were very busy. But people's eyes and mouths seemed to be glued or sewn up. These people were communicating with each other with their minds, as they were unable to do so verbally. Jackie and I knew something was going on but we couldn't speak about it as they would realise we knew what was happening.

We saw a man who was on his own. As we looked, he began to change and appear like the others. His eyes were half closed and his mouth was shut. He acknowledged us by saying, "Hmm…"

Jackie and I suddenly split off into opposite directions and I spoke to the man. I told him about Jesus. He bent over as if in pain as I carried on speaking the name of Jesus over him three times.

Suddenly, his mouth opened as wide as it could go as he yelled, "Aargh!" His eyes opened at the same time and it was as if he was then one of us – a Christian. He had been set free from his blindness.

I then found myself with Jackie in a huge garden. There was an enormous detached house set within it and we were hiding from the weird people with their glued-up eyes and mouths.

Flying above us, there were two huge eagles, black like ink. When they landed, they turned into dogs with red eyes. These creatures watched the people all the time and communicated with them. They looked like Egyptian Sphinx dogs.

Then the door to the huge house opened and a woman came out. She looked around constantly as if she was expecting something or someone.

There was a long outbuilding near the house and the two Egyptian Sphynx dogs sat on the top so that they could see everything in all directions.

Jackie and I were hiding in the bushes when someone appeared to walk down the long path towards the house. They looked straight in our direction, stared right at us, but didn't seem able to see us. Jackie even stood up in plain sight, but the person looked past her.

She turned to me, bewildered. "They can't see us," she said. It was as though we were hidden in Christ from the darkness that surrounded us.

I know dreams don't always have any meaning but I realised this was a spiritual dream and did mean something. The beings with glued eyes and sewn mouths weren't Christians and there were many of them. At the time, this seemed to indicate that the church was being blinded and robbed of freedom by the enemy. People were entangled and were going along with the deception. Little by little, Satan had been turning them against each other and he was laughing. He'd tried to pull me in too when he could, but that was when I drew nearer to God.

It's sad but true that in the world we live in today, people are being deceived and blinded by Satan and his tactics.

# 19

# I WILL CHANGE YOUR NAME

Along with great spiritual highs, there also came the dark and heavy times.

Despite having divorced Sean, he still had a big impact on my life as he continued to cause trouble within my family. Following months of abusive phone calls, threats, sending taxis to my parents' home at all hours of the night just to get them up out of bed, things had finally come to a head.

My brother Sam had just finished work and was settling down to watch television when he received a call from Sean, taunting him for being a coward.

Following the call, Sam got a taxi to Sean's house, only to hear the sound of police sirens when he got there. Sean had rung the police beforehand ready for when Sam arrived. He wouldn't answer the door, but continued shouting abuse at Sam from the other side.

This was all a game to Sean, who took pleasure in goading my family and trying to set my brother up.

The following day, the police arrived at my parents' house having received a complaint from Sean. I showed them the file I had to take Sean to court. I told them about everything he was doing. They said they knew there was more to it and just told my brother not to go near him again. They were going to tell Sean the same thing: to leave us alone.

Determined to punish and cause hurt to my family, Sean took my brother to court for damage to his front door. This was a horrible experience as Sean's solicitor knew we'd been set up and didn't really say anything in his defence. Sean didn't even show up at court, so the case was thrown out and Sam was free to go.

> *"You are my strength, I watch for you; you, God,*
> *are my fortress, my God on whom I can rely. God*
> *will go before me and will let me gloat over those*
> *who slander me."*
> Psalm 59:9−10

I'd begun to feel that I'd be tormented forever by this man. Then, one day, I was doing my housework when, through my tears, these words sprang into my mind:

**I will change your name. You shall no longer be called: Wounded, Outcast, Lonely or Afraid. I will change your name. Your new name shall be Confidence, Joyfulness, Overcoming One, Faithfulness, Friend of God, One who seeks my face.**

I didn't know where these words were from so I asked my friends, Stanley and Jean. They told me they were from a song. I didn't know this and when I heard it sung for the first time, I cried.

This was my God. He'd spoken to me directly through the words of a song I had never heard before. His Spirit was speaking to deep within me.

When Jackie came to see me, she saw how upset I was, as the ongoing problems with Sean were relentless. I was struggling to forgive but I knew I had to as Jesus had forgiven me. It was only by believing that scripture that I was able to keep going.

In fact, I was struggling so much inside my heart that I'd written out some scriptures and words from songs:

"You have broken chains that bound me. You have set this captive free."

"My chains are gone, I've been set free."

I'd put these verses up all over the house to remind myself that Jesus had released me from my own imprisonment in my mind.

It was a very difficult time. I forgave Sean every time he did something, but a part of me wanted to run away. Only, where would I go? I had two children who were also his children, while he had a new wife and another couple of children. So why did he still bother to torment me and my family?

Jackie prayed with me and I began to feel calm and peaceful again. Then, all at once, she started to laugh. I opened my eyes to see her looking over my shoulder. I could feel a beautiful presence but didn't know what she was laughing at.

"Can't you see them?" she said, pointing. "They're right behind you."

Jackie could see angels. I could feel them but she could actually see them.

I felt peaceful and sleepy, and Jackie put on her coat and started to leave. As I walked her to the door, she told me the angels were still with me.

"Two of them are going up the stairs now," she said, "but there's still one behind you." And she walked off down the path.

I had a beautiful sleep that night. When I got up the next morning, as I was walking down the stairs, I couldn't believe my eyes.

I saw three large, white feathers.

There was no explanation. I was the last one to shut the front door and go to bed, and the first one to get up.

I know that angels were with me.

Of course, Jackie was the first one I rang to tell.

"I know," she said, "I saw them. Three of them."

*"For it is written: 'He will command his angels*
*concerning you to guard you carefully'"*
*Luke 4:10*

I discovered that, the closer I grew to God, the more spiritual dreams I would have. I'd always been a dreamer, but I noticed a difference to my normal pattern of dreams.

I realised that, whenever I was frightened, upset or worried, I would have this recurring image of myself as a young girl, running away from something – but I could never see what I was running from. I looked different as I had blonde, curly, shoulder-length hair and I was about eight years old. I was also wearing an old-fashioned style, long dress with a white apron over it, and was in a place where it was quiet, apart from some background noise. I didn't know what the noise was. It was nice, though. I was high above the clouds on hills. There were no roads, just bumpy fields and green and yellow grasses, and I was running to God. I looked over my shoulder at what was behind, but I felt safe.

I always want to be in that beautiful, safe and secure place.

The picture returned many times in my life. It would stay in my mind until I'd fallen asleep – which was always the best and most peaceful sleep ever.

# 20

# FORGIVENESS

I had forgiven Sean over and over again and God had forgiven me.

I hoped things would settle down, and they seemed to for a while. We were able to speak civilly to one another when he brought the boys back.

Again, though, this was short lived, and I still don't know to this day why he continued to create problems and upset my family and me. But I had to go on forgiving as God forgives us.

I'd learnt that God can heal any burden, and this is what I discovered: to forgive doesn't mean I had to be a doormat. Forgiveness has consequences.

I had always forgiven Sean, but the more I did, the worse my pain became and I could never understand why this was. I thought I was doing the right thing in forgiving him, but then, after speaking to leadership and other Christian friends, they told me forgiveness also released me from the devastating effects of un-forgiveness – of not letting go.

I also discovered this, which sums up a lot about forgiveness:

Forgiving others is a direction from God. It may seem to be a choice, and in one sense it is. But God has been very clear about forgiveness. He has given us specific direction in numerous scriptures, all of which can be summed up in just one word – forgive!

*"And when you stand praying, if you hold*
*anything against anyone, forgive them, so that*
*your Father in heaven may forgive you your sins."*
*Mark 11:25*

*"Do not judge, and you will not be judged. Do not*
*condemn, and you will not be condemned. Forgive,*
*and you will be forgiven."*
*Luke 6:37*

God is saying that it's in our own best interests to forgive! He's not talking about the best interests of the person who needs to be forgiven. *We* are the ones God is trying to protect. *We* are the ones who receive the most benefit from forgiveness.

A spirit of un-forgiveness complicates and compromises our daily walk with God. Forgiving others releases us from anger and allows us to receive the healing we need.

The whole reason God has given us specific direction is because He doesn't want anything to stand between us and Him. God's love for us is beyond our comprehension. Forgiving others spares us from the consequences of living out of an unforgiving heart.

If you're struggling to forgive someone or to let go of a past hurt, please remember that God can heal you in this and He will carry your heaviest burden. He is the restorer of your soul. He protects and defends you, His child, if you let Him.

He knows you better than you know yourself and doesn't want you to carry un-forgiveness or burdens that separate you from Him.

Remember, when Jesus was on the cross, He cried: *"Father, forgive them, for they do not know what they are doing"* (Luke 23:34).

Jesus died to take all our burdens – our sins – and He forgave us as we didn't know what we were doing when we hung Him on a cross and left Him there to die. And He still does this today. He went to the cross once and for all, but not for us to continue to carry our burdens and un-forgiveness. Only He can do this.

When we struggle to forgive, we need to ask Jesus to forgive us and the person who has hurt us. This in turn releases something in us as we speak these words out of our mouths.

I struggled constantly in this area for many years. I ended up writing out verses from worship songs to remind myself that Jesus forgives me – but I also had to forgive those who'd tried to murder my brothers, and my ex-husband who was persecuting me:

**"The vilest offender who truly believes that moment from Jesus a pardon receives."**

**"My chains are gone, I've been set free, I rose went forth and followed thee."**

**"You've broken chains that bound me, You've set this captive free."**

**"My chains fell off my heart was free…"**

Jesus wants to release you and set you free to live out and enjoy all that He has promised you.

# 21

# DISCERNMENT AND INTERCESSION

Things at the church didn't change and the division was still ongoing. Many of us believed that God was unhappy and, though some of us were scared to say it, we felt that He had taken His hand off the church.

I felt torn because I loved the worship music, the drums, guitars and singing but, during my quiet times with God, I felt a deep sorrow and sadness, as if He was grieving for His church. I brought this to the leadership team who were already aware of it. They said I was like an antenna, picking up things both good and bad.

Throughout all this chaos within the church, I felt moved by the Holy Spirit to speak directly to another of the team about his ongoing battle to step up into his next role in leadership. Al was stunned when I talked to him as he hadn't spoken to anyone about this. But he was encouraged after chatting with me and asked me to continue to pray. He called me his prayer warrior. Years later, he became an ordained minister looking after his own church.

Just before June 2000, I became aware of a burden to speak to close friends about what God had put on my heart. They said they'd heard the same from God. We felt there was a heavy, spiritual darkness that was becoming heavier.

The church building was over a hundred years old and in desperate need of repair. Sadly, during my prayer times and when I prayed for a new church, I really felt that the building would be knocked down and that it would be many years before a new one would replace it. It wouldn't be in the same place either, and it would cost a lot of money. The word "consecrated" kept coming to my mind but I didn't know what it meant then.

The church had been raising funds for a new roof that would cost hundreds of thousands of pounds, but God kept putting on my heart that the roof wasn't important. It was hearts that needed repairing; hearts that needed to repent and turn back to Him. God wanted our eyes fixed on Him, not on material things.

This became more apparent to me each time money and funding were mentioned. Also, the money seemed to get lost in high interest ranks or not meeting deadlines to achieve certain amounts, so we never had enough.

I was very humbled and upset as I cried bitterly when I felt the depths of God's sadness for His church. All He wanted was for His church to come back to Him.

"Why can't you listen and see? Why all this mess? Why don't you ask me if this is what I want?" This is what the Lord put on my heart for us all.

The few of us who were aware of God's sadness continued to pray. But I also knew God was speaking to me in a new and more in-depth way. He had given me a new gift of intercession that I hadn't recognised.

There are always going to be times when we get it wrong but God knows this, and all He asks is for faithfulness and obedience from His children. This is how we learn and, like children, we grow the more we use the gifts He gives us.

# 22

# FOCUSING ON AND TRUSTING JESUS

My dear mum had been diagnosed with multiple myeloma, a rare form of cancer in the cells that produce bone marrow. She'd become very tired and was not at all her normal self.

Daily trips to Clatterbridge hospital for mum's treatment made her all the more tired, although we were lifted up when we listened to worship songs. We enjoyed new worship songs and old hymns that my parents knew. They soon grew to like Dave Bilbrough and songs from Vineyard and New Wine. Both my mum's and my dad's faith was strengthened as I talked endlessly about how Jesus was doing things in my life and revealing things to me. I think they were relieved to see the positive changes in me.

My sons enjoyed going to church too and would help out whenever they could. The vicar once said about Joe, as Joe pushed a large wheelbarrow around the church grounds, removing all the rubble and debris: "He's full of confidence, he is. He'll make a great builder." Little did any of us know that Joe would become a professional plasterer as well as working in the building trade.

Sadly, Sean got up to his old tricks again. There were more phone calls to my parents' house at one and two o'clock in the morning – phone calls wishing Mum was dead. Pizzas and taxis would arrive once more at all hours of the night. Sean knew Mum was poorly and needed her rest. It was horrible. *Forgive*?! How on earth was I supposed to forgive him? I found myself crying over and over again.

Again, it was to scripture and lines from worship songs that I was drawn back. But they didn't stop my tears or the anger from rising up in me. And I wasn't supposed to say anything to him as this only made things worse. He'd smirk and deny everything, telling me I was paranoid.

"Jesus!" I'd cry. "Help me! What am I supposed to do?"

My parents would tell me, "Leave it, Pam. He's got nothing better to do. If he's doing this to us then he's leaving someone else alone."

The old me began to rise up again as both Mum and Dad's health worsened. I had so much anger towards Sean. I felt frustrated and I didn't know how to vent it all as my parents' reaction was so laid back – as if they weren't bothered about this cruel taunting.

But I did have good friends who supported me and prayed into these situations every time they arose, which seemed to be endlessly, and this helped.

"**Faithful one, so unchanging**
**Ageless one, you're my rock of peace**
**Lord of all I depend on you**
**I call out to you, again and again**
**I call out to you, again and again**

**You are my rock in times of trouble**
**You lift me up when I fall down**
**All through the storm**
**Your love is the anchor**
**My hope is in You alone."**     (*Brian Doerksen*)

The words of this song shouted out in my mind as big tears ran down my cheeks. I was trying to get on with housework but my heart ached with the pain and sadness of Mum's illness and with Sean's cruelty.

"Will he ever stop, Lord?" I asked.

There was nowhere to turn, only into the loving arms of my Father God, who was clearly showing me He is my rock in everything.

I cried out to Him again and again and He always lifted me up but, each time, a little closer to Him. His beautiful embrace always brought more tears, but tears of joy. I knew I was drawing nearer and nearer to my amazing God.

Wasn't this what I'd been asking God for all of my life? Looking back, I can see how He was moulding me, shaping me into the person He created me to be. But I had to keep my eyes focused on Him and not on my problems. This was hard because the problems were constantly there. It was something I had to learn how to do as I went through every trial.

In the midst of this, I found I was being burdened to pray for the church again. Things were ongoing that weren't pleasing to God and, once more, I spoke with the elders. I felt God wanted the church to repent and come back to Him and, if it didn't, there would be consequences. Despite the fact that this had been going on for a number of years, nothing was getting resolved.

It seemed to me that the Holy Spirit was grieving for our church. I'd never felt burdens as heavy as this and I knew Father God wanted me to speak up again.

In praying, I again had the feeling that the building needed to be knocked down and rebuilt with new foundations. It was very cold and the roof repairs had turned out to be too expensive. A rebuild would be cheaper.

As time went on, I felt a difference in the church meetings and services. Was the Holy Spirit still with us? But all I could do was pray and take it to the leadership.

Looking across the road to my church one day, I was suddenly filled with a huge awareness that I would be leaving it. And almost immediately, I felt there would be another family for me somewhere else, but I had to let go of this one first. There, across the road from my home, was the church I'd belonged to since I was a little girl. But somehow, I didn't feel as though I belonged there anymore.

I prayed and discussed this with my home group. They said, "Maybe God does want you to move on."

Although I took this on board, I continued to pray for God's guidance as I was afraid. And the fear grew when things became clearer. God began to show me He wanted me to move out of the area completely. To Southport!

Sam, my brother, didn't know any of this when he asked me, "Have you thought about moving out of Bootle, Pam? It's changing around here and not for the better. Don't forget you have two little lads to bring up."

I was terrified. Terrified of the unknown. I'd always been very close to my parents and, here I was, thinking of moving nearly twenty miles away. How would I manage? And how would they manage without me now they were both ill?

Although I prayed for about twelve months, asking God to confirm this to me, I was still afraid. I knew deep down it was going to happen. I was going to leave Bootle, the place where I'd grown up and spent most of my life. I had a lot of good memories but a lot of bad ones too. And our God is a God of love and grace. He knew my fears and concerns over things changing for the worse in the area, and over leaving it behind. He also knew when I'd be moving on.

After lots of prayer, my brother Sam, who'd been looking for a house in Southport for us, found one. I went to view it in Churchtown. It was lovely. I handed in all the documents required by the estate agents, who said I'd hear back from them shortly. But a few weeks went by and I didn't hear a thing.

It was odd. I really felt this was the house God wanted us to move into, so when I eventually got in touch with the estate agents and they told me I wasn't a suitable candidate and someone else was moving into it, I couldn't believe it!

I also couldn't let it go. I tried to contact the owner of the house by post and I got a reference from my local MP, too, as well as continuing to pray. I could just feel in my heart that I was supposed to live there with my boys, despite what was happening.

The days passed and I had a vision of myself coming out of a church in Southport. I could see what the church looked like in the vision. It had glass doors and a large patio area, and I was smiling and happy as I stepped out of the building. I knew this would be the church where I would worship in the future.

I told Stanley and Jean of this vision when they were looking for a church in Southport for me, one similar to my church in Bootle, which was Church of England. The vision seemed to keep me focused and I tried to keep positive about moving into this particular house. Stanley couldn't believe it had fallen through either, as he too felt it was where God wanted me to be. He told me that the only thing he could think of was the story of Abraham and Isaac, when God tested Abraham and told him to take his son Isaac up a mountain and sacrifice him there.

I didn't really understand what Stanley meant, but I listened to him anyway.

By now, it was July 2001 and I couldn't stop wondering when we'd be moving. I'd never stepped out in faith like this before. I knew God would move us but the time was running out. The schools finished for the term at the end of July, and here we were still praying for a school for my boys in Southport. I'd even told their current school they'd be leaving when the term ended as we were moving away.

Friends prayed for direction for us as they knew I had to get the boys into a new school for September. One of them spoke to me about Nehemiah building the wall in forty days, and how people helped in different ways. She said that when one person becomes weary, there are the others who can help and hold them in prayer.

My friends prayed and told me, "If this house is from God, it will happen."

More time passed. Then, one day, out of the blue, I received a phone call from the landlady of the house I'd viewed in Churchtown. She told me she'd gone to the house by chance that day and had found my letter on the floor with some other post. She said she wouldn't normally have been there.

When she heard my story and how I had been treated, she was shocked. She said she wasn't comfortable with the tenants the estate agents had offered the house to, and she offered it to me immediately.

I got the keys that week.

When I looked properly at the story of Abraham and Isaac in Genesis, I now understood what Stanley had meant. I knew this was the house God had set aside for me and my boys. It would be a home for my mum in the future too. God is faithful and had been testing me. He wanted me to trust Him that He was working all things for my good.

> *"Sometime later God tested Abraham... 'Take your son, your only son, whom you love – Isaac – and go to the region of Moriah. Sacrifice him there as a burnt offering on a mountain I will show you.'"*
> *Genesis 22:1-2*

**God never wanted Abraham to take his own son's life. He simply wanted to test Abraham's faith – his love and obedience. And God stopped Abraham before any harm came to Isaac.**

**God is in control of everything when we submit to Him our deepest desires. Very often He has planted them inside us anyway.**

At long last, there I was getting ready to move into my new home in Southport. This became easier as I realised God was truly leading me. And so I began an even deeper walk as I trusted in Him.

I recall thinking in days past, did I ever see myself moving out of Bootle? And if I did, where would I go?

I also thought I'd never leave my church because, again, if I did – where would I go?

This all had to happen in God's perfect timing.

# 23

# NEW MOVE

As I packed up my car in Bootle ready to move things to my new home in Southport, I saw Anthony. He was a doorman from my past who I used to know. I hadn't set eyes on for many years.

To my complete surprise, he said, "All right, Pam? My daughter lives just there."

He pointed towards a house just a couple of doors away. "I've seen you loads of times," he said, "but I didn't know whether to say hello or not."

Anthony knew I was taking my ex-husband back to court. He went on to tell me that Sean had offered him a large amount of money if he'd lie in court to say that I'd asked to get him killed.

"I know I didn't treat you very nice in the past," he said, "and I'm sorry. But I know you're a good mother and I just thought you needed to be aware of what he's trying to do. He's trying to take your boys off you."

"*What*?" Alarm bells went off in my head. Was I hearing right?

I couldn't believe what this man was saying and I asked him if he'd put it down in black and white as evidence against Sean for me to take to court. He said he would, and he did.

I went to bed that night, thankful that I was moving out of the area. But I was also aware of a niggly feeling that my past would never let me go. I felt somehow ugly and unclean.

That same night, I dreamt I was rising up out of a huge, upright, tub shape, like a barrel. It was filled with warm liquid. I was wearing a golden gown and there was a luminous white light all around me. Drops of gold oil showered me from above.

When I woke up, I felt the most beautiful presence I'd ever felt. I was cleansed and purified – as though I'd been baptised without physically going into water.

Then the Lord spoke to me: "I have washed you whiter than the whitest of snow. You are pure, washed clean and cleansed. You are clothed in white. Your past has gone and your sins are forgiven."

Oh, how I cried with joy and the knowledge that things were going to be all right. I was hearing from my Lord Jesus. He'd come to me in a dream. I was not only forgiven, I was made clean – as I had read many times in His Word. I knew God had been working in me but this was something totally different. He was working in areas of me that I never knew existed.

"Thank You, gracious and merciful Father!" I cried.

*"Come now, let us settle the matter,' says the* LORD.
*'Though your sins are like scarlet, they shall be as white as snow..."*
*Isaiah 1:18*

*"The one who is victorious will, like them, be dressed in white. I will never blot out the name of that person from the book of life, but will acknowledge that name before my Father and his angels."*
*Revelation 3:5*

*"You will surely forget your trouble, recalling it
only as waters gone by."*
*Job 11:16*

We were now in our new home. It was a beautiful place and I felt secure. I knew my Father God was beside me in everything. I didn't worry that I lived further away now from my parents or that I'd have to go out shopping on my own in a new town. I had my car and I could still drive to my parents' home in Bootle and take them to hospital appointments. Things just slotted into place. The only problem seemed to be finding a new school for my boys, which was tricky as we'd moved during the school holidays.

Sean knew we were moving away. He mocked me when I told him that God would provide everything we needed. He laughed and said, "What? Do you think He's gonna put a letter through your door just inviting the boys into a school?"

I'd approached various schools but had been told there were no spaces. Yet I trusted that God would provide somewhere near to our home. And, sure enough, he did.

Over the last few months, a court welfare officer had been involved with us before we moved to Southport, due to Sean's behaviour. Joe was at an age where he didn't want to see his dad, and Sean would play both boys off against each other.

The court welfare officer assessed both parties with our sons and agreed that Joe didn't have to visit his dad, as Joe got upset over this. However, she also made a mistake. When she sent a copy of a letter to Sean, she left our new address on it. Sean wasn't supposed to have our address because of the ongoing problems he caused. She told the court what she'd done but emphasised that she didn't want us put under any more stress by having to move again, as we'd been through enough.

I soon discovered my new church: Christ Church, Southport. It was the vision I'd had where I'd seen myself walking out of the church building, smiling and happy. I was so excited that I told nearly everyone I met how God had brought me to this church through a vision, as I'd never seen it in reality before. I also told them that God had moved us into Southport.

I was on fire for my Jesus. I knew He was in everything with me. He was my rock. Yet, still, it wasn't long before the old struggle of unforgiveness returned again.

My heart felt as if it was broken as I prepared to go back to court. I knew Sean's plan to try to take my boys from me, and dread filled my heart. I had Anthony's statement to back me up on this, but this was my old nature coming through: I was trying to rely on people. What I had to do was turn to the biggest source of help, which was Jesus.

As I spoke to friends at my new church, they prayed for me and told me that the enemy would try to break my peace – break *me* – but that I needed to forgive Sean over and over again.

They were right!

I remember a feeling of sickness surging through my body as I prayed that I could forgive him, and myself, too, for feeling the way I did. I also prayed for God to forgive him and I sobbed as I prayed. I kept looking at my little plaques that I'd made, with verses of scripture and worship songs on to remind myself what Jesus had done for me.

When I appeared in court, my hand clung tightly to the large wooden pocket cross a friend had loaned to me for reassurance.

A lady came to see me.

"Where's my solicitor?" I asked her.

"She can't make it," the lady replied, "but don't worry I'm here to support you."

The lady then explained that I'd have to go into the same courtroom as Sean. I immediately felt intimidated and I told her he'd lie and smirk as I spoke.

How wonderful my God is! He knew what would happen as He'd planned it all for my good. And He turned the situation right round. I didn't even have to go into the courtroom. The judge looked at the whole picture and did it all behind the scenes. I didn't have to come face to face with Sean. I didn't have to see him that day.

How elated I felt as I knew justice was done in this situation. But, as things were ongoing with him, I did find I slipped back and forth between feeling uplifted and swamped. My emotions were all over the place. It was hard to stay focused on Jesus as much as I wanted to.

I was under the domestic violence unit and put in touch with S.W.A.C.A. – Sefton Women's And Children's Aid. They supported me through a lot and, with my walk with God and help from my family, I found myself being built back up again. I discovered I didn't have to be afraid of Sean anymore or intimidated by him. He couldn't hurt me. My phone was connected to a special number, which meant that the police would come out immediately if he turned up. There was other support available to us too, which was very helpful.

My brother Sam had always said that he'd get us a dog if I moved into a large enough property. So, off we went to look for a black Labrador.

Bob came from a litter of nine pups, all born outdoors. The owner said, "The one who follows you is the one for you."

There was a bitch who kept close to my heels and Bob who was on my other side. The bitch ran off and Bob decided to stop and urinate on my foot. Everyone laughed and told me he was the one I should get.

Joe and Mick were delighted with our new family member. He brought so much joy and laughter into our lives.

When the boys couldn't find their school shoes and I blamed them for not putting their things away, I'd often find them under the bush outside or hidden under my bed, where Bob had taken them. There were times when I heard the lads laughing uncontrollably upstairs in their bedroom. With all the banging about that was going on, I thought they must have their friends up there. But it would turn out to be Bob who was bouncing around and having fun with them.

Often, he'd even bring their washing down the stairs in his mouth, then run back up to get the next lot. He was a beautiful dog and it was wonderful for me to see my boys so happy with him.

# 24

# LETTING GO

School in Southport wasn't an altogether happy time for Joe and Mick. Because they came from Liverpool, some people made life difficult for them. Especially for Joe. I remember being so glad when his school years were behind him.

Life became something of a juggle. There were problems at school to deal with, and I was also travelling back and forth to Bootle every day as both my parents were becoming more unwell. Dad had C.O.P.D (chronic obstructive pulmonary disease), which affected his breathing, and Mum had multiple myeloma. They both ended up in hospital at the same time and, between my three brothers and myself, we managed to visit them regularly.

My brothers helped me with my sons. They'd collect them from their school and take them back to Bootle, or stay with them at our Southport home until I returned.

We managed the situation as best we could between us, as we watched our parents deteriorate before our eyes.

Things came to a head when Mum was taken into intensive care. The doctors told us she was very, very poorly with pneumonia and they didn't think she'd recover. At the same time, Dad was delirious with his illness and the medication he was on. He was very sick too and kept asking us why we weren't with Mum.

"If anything happens to her that you're not telling me about, woe betide you," he'd say. Despite how ill he was, he knew something wasn't right.

It was difficult to know what to do for the best. Doctors and nurses told us it would be better not to tell either of our parents about the other's deterioration as the shock could kill them. But keeping them in the dark about the seriousness of each other's conditions was one of the hardest decisions we'd had to take.

Suddenly, Dad took a turn for the worse with pneumonia and he ended up in intensive care too. Both our parents were in the same place at the same time without either of them knowing.

It was heart-breaking to watch the decline of these two beautiful people, who meant the world to us all; who'd given up everything for us and who'd supported us for all these years. But we couldn't shed tears. We had to be strong and act as if the other parent was OK when they weren't. Oh, how I cried inside as I tried to be strong for my younger brothers, although two of them were settled with their partners. It was Sam we had to really look out for.

I remember when the doctors called us in and told us Mum wasn't going to make it — it was just a matter of time. Jason and I sat outside in the corridor, bewildered.

Then, all at once, he spoke out: "No, Pam, God isn't cruel. He's not going to take both our parents away together and leave us as orphans. No, not now."

Wow! Why hadn't I thought of that? God is good, but, just then, where was He?

That's when I seemed to realise I had to think differently. Our parents weren't going to leave us behind like this. They were only in their early sixties — we would have time to see them again. Both Jason and I began to pray right there in the corridor of the hospital.

The days all seemed to merge into one. I think the only time I let some tears flow was when I was driving home on my own late at night. But I still had the boys to think about. I had to be strong for them so there was a time limit on my tears.

I can't remember exactly how long my parents were in intensive care but it was for a couple of weeks at least. Then, on one visit, my dad had had a turn around. He was eventually put back on a ward and became strong enough to know what was happening with Mum. He wasn't happy that we'd kept this from him but he understood, and then he demanded we take him to see her immediately.

The staff were amazing. They wheeled Dad, in his bed as he still wasn't allowed out of it, to Mum's little side ward in intensive care. As he held her hand and loved her and told her she'd come through this, all the staff were crying. Those moments were so precious. And slowly she came round and recognised him.

"Woe betide you if anything happens to her..." Dad warned us again. But we knew this was because of his hurt and anger that she was ill.

Eventually, Mum did make a slow recovery. The staff said she was a miracle as she bounced back. She was asked to put her experiences in hospital in a hospital magazine, but she didn't want to go over it all again. She just wanted to go home to her family.

My parents were both finally allowed to go home. They'd recovered from pneumonia but they still had to take it easy. Mum had to have chemotherapy tablets for the multiple myeloma.

Sadly, they began to find the house they'd lived in for most of their life together more difficult to manage now and, because of this, they needed to move into something that would be easier for them. But we were at least able to spend two lovely months more with them in the family home where we were all raised, before they moved into a little bungalow in Crosby. It was part of a sheltered housing scheme.

Sam and I decorated it and got it all ready for them to move into. It was only small, but it was plenty big enough for the two of them, they told us.

They'd lived in the bungalow for just a few days when Dad became ill again. Mum rang me and said his breathing wasn't too good. I'd dropped the boys off at school and I drove down to Crosby straightaway.

As soon as I saw him, I knew Dad's colouring wasn't right. The people from the sheltered scheme had already rung for an ambulance. Dad was admitted to hospital where he deteriorated again.

Dad told me he wasn't going to come through it this time. "I always told you I'd go before your mother, Pam," he said. "But, shush, don't tell her."

It was the beginning of December and I told him that we'd have Christmas dinner at our house. He smiled at me and said, "See what happens, love. I'm not going to be here, but I want you to look after your mother for me."

"Don't be talking like that, Dad," I said. "You will be."

But I had this feeling of doubt in my heart this time that he was right. And the feeling wouldn't go.

I left the cubicle when Dad was put on a CPAP mask to help him breathe. As I did so, I noticed some leaflets, and one of them seemed to jump out at me. It was about bereavement.

At 11.30pm, Dad was eventually put on the chest ward after thirteen hours of waiting on a hospital bed in a side ward.

He told me I'd been his right arm over these last months and was glad that I'd settled down. He said he knew I'd be all right but I was to make sure Mum was all right as well.

"I'll bring her to live with me, Dad," I said. "You can come and live with us too."

Dad smiled. "No." As he drifted in and out of consciousness, he told me he loved us. I hugged him and kept praying for another miracle. But I knew that the only miracle would be when he was set free to breathe without any aid. Dad had lived for fifteen years with an oxygen cylinder and a nebuliser machine, when he'd been told he'd only live for five. He was already a miracle. As I continued to thank God for him and for the precious months we'd had together, God brought us closer.

I kissed Dad goodnight and got home at 1.15 that morning. At 3.00am, the phone rang. It was the hospital.

"Can you come quickly?" a voice said. "Your dad has deteriorated." His oxygen levels had dropped very low.

Up and dressed and back on the road, I prayed that God wouldn't take Dad away until I'd seen him again.

All of a sudden, I saw a vision of three strong, warrior-like men, partially dressed, kneeling down and holding big dented shields. And there seemed to be two or three very tall, slim angels clothed in light and long, white gowns, with wings that appeared to be tightly closed. They were in between heaven and earth, waiting.

I saw this at 3.40am.

"Oh, no, not now Lord!" I cried. "Please don't take my dad, please..." I knew they'd come for him.

I arrived at the hospital at 4.00am and they told me Dad had suddenly settled down twenty minutes before I got there. That would have been at the time I cried out to God when I saw the vision.

**Angels are very active in the Bible and are used by God as messengers, warriors and servants. Angels had many functions too. They praised God (Psalm 103:20), served as messengers to the world (Luke 1:11–20, 26–38; Luke 2:9–14), and watched over God's people (Psalm 91:11–12).**

I believe that the angels and warriors I saw had come to take my dad home.

Dad was tired of fighting, he said. The angels and warriors had come for him, but he hung on until we were all there with him; all his family.

When Mum went to the bathroom, Dad said, "Pam, make sure you look after your mum. I'm not going to be here and you know that. They came for me last night. Now, don't tell her about this conversation, do you hear me? You know what she's like. She'll worry and she isn't well herself."

I understood exactly what he meant. I told him what I'd seen in my vision and explained what had happened.

Dad already knew.

He seemed to pick up after that and we were all hoping he might be able to come home. Although deep down in my heart I knew this wouldn't happen.

As evening approached, he began to deteriorate more. He'd told us he'd been in and out of hospital all his life, and he was tired of it now. He wanted to go.

I held his hand and asked him to pray with me inside his head. I told him to squeeze my hand when he'd repeated my prayer. He did this.

And Mum, my brothers and other family members were with him when Jesus took him home.

*"...in all these things we are more than conquerors through him who loved us. For I am convinced that neither death nor life, neither angels nor demons, neither the present nor the future, nor any powers, neither height nor depth, nor anything else in all creation, will be able to separate us from the love of God that is in Christ Jesus our Lord."*
*Romans 8:37–39*

My aunties and uncles couldn't believe what I told them about my faith and the vision I'd had. But they knew something must have happened because of my supernatural strength that only came from Jesus.

At Dad's thanksgiving service, I didn't stop telling people about where we go as Christians when we die. Everyone said they'd never been to a funeral like it. Considering it was a funeral, it was lovely.

One of my aunties was really encouraged and said she wished she had my faith. Thankfully, she does now, and I send her lots of Christian CDs and literature to lift her spirit.

Losing Dad was hard for us all. I loved both my parents dearly and I kept my promise to Dad and moved Mum in with me and my sons.

I didn't want it any other way as I wanted to look after her. There was plenty of room for us all. God had provided a big enough house – He'd had His hand on it for us when we moved to Southport.

Mum missed Dad so much, it broke her heart. They'd been married for over forty years. It broke my heart too, watching Mum struggle in her grief and with her own illness.

It was very difficult for me to grieve over my dear dad as I felt I had to be strong for Mum. So I tried to keep back the tears. It was when I had a few minutes to nip out to the local shop on my own that I'd cry in the car.

Joe took his grandad's death badly too. He went off the rails and it was difficult to help him as we couldn't even speak with him about it. He'd get angry and lash out. He didn't know how to cope with or handle his emotions. He was only sixteen so was already in a turbulent time.

One of our friends was a bereavement counsellor and she spoke with him and tried to help. Mick was only twelve years old at the time and he didn't really understand everything that was happening.

I rarely left Mum on her own. She was losing her confidence and became scared that something might happen to her when I was out. I did my best to reassure her, telling her where I was going and how long I'd be, which would be around twenty minutes at the most.

But, as time passed, Mum's illness made her weaker, and she was growing more ill as a result of her treatment. Life was a hard struggle. Jesus, the church and the house group were the only things that kept us focused.

We had a weekly Bible study group that was held at our house. Mum would come to this group too and was such a blessing to many of the girls who came. We all enjoyed practising the gifts of the Spirit as we studied the Bible. We became close, too, and I loved having Mum in the same home group as me, knowing I could still look after her if she wasn't well.

I remember Mum's friend, Joanne. She belonged to our church. I was talking to her about men on one of her visits to Mum, as I was missing their company and having someone to love.

I told Joanne and Mum, "I've asked God to let me know who the right person is that He has for me, by getting him to ask me to marry him in church. I love Jesus as He's brought me through so many storms in my life. And this man will know how much my faith means to me so there's no better way than to get engaged in church. This way, I'll also know he's the one God wants me to marry as he'll be a gift from God."

They both laughed and said, "Well, yes, that's right."

Sam had now met a lovely woman, Deb, who was keeping him on the right track. He was devastated when we lost Dad and knew Mum was terminally ill. And Deb did make us laugh, but she kept nothing back either. She'd be direct with you yet without wanting to hurt you. Sometimes it would sting when she said something, but she was a good woman.

Sam and Deb would come to stay with Mum and my sons from time to time, if I had a night out in Liverpool. It was a good release, dancing the night away, although I didn't drink alcohol anymore. I'd stopped drinking when I realised God didn't want me to get drunk. It was funny when I reflected back to a time I'd asked God to give me signs if He wanted me to stop drinking. He'd certainly done that.

Although lots of sadness surrounded me, I still had happy moments with my family and friends.

And there were moments when God spoke to me too; when He told me I was becoming the person He'd created me to be; that I was unique and His new creation.

At long, long last, things also seemed to settle down a bit with Sean. He wasn't persecuting me in the same way he'd done for so many years. There was even a time when he began to speak civilly to me again and he invited me to his wedding. I didn't go – only to pick up the boys from the evening reception. But when he offered to mend my car when it needed fixing, I really did think things were taking a turn for the better.

However, I soon discovered that he wanted me to start dropping the boys off at his home in Wavertree. I did help out from time to time – until I discovered that he was trying to get them into a school near to where he lived. He was always plotting something to try to take them away from me.

On many occasions, Mum must have seen the stress that took its toll on me as she'd say, "It's too much for you this is, Pamela. You haven't got your own life. I shouldn't be here."

This would upset me, and I'd tell her that I wouldn't have it any other way. If I had to do it all again, I would.

She seemed to be reassured and I added in all the positives about her being with my sons and me. I also told her what Dad wanted for her.

One day, the vision came to me again of the derelict building.

I discussed it with Mum and she told me, "The boys are getting older now and they can stand on their own two feet a bit more." She mentioned that Mick only had a couple more years left in school and God would bring this vision to me again at the right time. Mum told me God was getting me ready.

Then, she reminded me of the time we'd given furniture and other things to Argyle church. They helped the homeless people in Southport there. As she did so, I could feel something drawing up inside me – something big, but I didn't know what it was.

Mum was taken back into hospital again around 6 June 2004. She was sixty-six.

That's when I had another vision. I saw my mum in a bed wearing her night clothes. The bed was on a grass verge in the countryside and it was a beautiful, bright day. There was nothing to see, just a long, narrow, winding road.

A man stood beside the bed next to Mum and there was light all around as he offered his right hand to her. She got up out of the bed and glided across the road. Her feet didn't touch the floor but it looked as though she was walking.

I stood at the foot of the bed. On the other side of the road, there was a man with his hand held out, waiting for Mum to cross over and telling her, "Come and see…"

Mum was smiling and couldn't wait to go and see.

There were beautiful, green hedges, all perfectly cut approximately waist and chest height. I jumped up and down at the bottom of the bed as I wanted to see what they were looking at.

I was told by the two men: "You're not supposed to see this yet. Wait there." I couldn't see their faces properly as they were lit up, but I knew they were smiling and laughing.

I kept jumping up and down at the end of the bed. Again they told me I wasn't meant to see yet – I couldn't cross over as it wasn't my time.

As I jumped up to get a peek over the perfect bushes, I saw what looked like a gigantic city. I seemed to be looking down on it as if it were in a valley. I glimpsed many gold, bronze-domed and different-shaped rooftops. I spied sapphire-blue gems and diamonds that were outstanding in colour. I'd never seen anything like this before.

Once more I was told: "You're not supposed to see this yet."

Mum had now crossed over the road and I could see her face. She was gazing in awe at something.

"Wow, look at this!" she kept repeating. I still couldn't see and she never looked back at me.

I remember there was a number three in this vision and I felt the words, "The New Jerusalem". I didn't quite understand it until I read the book of Revelation:

> *"Then I saw 'a new heaven and a new earth,' for the first heaven and the first earth had passed away, and there was no longer any sea. And I saw the Holy City, the new Jerusalem, coming down out of heaven from God, prepared as a bride beautifully dressed for her husband. And I heard a loud voice from the throne saying, 'Look! God's dwelling-place is now among the people, and he will dwell with them. They will be his people, and God himself will be with them and be their God.'"*
> *Revelation 21:1–3*

When I was praying later on that day, I asked God to empty my mind of everything but Him. I then saw a huge beach stretched out before me. There was no water; no footprints.

I was aware of an obstacle to my right-hand side. I looked down at it and asked God to remove that too. It didn't go. So I asked Him to remove it if it wasn't from Him – for Him to remove anything that wasn't from Him.

Suddenly, I was even more aware of it. Then I felt the Lord say: "It's your heart."

As I looked down, there were lots of what looked like gold and silver necklace chains all ravelled up together, and I heard the Lord say: "Treasures."

*"For where your treasure is, there your heart will be also."*
*Matthew 6:21*

I received nothing more from these visions, except that I knew I had to tell Mum's friends and family to visit her while she was still with us. I felt Mum would be going home to her Saviour Jesus very soon.

My mum was deteriorating quickly now and I tried to keep strong. I was so thankful that my Jesus was in all of this. Where did my strength come from? Only from Him. He held me so close that I knew He was carrying me.

I thought back to the time when I lived in Bootle – when I felt I could never leave there or be alone. I didn't think I'd be able to manage at one point. But one thing I'd discovered was that I had to step out in faith; faith to learn to lean on Jesus alone. And the rest would follow.

This was so true. I had learnt to lean on Jesus, who was my rock, my shield, my sure foundation. I'd learnt that I needed Him in every area of my life. I was standing on His promises, not on man's. I'd learnt that, through all things, He would provide for and sustain us. I was on a new walk that I hadn't really noticed until quite some time after it had begun.

My mind also kept returning to the vision that I'd had on and off for the past fifteen years or so, of the derelict building and the homeless people. I thought this would stop once I moved to another area. How naive of me! What was I trying to do – run away from it?

My brothers looked after my sons as I repeatedly travelled to Fazakerley hospital. We were in the same routine as only eighteen months before when both my parents were in intensive care.

"Lord Jesus, please heal my mum completely!" I cried out from the hotel hospital bed, where I stayed one particular night alone.

Tears flooded down my face and I felt this was the first cry I'd released. I was on my own so I could do this now.

I begged my Lord to heal Mum completely from cancer. I asked Him to speak to me when I would open His Word. The story jumped out to me as I read about Jesus raising Lazarus from the dead. I cried and cried as I put my trust in Him regarding everything about my mum.

And I felt Him tell me to let her go.

*"Jesus called in a loud voice, 'Lazarus, come out!'*
*The dead man came out, his hands and feet*
*wrapped with strips of linen, and a cloth round his*
*face. Jesus said to them, Take off the grave clothes*
*and let him go."*
*John 11:43–44*

I felt stronger the following morning as I visited Mum in intensive care again. I knew I had one thing to do.

"Oh, wow!" I exclaimed as I went into Mum's little side ward, the same one she'd been in once before. I could feel there was something in the atmosphere. I could see people had come for her. They were above her bed, by her headboard, waiting for her. It was so peaceful; so serene. I'd never experienced anything like this before.

I thought back to the vision I'd had before Dad went home to be with Jesus. God had prepared me for that too.

"Can't you see them?" I asked my brothers, who were at Mum's bedside, holding her hands.

They looked at me and said nothing. I told them there were angels there and people who were waiting for Mum. I told them it was beautiful and they needn't worry. I don't think they took any of it in as they were too upset.

Mum lay there with the CPAP mask on. She'd developed pneumonia and the mask helped her to breathe. She didn't like that mask at all. She said it made her feel claustrophobic.

I knew it was time to contact Mum's friends. The number three I'd seen in the vision I realised meant three weeks. It had been three weeks now since I'd had those visions, and I knew God was preparing a place for Mum. But He was also preparing me to let her go. As she drifted in and out of consciousness, I knew she was going home to be with Jesus.

Mum came round and we sat and chatted with her. She kept taking the mask off to talk in between breaths. I told her that her friends were coming, along with Richard. Richard was a minister and he visited Mum in hospital.

When Richard arrived, he asked her what she'd like to hear him read from the Bible. She told him to just open it at any page and see what God wanted to say to her.

Richard did this, while the nurse began to take different tubes out of Mum's body.

"It's the story of Lazarus," Richard said. "Would you like me to read it?"

I couldn't believe that he'd randomly opened the Bible and it was the same message that God had given me the previous night.

I told him and he began to read, and it was as if the Lord was speaking to us there and then.

Richard told Mum that Jesus was preparing a special place for her and she'd be made completely whole and totally free. We knew what he meant as he went on to speak about taking off the grave clothes.

Mum understood too. These words were so special to her.

One of Mum's friends, Joanne, called to say she couldn't make it that day but would be able to come in a couple of days' time. Soon afterwards, she rang me back to say God had prompted her to come and visit that day urgently.

As other friends visited her too, they could feel the atmosphere in the room. They knew this was the day she'd go to be with Jesus.

When everyone else had gone and it was just my brothers and me with Mum, she sat up all of a sudden and said very clearly, "Pamela, let me go!"

I broke down crying as this was the thing I knew I had to do. I had to let her go.

Jesus had put that on my heart the night before.

I held her hand and said, "All right, Mum. But think of Jesus. You'll be going home to Him now, don't forget that."

As the tears streamed down all our cheeks, I prayed that Jesus would reveal Himself to her to take her fears away.

We'd been through all this only eighteen months before with our dear dad, who was only sixty-two.

Mum's last words were... JESUS.

*"My Father's house has many rooms; if it were not so, would I have told you that I am going there to prepare a place for you? And if I go and prepare a place for you, I will come back and take you to be with me that you also may be where I am. You know the way to the place where I am going."*
*John 14:2−4*

# 25

## VULNERABLE TIME

Our home felt so different without Mum.

Bob, our beautiful Labrador, sniffed at Mum's clothes when I was sorting them out. I cried when he put his head on them and whined, looking up at me with his big, sad eyes. It was as if he knew she wasn't coming back.

Life went on around us and I sobbed when I was alone. But I still had a peace in my heart, knowing that both my parents were with Jesus. He was the one who gave me strength and calm amid life's ongoing storms and battles. I'd learnt to trust Him in every area of my life so I wasn't going to turn away from Him now. He was carrying me through and I needed Him all the time.

Whenever I had a decision to make, I'd think, "Oh, I'll ask Mum or Dad" — then I'd remember they weren't there. It was hard as the reality set in that they were never coming back. But I also remembered God's promises: they were with Jesus and I'd see them again one day.

When Mum was ill, she'd told me to take the boys on holiday abroad for a break. I could never leave her to go on holiday and she was too ill to go away herself. But she'd been persistent in this and had told me to go once she'd gone home to Jesus.

As I knew this was her wish, Joe, Mick and I went to Zante, a little Greek island, for a week.

I felt vulnerable, alone in another country, with my boys to protect. What was I doing there? It was all a bit of a blur. Mick was still young and stayed with me, but Joe was older. He was sixteen and more independent, and he wanted to do things for himself.

Albanians had come to this beautiful island and were causing a lot of problems for the Greeks. One day, a man followed me from another hotel swimming pool back to our apartment complex. I soon discovered what was going on. This man was a well-known Albanian gangster who preyed on tourists by following them or befriending them. Then, while he distracted them, other Albanians would break into their rooms and steal their belongings.

Joe had done some investigating and found this out from bar staff. They'd recognised the man who had followed me as this same gangster.

At first, I thought Joe had been watching too many TV shows, but I discovered it was true. Thankfully, I never saw the man again as I think the bar staff intervened.

*"The Lord will rescue me from every evil attack*
*and will bring me safely to his heavenly kingdom.*
*To him be the glory for ever and ever."*
*2 Timothy 4:18*

When we got home, Mum's cousin came to visit from Australia. He was a retired minister and it was lovely to see him.

I told him of the visions I'd had before my parents went home to be with Jesus, and he said I mustn't worry if I never had visions again. He told me that not many people experience this. He also said he knew my heart was for people, and that what I'd seen in the vision of the beach was my heart and how I looked after my parents, as they were my treasure.

This really touched me and I did indeed treasure the memories of my lovely parents.

As with my dad, Joe had taken losing my mum much harder than Mick. Losing both grandparents within eighteen months of each other had a massive effect on him and being in his teenage years didn't make it any easier.

I wondered what we'd do now as I had to go out to find full-time work. I'd been Mum's full-time carer and had a small job with the local chemist collecting prescriptions once a week, which helped financially. But now I knew I had to go out and find something more.

Joe had left school and Mick was in his last couple of years there. I felt life was always very difficult for us. We never seemed to have a break from any problems. They just rolled into one another from every angle.

I remember coming home from shopping one day. I'd just walked in through the front door and put my bags down when I had this very strange feeling. I was suddenly alone. On my own without God. Everything felt horrible; empty; scary. I felt sick. It wasn't right. There was no direction. Nothing to keep focused on. Everything seemed manic. Where was I? Who was I? There seemed to be a darkness. Was God real? Where was He?

But then it hit me. I suddenly felt the warmth of God's love. His protection. I was a child of God. God was real. Jesus was my Saviour who'd died and risen again for me. Nothing could separate me from Him.

I believe that Jesus revealed something to me then. He was showing me that life without Him is empty. It's meaningless and there's no direction. I believe He showed me that, through every trial I had been through, He'd been beside me, guiding and protecting me. And not just me but my family too. That momentary emptiness I'd experienced was a glimpse of life without Jesus.

So, despite the endless heartache and trials I seemed to be going through, God was in them with me.

He is faithful and true to His promises.

> *"The* LORD *himself goes before you and will be with you; he will never leave you nor forsake you. Do not be afraid; do not be discouraged."*
> *Deuteronomy 31:8*

I'd come to a point in my life where I once again asked God about relationships and me.

I'd received a phone call from Anthony, who I'd last heard from him a couple of years earlier around the time I'd moved to Southport, after he told me my ex-husband was trying to take my sons off me. I wondered how on earth he'd got my phone number. When I asked him, he told me Sean had given it to him. That didn't make sense either.

He went on to tell me he was in prison. He'd made a mistake and was paying the price. But he'd been inside for a while now and was due out on parole. He did get time home from prison, but he had to go back in later the same day or the next.

I couldn't work out what was going on. What did God want me to do in this situation?

Anthony said he'd been serving a sentence and would tell me about it when he came out of prison, as he didn't have long to use the telephone. Then he arranged to meet up with me on his next home visit.

Although I was growing deeper in my faith, I still had a soft heart. Anthony knew this somehow and played it to his benefit.

I don't know what I was thinking of when I began to meet up with him. I didn't want a relationship with him so why was I going along with it? He told me he'd been caught with guns in his car but said he was just taking a package to someone. Foolishly, I believed this for a short time.

I'd meet up with him and take him to see his family and friends on his days out of prison. At least, that's what I thought I was doing as I sat waiting for him in the car. However, when he kept me waiting for nearly half an hour one day, that's when I found out it was a set up. I was being used. I was his get-out-of-jail card – not involved in the criminal world, somebody who went to church – which was the opposite to his normal lifestyle. I was the one who made his visits seem all above board.

Anthony would never change. He was in prison for carrying firearms for gangsters. There'd been no "mistake" on his part about that. So, there I was, sucked in by this man. And Sean knew all about him when he gave him my telephone number, putting me and my boys at risk again!

I felt so foolish when I looked back at things. I'd been telling Anthony about Jesus and what kind of life he could have. I'd sent Christian literature for him to read while he was in prison. But for him, this was just about getting a quick release.

I knew he must have been released when the contact stopped. He didn't need me anymore.

Anthony had mentioned that he'd like us to have a relationship when he came out of prison, and I'd told him I didn't want this. I was glad when I never heard anything from him again!


Last time I'd been in full-time employment was before my sons were born. And since then, I'd been Mum's main carer. Now the time had come for me to go back out to work, I wasn't quite sure what kind of job to look for.

I prayed and had to act quickly as things were different now. I had to bring extra money in.

On top of this, I was concerned that the rent would be increasing in the house where we'd lived for the past three and a half years and we wouldn't be able to afford it.

I knew I liked art, but I felt there wasn't much scope in this direction for me, as everything was computer-generated now and I knew nothing of computers. One thing I was sure of, though: I was good at looking after people. So this was the direction I decided to take, and I got a carer's job with a lovely company called Crossroads.

I'd been working with them for only a short time when my landlady told me the rent would be increasing on our house. I knew I wouldn't be able to afford it so I told her. She was lovely and understood our circumstances.

I'd been praying for a short while about this and had started to pack things up.

Joe and I sat in my bedroom, asking God to provide a new home for us. We prayed that He'd do this quickly, so we didn't have to bid on lots of properties and struggle or worry. We even asked Him for a letter just to pop through the letterbox, offering us a house. Although I'd had my name down on the council housing list for many years, we knew how difficult it was getting a house in the Southport area. We were asking for a miracle.

Sean still had some contact with our sons, who'd mentioned to him we were looking and praying for a new house. He'd mocked us the way he'd done over finding the boys a school in Southport: "Do you really think God is just going to post a letter through your letterbox?"

After Joe and I had finished praying, I went to collect the post. As I opened one particular letter, I couldn't believe my eyes. It was from the housing department. There were some newly-built houses available and I was being offered one in Ainsdale. I had to contact the office that same day if I was interested.

Joe couldn't believe it either. We laughed and thanked God for His provision and timing as we remembered his dad's words.

Our God is amazing. He keeps His promises and His timing is perfect.

*"And without faith it is impossible to please God, because anyone who comes to him must believe that he exists and that he rewards those who earnestly seek him."*
*Hebrews 11:6*

*"And my God will meet all your needs according to the riches of his glory in Christ Jesus."*
*Philippians 4:19*

*"So do not worry, saying, 'What shall we eat?' or 'What shall we drink?' or 'What shall we wear?' For the pagans run after all these things, and your heavenly Father knows that you need them. But seek first his kingdom and his righteousness, and all these things will be given to you as well. Therefore do not worry about tomorrow, for tomorrow will worry about itself. Each day has enough trouble of its own."*
*Matthew 6:31–34*

*"For the LORD God is a sun and shield; the LORD bestows favour and honour; no good thing does he withhold from those whose way of life is blameless."*
*Psalm 84:11*

Our new home meant we had to downsize. This would be a different living experience for us, but it was so lovely knowing that our God had taken all the difficulties away. He knew what we'd already been through.

I continued to travel to church in Southport, which was only four and a half miles away. My sons had stopped going. They were more interested in going out with friends and their girlfriends than to church. But they still had their faith and I didn't want to force them. I'd tried that and hadn't really got anywhere. So I entrusted them to God's loving hands, having faith that they would return one day:

*"Start children off on the way they should go, and
even when they are old they will not turn from it."*
*Proverbs 22:6*

I had to believe this as it was what I'd been taught earlier on in my walk in the Christian faith.

We settled into our new home and I found that my hours at work had been decreased. The company I was employed by had been privatized. Most of the work was now south of Liverpool. Eventually, my hours with my clients in Southport grew fewer and fewer due to the privatisation, and I was soon looking for alternative employment.

The more I prayed, asking God what I was to do next, the more the same vision would come back to me, over and over again: the cracks in the walls, doors hanging off hinges, a rundown building…

I knew God was trying to tell me something, so I began to do some research, looking for a building in Southport – the one that I'd seen in my vision.

I looked at other projects to do with buildings and soon found God was speaking to me more and more.

During my prayer time, apart from looking for a building, it seemed this project was about opening doors to homeless people. I only saw part of this vision and I knew there was an awful lot more. I hadn't yet seen the full picture. I suppose if I had, I would have done a Jonah and run the other way!

This seemed a huge project.

"Is this real, Lord?" I'd ask, over and over again. "Is this what you're asking me to do? Where on earth am I going to get money to buy a building?"

I tried to tell myself that I was just kidding myself – dreaming, maybe. But I knew deep in my heart that the Lord was speaking to me.

I'd decided to go to an evening church service, which I didn't often do, but I felt the Lord prompting me.

"I've been to church this morning, Lord," I said, "and I don't know why you want me to go tonight too. I've got things to do for tomorrow."

The feeling wouldn't go, so eventually I got myself ready and off I went.

I sat towards the back and the sermon was about how God hates injustice. As I listened, the tears streamed down my face and the vision came to my mind again.

At the end of the service, a man named Phil spoke of a picture he'd had. He felt that someone there was hiding behind a mask or a big overcoat, and they didn't think they could carry out what God wanted them to do.

I listened intently as he went on, "God doesn't want you to leave here tonight until you've prayed with someone. Don't go home unless you've prayed about this."

Once again, my face was wet with tears, but I wasn't crying. I didn't know what was happening.

I didn't really know this man. It was a large church with a big congregation, but I had seen him there many times.

A friend asked me if I wanted someone to pray with me. A lady came over to pray, but I felt I needed to talk to this man. I wanted answers. Why were these tears streaming down my face? What was going on? I'd received a touch from God but there was more to it that I wanted to know. I couldn't just leave it at that.

I prayed that God would bring this man over to me if His message was meant for me – and He did.

Phil walked up and sat beside me. I told him what had happened when he spoke and, just before I told him of my vision, the man in the seat in front of me turned round and asked, "Are you Pam?"

"Yes," I replied.

"I see a picture and it's got your name on it," the man said. "But it's of a map. Your name back to front reads 'map'. God wants you to turn right round as He has your life mapped out, Pam. Step out as a matter of urgency to whatever He's telling you. Not later on down the line, but now."

The man's name was Rob and he is now an ordained minister, although he wasn't at the time. He was listening to God and he acted in obedience to what God showed him.

As soon as Rob said this, I broke down in tears of joy that my Father God was speaking to me through these people. How else would they know any of this? There were only a very few people who knew of my vision. My parents knew and they'd gone home to Jesus.

That's when I opened up and told them both about my vision. They said, "Wow! It can't be any clearer than that!"

"Oh, God, please help me!" I cried. "I never expected anything like this tonight. Help me to remember and to take it all in. It's blown me out the water!"

This was something big. God was moving and fast.

I spoke to my friend Deb and we prayed, but felt called to contact Green Pastures (a housing project). We then spoke to a couple of other close friends who also prayed with us, and God gave them a picture of a silverfish. This represented that God had brought Deb and me together to pioneer this project.

Although I'd had this vision for many years, God also gave me ongoing scriptures, too many to list, and readings from the United Christian Broadcasting book, which always had a word for me. These all seemed to corroborate the vision.

This one piece of scripture came up many times:

> *"Do not neglect your gift, which was given you*
> *through prophecy when the body of elders laid*
> *their hands on you. Be diligent in these matters;*
> *give yourself wholly to them, so that everyone may*
> *see your progress. Watch your life and doctrine*
> *closely. Persevere in them, because if you do, you*
> *will save both yourself and your hearers."*
> *1 Timothy 4:14–16*

During my prayer time when I was asking for wisdom, courage, strength, boldness and anything to help me do God's will, I heard the word "imminent". I also felt the Lord was saying to me: "I will bring the poor to you. I will burden your heart for them."

# 26

# THE VISION BECOMES REALITY
# GREEN PASTURES

At the time, Green Pastures was a small, but growing housing project. Based in a local church, they looked after the marginalised people of our town. I'd donated items to them in the past, but this was the only connection I'd had to them.

My friends and I prayed and asked God that, if it was as urgent as it felt, I'd get to speak with someone from Green Pastures within a week. The next day, I made a call to the church and briefly told them about my vision and what had happened in my church. They asked me to come in for an interview the following day.

"That's urgent," my friend and I both said.

I met Dan and Vick, who took my details and lots of information about who I was and why I was there. Dan and Vick said they'd pass all my information on to Pastor Pete, who wasn't there at the time.

Soon after this meeting, my friend Deb and I worked alongside Dan, who took us around the properties. There were lots of broken doors and walls to fix. There were lots of broken hearts and lives too.

We were ankle deep in urine, vomit, sputum, slime, faeces, fleas, used syringes. You name it we were in it.

We scrubbed out baths, toilets, sinks, floors, walls. We even found a kettle in the toilet covered in paper, faeces and other muck. No one could believe it when they saw how clean the bathrooms and kitchens came up, as we spent days cleaning these properties.

Was this what I'd bargained for? I didn't know. One thing I did know was that I was where God wanted me to be.

We played worship songs and sang along to them as we cleaned the properties up. We didn't feel sick and weren't in the least put off by any of the smells as we focused on worship.

I was still working but only part-time now and I was struggling financially. I could only just about make ends meet.

There was an advertisement in the local newspaper for bank staff at Southport hospital, so I applied. I knew I wanted to do something to help people.

I got the job and was due to start work in a few weeks' time. Part of me was really happy, but the bigger part of me wanted to work with homeless people. Unfortunately, Pastor Pete said there was no funding to put me in a paid position.

Deb and I had been working for Green Pastures voluntarily for almost six months now, and the hospital job came along a week before that six months was up. We'd been emptying flats, cleaning them, painting, furnishing and even carpeting them, and we'd thoroughly enjoyed it. We'd got to know people over those six months.

One place I was always drawn back to was Derby Road in Southport. I bought Christmas presents for some of the tenants, made apple pies for them, and I always found my heart being pulled back there.

One Sunday evening when Pastor Pete came to our church service to speak, he talked to me afterwards. "I know a great place where you can begin to grasp your vision," he said. "Derby Road."

My new job at the hospital was due to start, but I still felt sad. As I picked up my uniform on the Thursday evening, ready to start work on the Monday, I felt something was missing.

Off I went to tell Pastor Pete that I was about to begin my new role at the hospital. I said that meant I didn't know if I'd be able to work with them anymore as I had to be available for my job.

Pastor Pete smiled a big smile that lit up the whole of his face. "Would you like to work full-time with us?" he asked.

"Would I?!" I exclaimed. "Of course I would!" I flung my arms round him. I felt as though something exploded inside me as he spoke; as if I were at home again.

Although I was given an income, I still had a shortfall of £400 per month and Pete told me this was a massive leap of faith.

"Go and do what God has called you to do," he said, as he told me Derby Road was my vision.

In my prayer time, I saw a bright white light over these buildings and I believed God was going to transform this place. God had also told Pete to go and claim back what was rightfully God's about Derby Road.

> *"Be careful to follow every command I am giving*
> *you today, so that you may live and increase and*
> *may enter and possess the land that the* LORD
> *promised on oath to your ancestors."*
> *Deuteronomy 8:1*

When I thought about Derby Road, it made sense. The vision came back again; the cracked walls, doors hanging off, the broken people. God had been revealing a little more to me each time I saw it as I worked alongside Green Pastures. He wanted me to go in and turn the place around. What I'd seen for so many years was now clear. God wanted me here.

In my vision, there were approximately seventeen flats. Each tenant had their own flat with their own front door under one roof. I was to help them with life skills, build relationships with them, and build them up to move on physically, spiritually and mentally. I was there because Jesus loved them and I had to tell them about Him.

This vision became reality.

It was too late to return my uniform to the hospital that evening so I returned it the next morning. The lady who interviewed me was very kind and understanding.

As well as reading my Bible, I would also read *The Word For Today*, which spoke greatly to me on many occasions.

Monday morning arrived and I was ready to begin my new role in Derby Road.

Just before Green Pastures bought the two Derby Road properties, there had been a double murder in one of the flats and, of course, this hit the news headlines.

There were seventeen flats between the two properties. They were big, old buildings and although I'd never had any experience of working with homeless people, most of whom had drug and alcohol issues, I had my own experiences of life and, most of all, this was where God wanted me to be.

My first job was to renovate one of the flats and turn it into my office, and the following is a list of just some of the supportive things we did, as God revealed more and more of my role as time went on:

- Arranged and took residents to hospital, dental, G.P. appointments.
- Filled in assessment forms.
- Assisted with bathing and personal care.
- Cleaned and decorated flats to get them ready for new residents.
- Haircuts.
- Trips out.
- Took some residents on holiday.

- Prison visits.
- Liaised with other organisations, e.g. social services, police, rehab.
- Filled in forms for housing benefits, D.L.A., other benefits etc.
- Taught life skills.
- Served meals.
- Moved tenants on as they progressed.
- Supported the vulnerable in court.

In the beginning, it was very difficult trying to keep "visitors" off the property. Deb, my friend, helped me out most days. She supported me in my vision and the church often sent volunteers round whenever they were available, to help with jobs like cleaning the forecourt up, painting, D.I.Y etc. A lot of contractors didn't like working there as many of the tenants could be aggressive or violent, and they might have their tools stolen. The flats weren't the cleanest of places either, due to tenants' chaotic lifestyles, so we had to rely on any help we could get.

The volunteers were great. They had a real heart for the people we looked after and they got on well with the residents, which was important in this type of work. Some of the tenants were real characters too. I could write another book on the things that went on.

There was a lot of work to be done at Derby Road. One of the main problems was visitors. Most of them were people who lived on the streets and they came to target the most vulnerable who lived there.

One man, who was in his seventies, would often be found wandering around the seaside resort. When I asked him why he was never home, he told me that some of the women who had drug issues would come and target him for money. They'd steal anything they could from him and sell it to buy their drugs, but they'd also use his home with their friends to take their drugs, mainly heroin.

I quickly got to know exactly what was going on. I discovered that the "visitors" knew when the residents were due to collect their pension or benefits. They'd hang around the main post office where residents went to collect their money and ask them to loan it to them. If they refused, tenants would be beaten up or mugged, and the money stolen from them.

This made me very angry and upset, but I'd only find out they'd been robbed once they'd returned to their flat.

It was very difficult as we didn't always see "visitors" sneaking into the property. Either Deb or myself were constantly having to leave whatever we were doing, as a resident would call into the office to tell us people were in the flats and someone was being beaten up and robbed.

We did speak to the visitors and would help them in any ways we could and they knew this. But they also knew the law. They tried to turn it against us by telling us that we had no right stopping visitors, although we soon picked up what we could and couldn't do. We liaised a lot with the police and police community support officers (P.C.S.O.s) and had their regular support. The police informed us that this premises was the number one hotspot for violence and crime in Southport. It was also said many times: "You'll never change this place. It's always been the same."

The police were called out to the Derby Road premises many times a day as there was always something going on – fighting, stabbings, stolen goods or drug raids. My panic alarm went off regularly.

On some occasions, an Irishman called Tony came to town. He was a bully and everyone feared him. He knew some of the residents and often beat them up, and would steal from them if he couldn't get his own way.

One particular time, his girlfriend Alana came to see me. She was a heavy drug user and we often prayed for and with her. She did give her life to Jesus but didn't change her lifestyle, and she had her children taken from her, as did many of the people we came across.

Alana was talking to me when Tony came into the office. She'd been telling me she was afraid of him and wanted to get away. He leaned over my shoulders and grabbed her by the neck, lifting her from the floor. I was stuck in the middle of the two of them, trying to push him back and telling him to leave her alone.

"You're strangling her!" I shouted to him, and I yelled that the police would be there any minute.

He grinned and put her down calmly.

The police arrived as my panic alarm had been activated.

Tony remained very calm and so did Alana, and the police told him to leave and to stay away. Alana didn't press charges and she eventually left too.

They stayed together, though, and left Southport to move in together, but returned a while later. We didn't see much of them then.

Although Tony was a bully, he knew exactly where he stood with me. He knew I was honest and straight with him and, if he caused trouble, he knew I'd call the police.

A lot of the visitors only ever came to steal, bully and hurt the residents and they called us "the God squad". When I'd turn up after they'd got into the building, they'd leave, telling the friends who'd come with them, "Come on, let's go. She's one of the God squad."

They did sometimes try to push it and ask if they could have five minutes. I'd say no as I knew what they were up to. Then I'd stay there chatting to them for a little while, before I told them their five minutes was up.

One day, I heard that a visitor was hiding in the building and the tenants were afraid. I marched into the flat to see three women and a man sitting there with the resident. I told them all to leave immediately.

The women asked, "Who are you?"

One of them answered, "Come on, let's leave it. She's one of the God squad."

It was as if somehow there was a secret fear of or respect for God's people.

"I'll leave in a minute," said the man.

"No," I said, and began to move his push bike into the hallway entrance. I could tell the man was high on something. "You'll have to leave now, come on."

I did get to know how and when to approach drug users. Understanding when or when not to approach them was vital as it determined whether they'd be violent or not. I also knew that God had given me authority and I needed to use it wisely.

As I moved the man's bike out of the flat on one wheel, it was standing up in front of me and I was behind it, against another resident's door. The man followed me out aggressively and shouted that I should watch my back as he'd come back for me. He yelled that I was dead and he wouldn't forget this. But as he snatched the bike from me, he wasn't able to control it and it rolled away down the stairs. I followed him to make sure that he and the women didn't sneak back into one of the other flats.

Once we were outside, the man continued to be abusive and confrontational towards me.

In the midst of this, I suddenly had the strange feeling that the Lord didn't want me to move – as if something like a glass dome had been placed over me. So I stayed put, exactly where I was, and watched this man head straight towards me.

He began to yell in my face and he tried to head butt me. I just moved my head backwards, not my whole self. He then tried to punch me in my stomach and sides. I stood there, staring at him. I couldn't see anything in the way, but he didn't seem able to touch me. There was an invisible barrier protecting me from his blows.

I stayed where I was and waited for him to stop. He couldn't see anything either. But he knew there was something there, in the way. He couldn't understand why his punches weren't touching me.

The next moment, a dog warden's van passed by and someone shouted out of the window.

The man panicked, probably thinking it was the police, grabbed his pushbike and cycled off the forecourt, still shouting that he'd be back for me.

It was only God's protection upon me that had kept me safe. When God calls you to somewhere dark like Derby Road, you have to listen to Him and not to yourself. Otherwise things can go dangerously wrong, as I soon found out.

I'd been involved in a car accident and had hurt my shoulder, so I took some time off work. But I knew there was plenty of paperwork to be done, so I thought I'd call into the office and pick some of it up.

I had a strong feeling that day that I shouldn't go to the office but I ignored it. The feeling wouldn't leave me, but I still insisted to myself that I was only going to pop in for my paperwork and come home. What was wrong in that? It wasn't as if I was going to stay.

I opened up the office and noticed a couple of the residents sitting outside the window in the warm sunshine, chatting away. I collected my paperwork, but when I turned round, I saw a man standing there who I'd never seen before.

I told him we were closed and asked him to come back the following week, or to go to Shoreline Church if he needed accommodation.

He seemed strange and was staring at me. I felt uncomfortable and again asked him to come back and I'd help him then, on my return to work. I tried to walk to the door, but he blocked me and pushed me back into the office.

I can't recall much more that was said but I do remember him pushing me onto the couch and standing over me. I yelled to the residents outside but they didn't hear me.

Suddenly, someone shouted in the hallway. The man turned instantly and headed towards the door to leave. I felt sick and my arm and shoulder were sore.

As the man walked off, the residents asked me what was wrong. I asked them who he was but they didn't know as he'd only just turned up. That's when I realised I should have listened to that inner, small voice and gone with my immediate feeling. It was God telling me not to go into the office. But I'd ignored Him.

Many months later, the same man turned up again for an assessment. Fortunately, I was with another member of staff. I briefly told her about him before we did the assessment, but he left halfway through it.

When he came for another assessment some time later, I discovered that this man had been convicted and charged with the attempted murder of two of his previous partners. He said he'd never had an assessment with us before.

The majority of people we assessed only told us part of the truth. But God had given me a gift in this area, and the truth always came out further into the assessment. I'd give people the opportunity to be honest. I'd tell them we knew they had criminal backgrounds but we needed to know the details so as to find the most suitable accommodation for them. This seemed to release a lot of tension for them as we never judged them. We helped everyone despite their backgrounds, even if it meant finding them alternative accommodation.

Deb and I loved Jesus and knew how much Jesus loved these people. We often told them about Jesus' love for them when they asked why we wanted to help them. They could never understand it and many of them were just the victims of circumstances.

Deb and I would stay there until late at night on most evenings to ensure the safety of the residents, as they told us that, when we'd gone home, the visitors would come and break into their flats. They'd kick the doors in if the tenants didn't open them and steal from them again or beat them up.

Sadly, this way of life was normal for the victims as well as for the perpetrators. They didn't know any different. So when we came along, "the God squad", it was strange for them all. No one knew what was happening, especially the visitors!

"Come on out," I'd tell visitors time and again as they tried to sneak around the back of the buildings to hide. "You have to leave immediately. We have a 'no visitors' policy here."

"I've come to collect my belongings from next door," they'd lie, but we soon became familiar with their ways to deceive us.

After a few months of me moving them on, they'd begin to get more fed up, so they'd hide out of sight and wait until I'd gone home.

When my friend had left, I'd continue working until late into the evening. Mick was now in his last year at school doing his exams and Joe was working. I felt this was when I could catch up on things that needed doing as there were never enough hours in the day.

Many times when I did this, I'd suddenly get an uneasy feeling and sense I was being prompted to leave. This was sometimes an urgent prompt, so I'd just drop everything and go immediately.

On returning to work the next morning, I'd soon discover why I'd been prompted to leave so urgently. There had either been a drugs raid, or someone had been injured through one of the visitors.

*"Whoever dwells in the shelter of the Most High will*
*rest in the shadow of the Almighty. I will say of the*
*LORD, 'He is my refuge and my fortress, my God, in*

*whom I trust.' Surely he will save you from the fowler's snare and from the deadly pestilence. He will cover you with his feathers, and under his wings you will find refuge; his faithfulness will be your shield and rampart. You will not fear the terror of night, nor the arrow that flies by day, nor the pestilence that stalks in the darkness, nor the plague that destroys at midday. A thousand may fall at your side, ten thousand at your right hand, but it will not come near you. You will only observe with your eyes and see the punishment of the wicked. If you say, 'The LORD is my refuge,' and you make the Most High your dwelling, no harm will overtake you, no disaster will come near your tent. For he will command his angels concerning you to guard you in all your ways; they will lift you up in their hands, so that you will not strike your foot against a stone. You will tread on the lion and the cobra; you will trample the great lion and the serpent. 'Because he loves me,' says the LORD, 'I will rescue him; I will protect him, for he acknowledges my name. He will call on me, and I will answer him; I will be with him in trouble, I will deliver him and honour him. With long life I will satisfy him and show him my salvation."*
*Psalm 91:1–16*

The words of Psalm 91 were so true and so relevant to every detail of my life at Derby Road. They summed up everything I went through.

Not long after I began work with Green Pastures, the Lord put on my heart to contact Ellel Grange. I called this a spiritual hospital. I was still feeling deep grief over losing my parents and couldn't look at a photograph of them without crying. I knew God wanted to heal and restore me.

After praying about timing, I contacted them and was told I'd have to wait a few months. If God wanted me to go there before then, I asked Him to arrange it – which He did: a cancellation came up.

Ellel Grange was very different, but I knew Jesus loved me deeply and, as we worshipped and prayed there, His presence was tangible.

There was another presence there too that tried to break me. During prayers, my ankles and wrists would swell up, but when I was prayed over, they seemed to go down. I knew there were a lot of people there who were mentally broken and had gone for healing, so the enemy was going to be active to keep them bound. But I also knew this was a time for me and Jesus. I needed to be set free from the grief and pain that I'd carried for so long.

I was there for three days and had prayers and counselling. I was set free from my ex-husband's soul ties, from the demons that told him about me. I was severed from soul ties from past relationships, boyfriends and my parents. I was set free from all curses that had been put on me and my family; free from generational curses.

Words are powerful and can destroy or build up, so when a lot of negativity has affected you and suppressed you, you live and act with that bondage and it needs to be broken. There is power in Jesus' name and when we trust Him and believe what His Word says, then we can live lives of freedom as we are broken out and severed from the enemy's lies and deception.

It was amazing really as I thought about how beautiful and kind my parents were. It's not bad to be like our parents, but our God made us unique. We're individuals who have our own personality. We're created in the image of Jesus Christ. My parents wouldn't have wanted me to be bound up in their sayings and doings. They'd have wanted me to be free; to be happy. I asked God to give me back all the pieces of me that He'd given me in the beginning; everything the enemy had stolen from me.

One thing my counsellor asked me to do was put on the whole armour of God every time I went to work. I was to ask God to tighten it daily and polish it to reflect on the demons in the drug users. She told me the enemy could see the light of Jesus in me, but I mustn't be afraid of him. I was also to make the sign of the cross on my hands if I had any contact with them. This would prevent any of Satan's network coming through.

"Ask God to put angels in front of you so the demons will see the angels," my counsellor said to me.

Another thing I should do was ask God for a shield of protection and a sword of defence if anyone came to attack me. I knew what she meant by this. In my line of work, I was very vulnerable to verbal and physical assaults.

I knew the demons in people would retreat when they knew I was standing on God's Word in this spiritual battle. So I wouldn't retreat and I wasn't afraid. I knew the enemy was coming into the land that God had given us, and *he* was the one who would have to retreat as God had told us to claim back Derby Road. That's what we were doing, but the enemy didn't give up. His plan was to steal and destroy!

*"Be alert and of sober mind. Your enemy the devil*
*prowls around like a roaring lion looking for*
*someone to devour."*
*1 Peter 5:8*

After the counselling, I was physically, spiritually and mentally exhausted. There was so much to take in and remember for when I returned to work.

As I depended more and more on Father God, I realised how much He had shielded me in my life; how much I relied on Him and had begun to live in deeper faith than I had never known.

Financially, I'd had to depend on Him as I prayed for guidance as to where the £400 per month shortfall was going to come from. And He'd graciously provided this through my church family and friends.

The more I got alongside the broken, lost people at Derby Road, the more my heart began to break. But I had to be faithful to God. After all, He'd brought me here to do His will. When we step out in faith, Christ promises to lead and doors will swing open all the way. This is what happened but I had to keep my eyes fixed on Jesus.

There were many fights on the forecourt – girls as well as men. The girls were worse. We'd try to ask visitors nicely to leave the premises, but suddenly they'd pull a knife out on one of the residents. It was a nightmare a lot of the time.

Dan called me "Can-you-just Pam", as I was always asking, "Can you just send someone down, please?" or, "Can you just do this, that or the other…?" There was always something I needed help with.

That name stuck with me throughout my ministry and, to this day, when Dan sees me he still calls me "Can-you-just…"


I was learning a lot in my ministry – very quickly too – and always had to have eyes in the back of my head. I loved it when I read things pertaining to ministry. I'd keep a note of them and type them out to remind myself of things I may come up against. This was something I read and kept from UCB Word for Today. It's been a great help in my life over the years:

*"God knew the specific purpose you were born to fulfil, so He provided all the gifts you need, including the environment required to put it all together. Then He looked at you and said, 'Very good.' Can you say that too? It's*

*important you can. Why? Because others will treat you according to how you treat yourself... Truth be it determines how far you'll go in life...*

1. *Never think or speak negatively about yourself, that puts you in disagreement with God.*
2. *Meditate on your God-given strengths and learn to encourage yourself, for much of the time nobody else will.*
3. *Don't compare yourself to anybody else. You're unique, one of a kind, an original. So don't settle for being a copy.*
4. *Focus on your potential, not your limitations. Remember, God lives in you!*
5. *Find what you like to do, do well, and strive to do it with excellence.*
6. *Have the courage to be different. Be a God pleaser, not a people pleaser.*
7. *Learn to handle criticism. Let it develop you instead of discourage you.*
8. *Determine your own worth instead of letting others do it for you. They'll short change you!*
9. *Keep your shortcomings in perspective – you're still a work in progress.*
10. *Focus daily on your greatest source of confidence – the God who lives in you."*

Many mornings, I'd return to work to find that the flats had been flooded. There was a young man who was constantly destroying the place. He'd break into empty flats and rip the copper pipes and tanks out of them, leaving water flooding the properties below. No matter how many times the police were called, he didn't care. He'd serve his time in prison, then come back and do the same thing all over again. I often wondered how long this would go on for.

Once when he was back in prison, Deb and I spoke to his girlfriend, who was in her late teenage years. She told us she was afraid of him as he'd often beat her up. She gave her life to Jesus but, soon afterwards, she left the building and we didn't hear from her again.

There was another woman, Jane, who was in and out of prison and addicted to heroin. She would always return to Derby Road when she was released. She was aware of the "no visitors" policy but I always found evidence she'd been staying there.

I spoke to her one day when she tried to sneak off the premises and my heart went out to her. I knew she came to stay where it was easy for her, but I also knew that trouble would come looking for her so she was endangering the other residents.

Although our hearts were to see people saved, we also had to be tough in a loving way. Most of the time, Jane was out of her mind on drugs. She'd previously had her children taken from her. We had good conversations with her if she happened not to have taken any drugs. She even gave her life to Jesus as she said she was sick of her lifestyle – in and out of prison, doing the same old thing over and over.

Jane became pregnant again and was worried her baby would be taken away. She was wanted by the police for theft and knew she'd end up back in prison.

She came to us one particular day, high on drugs. She told me she wanted to hand herself in and, when she came out of prison, she'd be off the heroin and this would give her an opportunity to start afresh.

We took her to the police station, where they were amazed at her giving herself up. She'd taken a lot of tablets that day, she confessed, so had to go to hospital.

Jane was in prison for a few months, and her partner found a nice little house for them and their baby for when she came out. She really did go on to give up her lifestyle of drugs and she did really well for herself. It was lovely to see. The local newspaper even wrote an article on her – how she'd given up drugs, become a Christian and had her baby. It was a wonderful story.

Sadly, Jane's partner William passed away after a few years due to his alcohol abuse. We'd worked alongside him and Jane to help them through their addictions. Dan and I had driven William to Nottingham Betel, a Christian rehab. He came back telling us there really was something very powerful that got them through their addictions there. He was talking about the Holy Spirit.

People we took to rehab often talked about how strong and powerful the Holy Spirit was, but I could never understand why they wouldn't accept the gift of Jesus. The sad thing was that many of the people we took to the Christian rehabs could cope initially with giving up drugs and alcohol but not with giving up smoking. They would dry out in the rehab, then go back to what they knew best – drugs or alcohol.

The months passed by and, as we worked, we always had worship music blasting out through the darkness. It was like giving the house a spiritual clean out. The more we worshipped and claimed back the flats we worked in, the stronger we became. We prayed in the premises daily and commanded any unclean spirits to be broken off us when we were leaving. This became a way of life for us as we entered into the darkness. It was still a dark place to work and we discovered how evil some people could be.

One woman, Kayleigh, who was in her forties, lived there with her partner. They were both heroin users. Often the residents would come into the office for a chat and tell us what had gone on the previous night.

This woman, I discovered, had a very dark side to her and I did fear her. She was the only person who made me feel like this when I was around her. It had never happened with anyone else. She was about five foot ten inches tall and a big lady. Her eyes always shone as though she was high on something, yet at the same time they were very dark. I didn't trust her at all and knew never to turn my back on her. There was something sinister within her and I was aware I needed to pray into this situation. I felt as if I had to stand my ground when I was near her, but also be very careful and not show any fear. I could sense demonic activity, mischief brewing up inside her. She would often glare at me with laughter in her eyes, intimidating me and trying to frighten me off. But I stood firm and trusted God's armour of protection to keep me safe. Her support worker was often weary when she came to visit her and would be relieved when I told her Kayleigh wasn't in the mood to see her.

Often, I'd hear Kayleigh screaming at her partner. Then I'd see him run out of the building, with huge black eyes or his face bleeding. There were times too when we wouldn't see him for days, but she'd come down to the office, high on drugs and in a cheerful mood.

She would ask us about our faith and told me she really liked the "Footprints" poem. So I made her a small plaque of this and she was very happy with it. I could never understand this as darkness and light don't go together. I knew the devil comes in forms of light and uses it to deceive people, but I prayed she would discover Jesus for herself. I also began to put words of scripture up in the hallways and they often went missing. Residents would take them into their flats, which was great. We were claiming ground.

> *"...go in and take possession of the land the LORD*
> *your God is giving you for your own."*
> *Joshua 1:11*

One evening, I was called out to Kayleigh. She rang me in tears, asking if I could visit her. It was around 9.30pm. When I got there, she was crying uncontrollably and told me Sam, her partner, had stabbed himself in the stomach and run off. She didn't know where he'd gone and she was worried about him. And she said she didn't want the police called as he didn't like them.

I stayed there for about an hour and prayed with her. Just as I was about to leave, Sam returned, clutching his stomach. He wouldn't speak to us and went into his bedroom. I heard him shoving things up against the door to barricade himself in.

"If he'd stabbed himself in his stomach, would he have been able to run off so fast?" I asked Kayleigh. She didn't reply, so I left them.

I saw Sam a few days later on his way to the shops, and called him into the office. Kayleigh and Sam's flat was directly above our office. I'd heard Kayleigh shouting to him, "You'd better not be going into that office. Get to the shops now!"

Sam had fear all over his face and things began to slot into place. He scurried out of the office before I could even speak to him.

It was one of the other residents who told me Kayleigh had stabbed him in his stomach. This was presumably why he'd barricaded himself in his bedroom – so she couldn't get near him again.

It was no wonder I felt so uncomfortable around Kayleigh. I could sense the evil in her as she made snide, nasty remarks to Sam and to other residents. She did the same to me one day and she threatened me. She was high on drugs and I knew then that I had to pray for God's quick intervention before something went drastically wrong.

Sometimes, Sam was terrified to speak to us as she'd beaten him up badly. He became very withdrawn and lied all the time when we asked him about her. She'd be at the top of the stairs, listening to see if he told us anything. I remember one time seeing his face swollen and black, round like a football. I couldn't believe it. Kayleigh had beaten him with an iron bar.

Some of the residents had seen Sam on the stairs with hardly any clothes on. He had a dog's collar round his neck and Kayleigh held him on a lead, hitting him.

Many of the residents knew what was going on. They'd been threatened by her, ordered not to say anything. Some of them were brave enough to come forward, however. Sadly, she would beat them too. Even the toughest of the men were beaten and humiliated by her.

I rang the police, social services, all the organisations I could find to try to help him and get some support. There were so many meetings taking place about assistance for him but he was still petrified of her.

Eventually, I got a breakthrough. There was a safe house for him out of town. We told Sam the news when we saw him going to the shop while Kayleigh was asleep.

At teatime, we shut the office down and took him to the safe house. We bought him lots of food and snacks and said we'd call in to see him in a few days' time, as we were arranging for his methadone prescription to be transferred. He was happy with this, and we told him Kayleigh would never find him here and wouldn't hurt him anymore. He told us many more horror stories of what she had done to him. At least we knew he'd be safe for now and could have a good night's sleep.

Two days later, we saw Sam coming through the front door. He'd misunderstood and thought we'd be visiting him every night. He was upset that we hadn't been yet.

Unfortunately, he ended up back in the same old rut – getting beaten up and bullied.

We built up great relationships with the residents and the Lord revealed more and more to me. As we finished one task, another would soon take its place. There were always lots of jobs to do on the buildings as the walls and doors constantly needed repairing due to the break-ins we had.

Two young sisters, who were tenants of Green Pastures in another property, often visited Deb and myself. They said they loved the atmosphere. We always had worship music on as we got stuck in, cleaning out the flats that were empty and painting them. They both became volunteers and we led them to the Lord. They began going to church on a regular basis too and always kept us informed of what was going on with the residents. One of them moved into the buildings we looked after as she said she felt safe there.

The chaos seemed to be calming a little but residents were still targeted. The visitors, who seemed to be the ones who had drug issues, still waited outside the post office for them and took their money. This made me so angry that I decided to take residents to the post office myself every time they were due to get their benefits.

Sure enough, the visitors would approach them, asking for a loan until they got paid. But I knew they never paid the money back. I'd come right out with it and tell them straight: "No."

They didn't know what to do when I said this. They weren't expecting it but they soon took the hint. Not only was I stopping them coming onto the premises in Derby Road, I was also the barrier that got in their way when they wanted money.

Despite this, I'd always make time for the visitors when they tried to sneak onto the premises, and Deb and I did build relationships with them. However, the residents, who mainly drank alcohol, had built up some confidence now and didn't want to have the drug users around. This was their territory and they'd begun to feel safe. So they started to stand up for themselves and there was some conflict.

It was March 2006 and Andy, one of the directors, told me someone was coming out to price up the cleaning out of an empty flat. The previous tenant had been sent to prison for a long period of time and his flat was full of used syringes, amongst other drug paraphernalia.

Andy told me, "You'll get on well with him, Pam, he's a Scouser like you. His name's Dave and I've told him to meet you outside Derby Road."

This flat was in a real mess. There were used syringes everywhere, on the furniture, carpets, in the fridge and bins.

Dave's business was Liverpool Cleaning Services (LCS) and they specialised in cleaning premises where normal cleaning companies wouldn't quote. Dave wasn't like the other workmen who didn't like coming to Derby Road. He took his time when he asked me about the place. He'd done many jobs for Green Pastures in the past.

We stood in the middle of this dark flat that smelled not very nice, and we talked. He told me his mum was ill with lung cancer and that he lived with his partner of ten years and had a four-year-old daughter. His daughter had been diagnosed with epilepsy and had many seizures. I told him I'd lost both my parents within eighteen months of each other but it was my faith that had got me through. He asked me about my faith and I shared more.

Dave and I must have spoken for about one and a half hours and the time flew by. He seemed a lovely man and had been searching for some kind of faith. He couldn't accept that this was all there was on earth and then you die. He'd seen signs for Alpha courses on the back of buses but hadn't known whether to go or not. And his friend had given him a book on Buddhism but he still hadn't read it.

This man was searching, but he wasn't a Christian yet.

I told him I'd pray for his mum and asked if I could pray for him before he left. He said yes and I did.

Praying was the most natural thing for me as I knew what my God had done for me. I didn't want to hide my faith from anyone. Jesus had set me free so I wanted others to know that the power that had set me free could set anyone free if they wanted it to.

When Dave had driven off the forecourt, I looked up towards heaven and said, "Oh, Lord, he was lovely. Why can't I meet someone like him?" But he wasn't a Christian.

Dave told me he'd contact Andy with a price for the job and I'd see him soon.

The days since our meeting passed by, turning into weeks and months, and Derby Road always had some kind of activity going on. We met so many people, from millionaires to the poorest of the poor.

Chris was a real character of a man. He was well known around the town – big, with a loud voice, and many people were afraid of him. His hair was wirey, he was unshaven and he always looked angry. He had alcohol issues, which made things worse as he marched through the streets when he was drunk. He spent many nights in the police cells.

Chris never showered as this was something he seemed to have forgotten how to do. And he never liked to part with his money either, even for the top-up of his rent. He kept it for his alcohol.

As time went by, Chris gradually started to trust me and would often come into the office wanting my attention only. He didn't like anyone else being in there. It was these times that were special for both Chris and myself, as I got to know this gentle giant of a man who had been bullied by Kayleigh. The reason he didn't want anyone else in the office was because he didn't want them to see he had money. He'd give his money to me to mind for him. Kayleigh used to steal it and knock him about. This cruel, evil woman had crushed him mentally and humiliated him. It wasn't just her partner she bullied and beat up. It was other residents too. It was so, so sad and wrong, and it had to stop.

The flats were beginning to take shape. But they still needed a lot of work that would take a long time, and we discovered there were fleas in the building so it had to be fumigated.

Seventeen flats needing fumigation! How was I ever going to get everyone out and keep them out so that the work could be done? Kayleigh never went out. How would I approach her? *How*?

I prayed that God would give us a nice day so that everyone in the buildings could be outside. I asked Him to intervene with Kayleigh as I didn't know how to pray her out.

In the end, the whole thing couldn't have gone more smoothly. It was amazing! God did it all.

The day was lovely – just what I'd asked God for. Every resident knew about the fumigating and off they went. Kayleigh disappeared without me even having to speak to her. It was incredible.

This was what we did with everything. We prayed. But, as we discovered, some things needed more prayer than others.

Kayleigh was becoming more difficult. She went against everything we were doing. Many mornings, I'd come in to find her stepdad, Don crying. Don was a Scottish gentleman who enjoyed his drink. He never hurt anyone and was a very quiet man. He told me she'd stolen many things from him, including his benefits. He had black eyes and bruising to his body. He didn't want to tell me who'd hurt him but I knew it was her as other residents had told me. Everyone in these buildings was afraid of her.

I prayed that God would move her out of the buildings, away from the other residents. I asked Him to stop her wicked violent ways. She ended up in hospital for a brief while with kidney problems. This wasn't what I expected, but the residents did get some peace, even if it was only for a few days.

There were lots of funny times as well as sad times. I remember once, when I was off work ill, that Chris told me he had a present for me.

"Oh, no, what's he got this time?" I wondered.

Chris had a habit of taking things from the local charity shop, then bringing them back to his flat or giving them away. I couldn't believe it when he told me he'd stolen a typewriter and this was my gift.

"It's to help you with your work in the office, Pammie," he said. "Save you all that writing."

I told him to give back all the things he'd taken, but he brought them to me instead. So, after a while of collecting them, I'd take them all back to the charity shop, who were aware of what Chris did. I tried to teach him that it was nicer to give than to steal. But he didn't see anything wrong in stealing something and then giving it away to someone.

Another time, he actually bought a hammer from a shop in town. He had it in a flimsy carrier bag and wasn't impressed when it fell through. He ended up carrying it in his hand and was arrested for swinging it through the seaside resort. We all laughed as he told us.

One summer afternoon, Chris had gone out for a walk around the seaside town. All the residents were sitting out in the sun when one of them came running into the office in a panic. It turned out that Chris had taken a bike from outside the train station and they were worried he'd get arrested.

"Chris," I said to him, "what have you got there?"

"It's a bike! Do you like it?" he exclaimed. "I only borrowed it."

"Yes, I do like it, Chris," I replied. "But just think of that poor person who can't get home on it now. He's probably been at work all day and wants to go home to his family. He's going to be very upset, isn't he?"

"But if I take it back, I might get arrested, mightn't I?" Chris pointed out.

"Yes," I said. "But just think what a good person that would make you, knowing you did the right thing in the end."

"Oh, OK, Pammie." He nodded his head. "I'll take it back now."

And off down the road he went.

It was after the weekend when I next saw him. He walked across the forecourt, heading back to his flat, very sober and quiet.

He soon came in and told us what had happened. He'd been arrested when he'd returned the bike and was kept in the police station cells over the weekend. It was for theft he'd been arrested, he said, not for returning the bike.

"See what happens when I do something good, Pammie?" he went on. "I get arrested. I even got arrested for buying a hammer – and I paid for it, I didn't steal it!"

He was so funny.

I'd been thinking of Dave and his mum and wondering how she was getting on, as I'd been praying for her. I'd been praying for him, too, to know Jesus. Three months after quoting for the job, Andy told me Dave would be starting work on the Monday and meeting me at 9am. The day came, and I pulled into the carpark beside him and got out ready to greet him.

Some volunteers worked with Dave and they were a great team. Everyone worked hard and got on well together.

I showed Dave the flat he'd be working in and he got on with it. The job should only have lasted a week, but Andrew kept piling different jobs on top. In the end, Dave was there for six weeks.

Dave was a lovely man and nothing was too much trouble for him. When he saw me wearing sandals, he asked if I went into the flats with them on.

"Most of the time I wear trainers," I told him.

The next day, he brought me a pair of steel-toe-capped boots to wear.

"I can't wear them if I'm wearing a dress," I said with a laugh. "I'll look funny."

"Better to look funny than get pricked by a sharp," he told me.

He was right. Many of the people who sneaked in at night were heroin users and used syringes. He gave me the steel-toe-capped boots to protect my feet. He was very considerate.

One morning, I had to go out to buy a kitchen sink for one of the flats. I'd told Chris the previous evening I'd go with him to the post office, as I knew there'd be people waiting outside to take his money from him. However, I wanted to pick up the sink before we went.

I also told Dave where I was going and said I wouldn't be long.

Dave rang me just as I was leaving the shop, warning me that Chris was in an aggressive mood and to be careful on my return. Dave had told him I wouldn't be long, but Chris wanted to know how long.

"I'll be back in five to ten minutes," I said to Dave.

Chris started counting and threatening Dave with what he'd do if I wasn't back soon. I could hear him, and told Dave to pass the message on to him that if he didn't behave, I wouldn't be going with him to the post office.

Again, Chris started counting. I could hear him getting angry.

When I returned, there was a chest of drawers smashed up across the car park. Chris had been throwing the drawers at Dave. They hadn't hit him, but each one had got closer than the one before. Someone had rung the police and they arrived just as I did.

The policeman got out of the car and approached me.

"Do you want me to come in with you?" he asked, as Chris came out of the doorway.

Chris walked over to my car and simply said, "Hello, Pammie. Can we go to the post office now?"

Dave and the policeman couldn't believe the change in this man's behaviour as soon as I turned up.

"No, I'll be fine," I assured the police officer, who didn't really know what to do. "He'll be OK with me."

Dave was amazed at the difference in Chris. He told me that as soon as Chris saw my car pulling up on the forecourt, he calmed right down.

I spoke with Chris in the office about his behaviour and said it wasn't acceptable. He apologised to myself and to Dave.

Then I walked into town with him and, sure enough, people were there waiting for him.

"No, he doesn't have any money to loan to you," I told them. "He doesn't have anything left after he's paid everything out."

Sadly, there seemed to be many demons around Chris. He came into the office one afternoon to pay his top-up rent. He seemed very calm and peaceful. Then, as we were talking, his voice changed. His eyes became like pin holes as he spoke and he grew very nasty and aggressive. I couldn't understand his language properly, but he did seem to quieten down when I looked at him.

I carried on speaking and the voice I could hear coming from him became agitated. Staring into Chris's eyes, watching for changes, I said firmly, "I'm speaking to Chris, not you. Now leave him alone. I'm talking to him."

Suddenly, Chris seemed to come back to himself. He began to speak as if nothing had happened. His eyes looked normal again.

I didn't realise at first what was going on – until the voice carried on speaking through Chris but I couldn't understand what it was saying. I just knew it was nasty, demonic and aggressive.

This was the first time I'd ever seen a manifestation like this.


Raymond was one of our volunteers. He was very good at woodwork and carpentry. He was a lovely, retired gentleman who offered his services by fixing things in our buildings.

Due to the nature of the work at Derby Road, we had rules for volunteers: they mustn't be left on their own on the premises as anything could happen.

When I arrived for work one day, Raymond came to see if there was anything he could do for us, and he told me he'd been to see Kayleigh a couple of days previously. He said he'd prayed with her and cast out demons.

"Oh, no!" I thought.

He went on to tell me she had my "Footprints" plaque up that I'd made for her. She'd told him she had a problem with alcohol and drugs and he'd asked if he could pray for her. She'd agreed.

What he'd done was great – but he'd been on his own in the building, casting out demons. And I felt very uncomfortable in my spirit with all of this. Praying for and with people was what we did on a regular basis, but what Raymond told me disturbed me and I didn't know why.

> *"Then it says, 'I will return to the house I left.'*
> *When it arrives, it finds the house unoccupied,*
> *swept clean and put in order. Then it goes and*
> *takes with it seven other spirits more wicked than*
> *itself, and they go in and live there. And the final*
> *condition of that person is worse than the first.*
> *That is how it will be with this wicked generation."*
> *Matthew 12:44–45*

One afternoon, when we'd been out to collect furniture for one of the flats, we returned to see an ambulance on the premises. Raymond and Don, Kayleigh's stepdad, were covered in blood. They were taken to hospital and received stitches for head and facial wounds.

Raymond had arrived at the building while we were out and had begun to fix a door on one of the flats when a visitor had turned up. Raymond had answered the main door to him but refused him access.

The visitor was Kayleigh's son. He then assaulted Raymond and his grandad, Don, who refused to give him money.

Raymond never volunteered his services again after that. And there were many similar incidents that happened.

I rang in ill one morning and spoke to Dan, who had already arrived at Derby Road to catch up with me. Dan was one of the workers who did the pastoral visits.

"I'll ring you back, Pam," he said. "Someone's been injured. Not one of the residents but someone who shouldn't be here." Then he hung up.

Dan always did his best to protect me from the ongoing chaos that surrounded me. He'd often grab my hand and shout to everyone: "She's going for her dinner now. She'll see you all later." Then he'd physically pull me out of the office.

The visitor who'd been injured had been let in by Kaz, one of the female residents. She'd also let in another male visitor. The two men had begun to argue and one of them had stabbed the other in his groin, then run off, leaving him bleeding and unconscious on the stairs.

If I'd been at work, I would have been there when it happened. This was one of the ways God always intervened and protected me.

I was beginning to see things in a new light too. I'd said I never wanted to be around drug and alcohol-related problems ever again, and here I was in the midst of them, but looking at them through different eyes.

Jesus was my rock in all of this. He was my strength and shield, my guardian in everything I faced there. I recalled Sue and my mum telling me a long time ago that Jesus would use all my experiences to help others.

I saw so many broken people who Jesus loved and wanted to restore. Sadly, not many gave up their alcohol or drugs, but they did want peace. Many of those we prayed with invited Jesus into their lives, but they still returned to the same lifestyle. The more I prayed for God to intervene and remove the ones who were causing problems, the more I saw God in action.

Kayleigh had been in and out of hospital and we visited her a few times when we could, taking in toiletries and new nightdresses for her. Even though she was wicked to the residents, I believed they all needed to be treated the same – with love.

As it turned out, Kayleigh never returned to Derby Road. I think she eventually moved out of town.

It was around this same time that I realised I hadn't seen Sam for a couple of days. I had a very strong feeling I should go up to his flat. I knocked on the door a few times but didn't hear anything.

Some of the residents said they'd seen him around town a couple of days earlier and that he may still be out.

No. Something wasn't right. I prayed and I felt I had to go into his flat. I rang Dave to share my concerns and I let myself in with the master key.

There was Sam, dead in the darkness of the flat. I felt as if something else dark lurked there too.

Dave told me to ring 999 and said he was on his way over.

This was the first time I'd found someone dead. I was so sad to see this poor man who'd been in turmoil, living in fear for his life. He wasn't suffering physically or mentally anymore now, but I didn't know where he was spiritually.

I don't remember much after that, apart from the police being there, asking me lots of questions, and Michaela, another one of our residents, asking what was for dinner after I'd just told her I'd found Sam dead.

Sam's lifestyle contributed to his death. It was thought he'd been dead for a day or two. The police didn't investigate any further and we never saw or heard from Kayleigh again. She'd disappeared a few days earlier.

People had their own ideas about Sam's death. Some thought Kayleigh had killed him; others that he'd died from an overdose. Others said he was in a better place now, away from Kayleigh. It was very sad.

Still, I had to pull myself together quickly. There were others I had to look after. And my emotions were everywhere. I had to think about them too. It's very strange when you find someone dead one minute, then the next you have to function and keep focused on everything and everyone else. Life still went on.

These people were tough. They'd lived rough and been beaten and left for dead themselves. They knew how life was; knew hard times as this was their story so why did I expect them to feel or react any differently? This was normality to them.

"Sam's at peace now," the police officers told me.

I certainly knew there'd be no more beatings from Kayleigh, but at peace? Where was he? Had he gone to be with Jesus? We'd told him about Jesus when we could and prayed – but where was he?

After Sam's flat had been cleared out, we painted it. The atmosphere wasn't nice in there but we continued to pray in it. We played and sang worship songs as we decorated, which changed the place. It felt clean. The darkness was gone.

Another flat was claimed back:

> *"...hear the decrees and laws I am about to teach*
> *you. Follow them so that you may live and may go*
> *in and take possession of the land the* LORD, *the*
> *God of your ancestors, is giving you."*
> *Deuteronomy 4:1*

The same scripture came flooding back to me each time we claimed back the flats, and some of the people too.

# 27

# THE DESIRES OF MY HEART

Dave was coming to the end of his work. We'd all got on well with him and he was accepted as one of us. And the volunteers were great girls. They had hard lives, but they enjoyed being with us. They'd think nothing of cleaning the dirt and grime from the muckiest of places, painting, and coming with us to pick up furniture for flats we were restoring. They had wonderful hearts, so it was lovely to see them give those hearts to Jesus and go to church when they could.

We did have to make our own fun at work sometimes, as it was mostly a difficult job. But when the volunteers and Deb and I would have a mad half hour, doing something like painting each other, it lifted everyone's spirits. I remember dabbing a bit of paint on Dave. He then grabbed me and rolled his paint-loaded roller right down my front. The girls couldn't stop laughing. We had to find a balance.

It was times like these that the volunteers loved working with us. We'd lost a lot of them due to changes in their personal lives. Some had gone to work for Green Pastures in other areas.

"Imagine if Dave worked with us on a daily basis?" I said to Deb one day.

We'd all chipped in and bought him a card and some chocolate to thank him for his work and for just being who he was. He shared his chocolate with us all and we mucked about, blowing the Maltesers into the air and catching them in our mouths, or throwing them into each other's mouths.

But there was something different happening here, I told myself. It didn't seem as if it would be the last time Dave would be working with us.

Dave asked me if he could pick up the work key from me at the weekend as he had to collect the rest of his belongings. He said he'd call round to my home on the Sunday.

Deb had been telling me that Dave liked me, but I didn't seem to believe it. I'd been let down so much in the past and I didn't want to make the same old mistakes I'd made so many times before. Anyway, my focus was on Jesus and His ministry. I had no time for relationships. Derby Road was the vision that God had given me to look after, and I wanted to serve Jesus and serve Him well.

I'd prayed months beforehand and surrendered myself – my life – over to Father God. I'd asked Him to make it clear if He wanted me to be alone for the rest of my life and, if He did, to take my sexual desires away from me, as I'm only human. I said a prayer along these lines:

*"Lord, if You don't want me to be in a relationship again, then so be it. I'm aware that You made man not to be alone but I don't know if You want me to be with anyone or not. If You want me to stay celibate, then please take my sexual desires away. And if You do have someone for me, please keep me pure for Him."*

I went home that weekend with a feeling that I would see Dave again. As Deb told me over and over again how he'd told her that he liked me, I was very calm about it all. I knew I had to listen to God and not to my own feelings. And Dave wasn't a Christian.

Dave called me over the weekend and arranged to come and see me on the Sunday. That's when he opened up and told me how he felt about me. I can't remember everything he said as I was somehow in another world, something I'd never experienced before in any relationship, and certainly not to this extreme.

Dave told me he'd been in an empty relationship for the past ten years. He'd stayed and tried to make everything work, but there was no love. He had plenty of money but that didn't buy happiness. They did have a daughter. She was the only thing that brought joy to him. There was no love in the relationship with his partner; no love from her.

Dave had told himself that he'd be out of it before the end of the year. He'd decided this before he'd even met me.

He went on to tell me that, the minute I'd got out of the car and smiled at him on the second day we'd met, he knew he was going to marry me. He didn't know how, why or when – he just knew that it would happen.

He knew, too, that this was God revealing Himself to him, as he felt a love for God and for me. And he understood that he had to walk away from the relationship he was in, despite what I thought. He didn't know if I was interested in him or not; he just knew he had to leave.

"I'm having no part in any breaking up a relationship," I told God, Dave and myself.

But Dave said he'd made this decision himself and, no matter what happened, he knew that now was the time to leave – whether I had any interest in him or not.

And that's what he did. That very night.

His mum was relieved as she knew how his partner treated him. She'd seen the hurt and upset in him as she worked in the same office as he did. And she'd heard the arguing and his partner shouting down the phone.

When Dave told me he'd left, I still didn't know what to do about anything – apart from pray. I discussed it with my closest friends and family, but I was aware that I had a peace that was beyond compare. I knew God was in this.

Dan told me he felt that God had brought Dave into my life. Dan knew I'd been through a lot of trials and he added that he wouldn't normally talk this way. But he'd prayed about it too and he felt God was giving Dave to me. Deb said the same.

I prayed a simple prayer:

*"Oh, Lord, help. Dave is lovely but I don't think he's yet given his heart to You. And I know this is the only way I can be with someone, from what You told me years ago about being with a man who loves You. Show me clearly what to do."*

God had given me this Bible verse many years ago when I was praying for the right man to come into my life:

> *"...she is free to marry anyone she wishes, but he must belong to the Lord."*
> *1 Corinthians 7:39*

But I still had this amazing peace about Dave, and it never left me.

Dave came to work the following day to tie up the loose ends and collect his tools. Before we left the office that evening, Deb, Pete – one of the volunteers – and I were discussing faith with him.

Dave sat there and prayed with us. He then gave his life to Jesus.

I didn't know what to do! It was an amazing time there in the office. As I looked into Dave's deep blue eyes, which sparkled with life, I knew God was doing something incredible. We all felt it. Dave really had made a sincere commitment and we praised God together.

These moments were very powerful and serious, but exciting too. As I continued to look into those sparkling blue eyes, God gave me the words "cherish" and "protect". I felt I needed to be gentle and guide Dave in his faith. I also felt we needed to protect ourselves spiritually and physically in our relationship – which was strange as we weren't yet *in* a relationship. But

I knew this was from the Lord. He wanted us to put Him first in everything and He would bless us immensely.

God then gave me the words of this verse:

*"Peace I leave with you; my peace I give you. I do not give to you as the world gives. Do not let your hearts be troubled and do not be afraid."*
*John 14:27*

I still kept things close to my heart as I pondered what was going on. I had a day's holiday coming up, so I took the time to pray about it.

My friend Dan came to see me and asked me to list reasons why I shouldn't have a relationship with Dave and reasons why I should. As it turned out, I didn't have one reason against, but many for.

Deb and I had booked to go away on holiday for a week and there was no better timing than the present. It would give me the chance to pray about everything as it was all happening so fast.

We spent the time mainly on the beach in Menorca and Dave rang me in the hotel room every night. It was always so lovely to hear his voice.

During one of my prayer times, as I lifted my hands in praise, I saw my Lord take hold of them and put them on His cheeks. It was so beautiful as He was happy and smiling at me.

I spent a lot of time in prayer and God gave me many Bible verses about my ministry. One section was Deuteronomy chapter 6. As I read it, He took me to other chapters of this book:

*"...be careful to obey so that it may go well with you and that you may increase greatly in a land flowing with milk and honey, just as the LORD, the*

*God of your ancestors, promised you."*
*Deuteronomy 6:3*

*"Love the LORD your God with all your heart and*
*with all your soul and with all your strength."*
*Deuteronomy 6:5*

*"See, I have taught you decrees and laws as the*
*LORD my God commanded me, so that you may*
*follow them in the land you are entering to take*
*possession of it."*
*Deuteronomy 4:5*

Reading these verses, I felt that God was speaking to me in my personal life as well as in my ministry with Green Pastures.

At the end of the holiday, Dave picked me up from the airport. It was wonderful to see him again. Then, a couple of days later, I was back at work. Of course, by now Dave had finished at Derby Road. We all missed him being around but life carried on as normal there.

The flats got sorted out and we were now liaising with police community support officers (P.C.S.O.s). They'd drop in to ensure things were functioning well and to see if there were any problems. Although there were problems on a daily basis, they mainly came from the visitors, and our hearts were to protect and look after the residents.

I wanted to see people changed; to show them that, not only did we care for them, but there was a God who loved them more than we ever could. As we prayed, God showed us more direction for the plans He had for the people, but He also showed me what He wanted me to do.

The Derby Road buildings were a stepping stone up from the streets. Residents lived here for approximately six months before being moved into other suitable accommodation once we felt they were ready. It depended on the individual. This was a place for vulnerable people, some of whom had drug and alcohol issues. Initially, we'd carry out an assessment to see if they were suitable for Derby Road or one of Green Pastures' other properties. We then filled in forms for housing benefit and any other benefit they may be entitled to. And from there, once we had everything set up, we moved them into accommodation.

On assessment, we discussed with potential residents the three-strike system for Derby Road. This was set in place with rules to keep out visitors. Alcohol could only be consumed on their own premises, not in the communal areas, and there were other rules too that they seemed to adhere to most of the time.

Unfortunately, we did have to use this system at times, when residents broke the rules by bringing in visitors and putting other residents at risk.

God supplied our every need. All we had to do was ask Him. We were given a new cooker and washing machine for our office. People donated everything from toiletries to clothes for the people we looked after. The more word got round about what we were doing in Derby Road, the more I received phone calls from people wanting to donate larger items of furniture. There was such generosity. I stored most of what we were given in my office, as I knew God had a home for everything. Nothing would be surplus to requirements.

It was amazing to see people who'd come off the streets with nothing but the clothes they had on their backs, and be able to house them and provide beds, food, clothing and toiletries, which we called a starter pack.

We also taught them that not everything in life is free, so some of them who were able volunteered their services and helped us to get flats ready for newcomers. It became like a community of people who looked after each other. Many did move on to better accommodation, but there were still people who loved it at Derby Road and remained there until they passed away. We would offer them something more suitable, but they felt secure and looked after with the setup we had in place. And when others decided it was time to go, their flats were never empty for long. There was always someone else who was homeless and in need of accommodation.

In the meantime, Dave kept in contact with me. We went for a walk on the beach one evening and took my lovely dog, Bob, with us. Bob was very protective but very funny with it. He insisted on walking between us.

We spent hours sitting under the stars on that beautiful, clear night, Bob in the middle. It was when Dave gently kissed me that I knew this was meant to be. Bob, however, had other ideas. I was his mum, and he began to tug at the back of my skirt, pulling me away.

We couldn't stop laughing.

"He's jealous," Dave said. "I've never met a dog like him!"

Bob simply wagged his tail and jumped up at me, nuzzling me for attention.

We drove home, me starry-eyed from the wonderful evening, which felt like something out of a romance novel. Then Dave came in for a cuppa before his twenty-five-mile drive home.

We walked in to find that Mick was still up.

"Where have you been?" he demanded. "I've been worried, you know."

"What?" I exclaimed. I was bewildered at his tone of voice. "Since when? Why didn't you ring me, then? You know I always have my phone with me."

Then, out of the blue, Mick blurted out to Dave, "Do you know she's had loads of boyfriends and girlfriends?"

"*What?*" I couldn't believe what he was saying, and I started to laugh as he named the same three men, over and over again.

Dave laughed too and said, "It's OK, I don't care. But I'm with her now so there won't be anyone else. And I'll look after her. You don't need to worry now."

I'd always been close to my sons. It was clear Mick didn't want his mum to be with anyone else as he thought that meant I wouldn't have the same close relationship with him and Joe.

I'd explained to him many times that God would have to give me a very special man if I was to marry again; someone who would love my boys as his own and look after me too.

Mick started to chat with Dave then, and got on well with him. But somehow, I already knew it was going to be all right.

That was the beginning of something beautiful between Dave and me. I was in another world in this relationship, so high I couldn't come down. It was incredible. I could be myself without worrying that I was going to be hurt.

Dave told me things that I only spoke to Jesus about. Jesus was revealing them to Dave as he spoke them out to me.

"I want to be the one to catch you before you fall down again. I want to be there before you fall," he said. "I want to be the one who catches the moths at night in your bedroom when you're scared..."

Words upon words. Tears streamed down my cheeks as he spoke them to me.

Where had this man been all my life? The question kept revolving in my mind until my Jesus gently reminded me: "God's timing – not yours."

Later that night, as I read the book of Esther, I fell asleep in God's beautiful presence, tired and tearful. When I awoke, I felt the Lord had put these words on my heart: "I have given you Dave and you've been asking constantly for confirmation."

All of a sudden, it was so, so clear.

I'd been so blinded and bogged down, I hadn't realised that God had given me the desires of my heart. I needed to finally leave my past behind and walk by faith.

When I realised God had given Dave to me, my eyes were once again opened.

I thought back to the time at Derby Road when Dave had given his life to Jesus; when I'd looked into his eyes and God had shown me that our relationship was to be.

We continued going to church together and felt the Holy Spirit move in us many times. We were attending Lytham St. Anne's, known as Ansdell Baptist Church, at the time, and at the end of one service there was what they called a "fire tunnel".

The fire tunnel was made up of two lines of people who prayed over individuals as they walked through. Dave and I had never experienced anything like this before, so we went back through again, feeling the power of the Holy Spirit upon us. It was amazing.

At one point, I felt as though God wanted to release me from something and, at the same moment, someone prayed over me and said, "God is healing your heart. He wants to heal all your past hurts and give you a completely new life." This is what I felt in my spirit, too, and I was in tears.

Before the service had started, a lady had told me to read the book of Esther in the Bible. She told me the name "Esther" meant "Star". Dave had said that he saw me as a bright, shining star when he first met me, and he continued to call me that from the start.

I told the lady I'd been reading the book of Esther as God had also prompted me to do this a few months earlier. I remembered the verses about her preparing herself with oils and perfumes, and I believed God was preparing me for something big too: my wedding day. He had been getting me ready all these years for what He was about to give me.

I met Dave's family and Dave's beautiful daughter, who was only five. They were lovely people and I got on well with them all.

Dave came to church with me every week. He went on the Alpha course and began to really grow in his faith. My brother Sam and sister-in-law Deb got on really well with him too.

One day in October 2006, when Dave had been a Christian for four months, Stu, our vicar, called him to the front of church. Just as Stu called him, Dave told me he didn't feel too well.

"I'll pray for you," I said.

"I think it's a good idea for you to come out too, Pam," Stu added.

I just sat there as there were three Pam's in our congregation. Stu repeated the invitation and I realised he was looking straight at me.

I pointed to myself with a question in my eyes and Stu nodded. "Yes, chop, chop, I'm talking to you, Pam! Come on, quickly."

My heart sank, just a little. "Oh, no!" I thought. "Why didn't he tell me he was going to call me up the front? I haven't prepared anything." I imagined he was going to ask me to speak about my work. I never liked speaking from the front of church. It wasn't something I was confident in.

I walked up to the stage in front of the two-hundred-strong congregation.

Dave began to grin at me. "Pam," he said, "I love you with all my heart. Will you marry me?" As he spoke, he pulled out a beautiful engagement ring.

I was so stunned I could hardly get the word out.

At last, "Yes!" I gasped. And I grinned to from ear to ear.

"I don't think anyone heard you, Pam," Stu said. "Can you say that again?"

"Yes! YES!" I was laughing with the nervousness of being on the stage and the total joy of Dave's proposal.

Our church family clapped and shouted with happiness and excitement, and we worshipped God together.

Stu was delighted for us and took a photograph. He told us it was the first time anyone had proposed to someone in his church in all his years of service there. He even sent the photo off to the local newspaper and they wrote a big article about us in the centre pages!

On the way out of church, my friend Joanne caught me. She was overwhelmed as her words tumbled out. "Pam – do you remember what you told me and your mum?"

I looked at her questioningly.

"That you will know if a man is from God," she continued, "if he asks you to marry him in church. This was your desire!"

Of course! Somehow, I'd completely forgotten! I flung my arms around Joanne. And I knew absolutely that God had given me this beautiful man, who was a Christian. I was on such a high – I still haven't come down!

Soon afterwards, Deb asked me to go to a wedding fair with her, so off we went. I floated around, eyes shining as I looked at everything on offer, and I let Deb do all the talking.

It was strange in one respect as I thought I didn't deserve to have a proper wedding because I'd been married before. I thought I should dress down and not wear a big gown. I mean, I knew marriage wasn't about what dress you wear to your wedding, but I was a romantic at heart and I wanted all of this.

Deb surprised me. "Oh, no, Pam," she bubbled. "You are a child of God. You are the bride of Christ – an heir. You're royalty. God wants you to have the best now."

"Yes," I said, as the reality of her words hit me. "I am a child of the living King Jesus and He does want the best for me. Does this mean I can wear a long bridal dress, then?"

"Of course it does!" Deb cried.

It was wonderful telling our families the news. My parents would have been so happy for me, and Dave's family were over the moon. They were beautiful people who warmly welcomed and accepted Joe, Mick and me. Kaz and Sue, Dave's sisters, treated me as if I was another sister of their own.

Dave's dad was also called Dave. (I called him "Dave Dad".) He was a carpenter and he made huge rocking horses and dolls houses, among other things. He'd been on TV when *Granada Reports* had interviewed him about his hobby. I always thought he had a look of a slimmed-down Father Christmas about him, especially with his white beard. He'd make us laugh and had plenty of time for us all.

Anne, Dave's mum, was lovely too – warm, loving, funny and kind. Although she was ill with cancer, she was a strong woman who kept the family on track. It was easy to see what loyal, faithful, genuine people they all were. They'd worked hard all their lives, and how extraordinary it was to know this was now to be my family too. I automatically loved them all and my new nephews as well.

My parents would have been thrilled to see how my new in-laws accepted us so warmly and lovingly. I missed my mum and dad, even though I knew they were now with Jesus.

Dave and I hadn't been engaged long when I was woken up by a dream one night, with the words: "Let no two things that are brought together by God be separated by man." This was a very powerful message to me and I totally understood it.

We discussed plans to marry the following year, in September 2007. But when we spoke to Stu, he said, "Why wait that long? Especially if your mum isn't well, Dave."

It was October at the time, and eventually we settled for the beginning of March 2007.

Because I'd been married before and divorced, both Dave and I had to go to regular meetings with Stu for a few weeks. It was at one of those meetings when Stu asked us where we were going on honeymoon. We didn't know at that point but I piped up: "Somewhere hot and erotic, I hope!"

Stu quickly changed the subject after that and I wondered why – until Dave leaned towards me and told me that what I meant was "exotic"!

It was difficult trying to focus on wedding plans as Derby Road demanded a lot of my time. Dave would visit me through the week as his office was in Liverpool and I was still living in Ainsdale then.

One cold November Sunday, his mum came over to visit. She knew I was a Christian and had introduced Dave to the Christian faith. We invited her and Dave's dad to come to our church with us as it was the Christmas lights switch-on parade and the streets were heaving with visitors. At the end of the church service, I prayed with Dave's mum. She cried and hugged me. I knew God had hold of her.

Afterwards, we went for something to eat and did some shopping. Dave's mum was looking for a wedding outfit. We then waited for the Christmas lights switch-on. We had a lovely time together and she was so happy when she came back to the home where she knew her son would be living.

"I know he's going to be all right now," she said. "I feel much better."

It was very sad to hear the story that Dave's mum went on to tell me. Her sister, who was once very close to Dave, had told her that Christians take all your money and Dave was getting involved in a cult. She'd fallen out with him when he'd left his ex-partner and didn't want to know him when he met me.

I was glad Dave's mum came to church to see for herself what we were all about. And she liked it too.

Sadly, Dave got a phone call at five o'clock on the following Tuesday morning to say that his mum had died: two days after she'd come to church with us. It was a very emotional and sad time. But I was so grateful to have met this lovely lady, and for the brief time I'd been able to spend with her.

# 28

# MARRIAGE

The first Christmas Dave and I had together was tinged with sadness due to the loss of his mum. So Dave's dad, sister and her family, my family and brother and sister-in-law all had Christmas dinner at my home. There were thirteen of us and we mucked in together and enjoyed it as best as we could.

The season passed quickly and, before I knew it, the end of January was in sight.

I was on my way home to get ready for church. I'd been out looking for tiaras and hair clips for my wedding day. It was dark and raining and I didn't know the area very well. I barely saw the Give Way sign as I overshot it.

I remember hearing this almighty bang as I felt my car hit something. Someone came to my aid, talking to me, telling me it was fine and I'd be all right. It was a man with a young boy. I could hardly speak. I couldn't see in front of my car as the bonnet was all squashed up.

I was taken to hospital in an ambulance with Joe. I heard one of the ambulance crew say something along the lines of, "It's broken. You'll have to use another machine." I was in shock and apparently my stats were so high that the crew member thought the monitoring equipment wasn't working properly.

The police came and breathalysed me in hospital. The result was negative, but the policewoman wasn't very nice to me. I was allowed home a few hours later.

I knew it was my fault as I'd overshot the junction. I hadn't spotted it until the very last minute when it was too late. A vicar and his wife were travelling across my path when I hit them, spinning my car up on the pavement backwards, then crashing into a garden wall and knocking it down. Thankfully, the vicar's wife in the other car had no more than a cut on her nose when her airbag went off. Other than that, both she and her husband were all right.

My car was a write-off. However, although my airbags didn't go off, I do remember feeling as if I had a cushion in front of me.

Looking at the state of my car, it seemed incredible that, apart from being in shock, I'd come through this totally unhurt.

Again, my God was my defender. My car was written off but I was alive. Praise Him!

> *"But I will sing of your strength, in the morning I will sing of your love; for you are my fortress, my refuge in times of trouble. You are my strength, I sing praise to you; you, God, are my fortress, my God on whom I can rely."*
> *Psalm 59:16–17*

Two weeks later, it was Valentine's day.

I'd come home from work feeling achy and tired. Our wedding day was approaching fast. With only two weeks to go, we still had a lot to do.

Dave had finished work early and, as it was Valentine's day, had come to my home.

"I've run you a nice bath," he said. "Get undressed and give me a shout before you go into the bathroom."

Understandably, I was confused. "But – why can't I just go in?"

"Just shout to me when you are ready," Dave replied.

So I did. I stood there in my dressing gown while he told me to close my eyes and he'd guide me into the bathroom.

"OK," he said softly. "You can open your eyes now."

It was beautiful. My small bathroom was dimly lit by the flickering flames of tiny tea light candles. There were bubbles to the top of the bath, glitter was scattered across them and rose petals floated on top. And on the side was a bottle of bubbly and a glass bowl of chocolate truffles.

Oh, how I melted! He was so romantic and loving, my husband-to-be.

"When you're in the bath," Dave said, "give me a shout and I'll come in and you can tell me all about your day."

I climbed into the beautiful hot bath and Dave returned and we chatted. He poured us a glass of bubbly each and we ate the chocolates together.

Gradually, I became aware of something.

"What's that smell?" I asked. "And that hissing noise?"

Dave's jaw seemed to drop in horror.

Before I knew what was happening, he'd hit me on the top of my head.

"Oh, no, Pam!" he yelled. "Your head's on fire! Stay there!"

I'd never had a candle-lit bath before and, because the wispy bits of hair around my neck were dangling down, they must have caught fire in one of the small candle flames.

I burst out laughing. I don't know whether through shock or relief.

"Why didn't you just stick my head under the water?" I said to Dave, who hadn't known what to do or how to react.

It was when I remembered I was getting married in only just over two weeks that I panicked, thinking I could have ended up with bald patches. When I told my hairdresser, she couldn't believe it. She said she couldn't find even a tiny piece of singed hair on my head. I knew my Jesus was looking after His bride!

I'd had my hen night with friends and it had gone well. It was Dave's stag night the week before we were to be married: two vicars, his dad, his friend and my sons. A nice, sedate night of playing ten-pin bowling and going for a meal. "What could go wrong?" he thought.

Well, nothing went wrong. Dave thoroughly enjoyed it. Until the early hours of the morning when he was woken up with severe chest pain and a suspected heart attack.

He ended up in hospital. The medical staff tried all sorts of things for the pain. Eventually morphine seemed to eliminate it. After further tests, it seemed it was related to an ongoing reflux problem.

With so many incidents in those days leading up to our wedding, it seemed that the enemy was certainly trying to destroy us.

Even the people we looked after said, "Are you sure you're meant to be getting married?"

Oh, yes – for certain. Satan wasn't having his way in this!

Finally, the day of our wedding arrived.

It was raining in the morning but I knew the sun would come out. And it did!

I woke at eight o'clock, feeling totally relaxed and in another world.

My bridesmaids arrived and began to get ready. Joe and Mick got up and asked me to cut their hair. So, there I was, giving them a haircut before even thinking about getting myself ready – typical!

Time was getting on. I was getting married at one o'clock. The trouble was, the lovely young lady who was doing my make-up was still attending to me at one o'clock, and my car hadn't turned up.

"Mum," said Joe, "I think I'd better ring the car people up. What's their number?"

At twenty past one, a car arrived. It wasn't decorated as it should have been. It wasn't actually the original car. That one had broken down. Yet despite everything, I didn't feel panicked. I felt God's beautiful presence with me all the time.

Meanwhile, in the church, Stu the vicar was panicking his socks off!

"Where is she?" he asked Dave.

Dave was calm like me. "Don't worry," he said. "She'll be here soon."

"Well, she'd better be quick. She has two vicars and a church full of guests waiting." Then, "I'm going for a cup of tea," he told Dave.

When I eventually arrived, I was nearly an hour late. The man driving my car told me he'd never seen a bride as relaxed as I was and he said no doubt my husband-to-be would be in a state.

"No," I replied, "he won't be. He knows I'll be there."

The service was better than I could ever have imagined as we worshipped and praised God. His beautiful presence was so great. Jesus was at the centre of our wedding day and I knew He would always be at the centre of our lives together too.

After a wonderful honeymoon in Thailand, it was back to work. The residents told me that Chris had planned to come to our wedding wearing a suit, but he'd missed us. He'd fallen asleep. When he woke up and realised the time, he'd headed off for the church but arrived just as everyone was leaving. It was funny as I thought I did see him wandering across the grounds.

Dave continued to run the family business with his dad but, eventually, they decided it was time to close it down.

I'd thought for a while that Dave and I should be working together and, after a lot of prayer, I began to recognise that God did seem to have this in mind.

As with everything, it was all in His perfect timing: one day, Deb decided it was time she moved on from Green Pastures.

Deb had been a great support to me in the vision God had given me, but she needed a better salary now. Soon afterwards, Dave was given the opportunity to look after Derby Road with me. We worked really well together, too, even though there seemed to be an endless amount to do.

Dave looked after the policing, as well as the DIY, while I took care of the social side.

By this time, we had two-way radios that were valuable to our work for security reasons. I also still had my panic alarm. However, it was embarrassing when I'd occasionally get a phone call from security to say it had gone off while Dave and I were having a "husband-and-wife" conversation!

"Pam," they'd say, "it's Sefton Security. Your alarm's gone off. Again." And they'd laugh as they told me!

# 29

# EMPOWERING THEMSELVES

As time went by, we decided through prayer that we needed to do something to prevent visitors breaking into the flats at the back of the buildings. This was a big project. We'd have to raise funds for wrought iron gates to put up in between the buildings.

We constantly had problems with people getting into the properties. One man, who had just come out of prison and kept breaking in, was very dark and dangerous. Many times I sensed this from him, as the things he said were evil. There was a younger man, Adrien, who lived at the back of the buildings, and he left due to this man's persistent, evil behaviour.

I mentioned to the tenants the possibility of a sponsored walk in aid of protecting their buildings. They were very happy with this idea and most of them offered to take part to raise funds. It was amazing – we knew it would be difficult for some of them as they couldn't walk far.

We did a nine-mile walk along the coast road to Formby, where one of our volunteers, Pauline, laid on a delicious lunch and refreshments for us all.

I pushed one of the residents in a wheelchair. He didn't realise the distance we were walking and was shouting for me to stop and let him out – but, as he did, his false teeth fell out! He settled down after that and chuckled every time we mentioned it.

Most of the people we looked after in Derby Road had travelled before they arrived with us and a lot of them didn't want to go out of their local area now. The flats were their place of safety in a strange kind of way. But the long walk was well worth it as we raised a good amount of money.

The man who manufactured the gates had an understanding of the work we did. He told us a story of someone close to him who'd died of alcohol misuse. He even knocked a lot of money off his bill, which brought the full cost to the amount we'd raised through the sponsored walk. We met many kind and generous people through the work we did.

One day, Pauline, who'd provided lunch for us on the day of the walk and who later became a very close friend, volunteered to make a dinner every Friday for the residents. She always cooked something wonderful – a shepherd's pie or lasagne. She even got her church involved, and the people who went there donated generously. There was a seemingly never-ending supply of toiletries, cutlery, crockery and clothing, and anything else needed to start the new residents off in their flats. There was even enough for new residents in other Green Pastures properties. These were ongoing donations from people all over the place, supporting the people we housed. God is so good.

*"Whoever is kind to the poor lends to the LORD, and*
*he will reward them for what they have done."*
*Proverbs 19:17*

It was Dave's and my first Christmas with the residents, together, and we asked them if they had any plans. Most of them would go to the churches for food supplies.

The Soup Kitchen was a great thing for the homeless and opened every weekend. It was run by Justin and Jill and they did so much for people, helping everyone they could, homeless or not.

I suggested to Dave that we open our office up for a party for our residents. It was a tiny place, a converted flat. But we emptied it out to make room for tables and chairs for everyone. Justin loaned us these and bought us a turkey.

Our kitchen was too small for us to be able to cook everything in it, but Pauline and her friend offered to cook the Christmas dinner for everyone and they supplied a fantastic meal – three courses: soup, Christmas dinner and a choice of desserts. Helen, one of our residents, had previously done a catering course and knew how to fold the serviettes in a fancy way. The tables looked stunning! Many of the residents did what they could to help us, so everyone had some input.

We made it clear that no alcohol was allowed in the office and if anyone was drunk, they wouldn't be allowed in. This was a big test for us all. But in the end, everyone adhered to this rule and we all had a fantastic time. We had party games, and pass-the-parcel went down especially well. Some of the residents didn't know how to play it – they'd never even heard of it!

From time to time, residents would end up in prison. Generally, we were the only contacts they had, so we'd go and visit them. We'd write to them too, as they were often afraid. They didn't want to lose their flat or the small number of belongings they had. But everything would be just as they left it on their return from prison and now they could see it through sober eyes. And it was good to see them clean their flats up when they got back, even though they were only clean for a short time.

Dave arranged to have CCTV fitted in the buildings. What a difference it made to the whole set-up we had. There weren't as many problems once everything was being recorded. Sometimes we used footage for evidence in court matters, and people began to see the lengths we were going to protect the residents. Finances were always difficult, but we worked hard to raise funds to assist with costs.

As residents came and went, we taught them life skills. Most of them would throw away their clothes instead of washing them. We'd been given a washing machine so there were no excuses, although they did complain, and rightly so, in the winter because they couldn't get things dry.

I asked each resident to donate some money towards the cost of a tumble dryer. Of course, some of them complained. They didn't want to part with their money. But after breaking the costs down for them, they agreed to it. Dave and I put £50 towards the new dryer too. It was the first and only thing that was bought. Everything else was donated. God always provided for us in every area, and we knew we were reclaiming back the land, which is what He'd told us to do.

And it wasn't just our own we helped. People who were homeless or who lived in other properties would come in to see us when they needed clothes, toiletries or food. If we had it, we'd give it.

Some people donated money if they had any spare and this was always a blessing as we put it right back into the work we were doing.

Even volunteers appeared just when we needed them. When Pauline, who'd been making a hot meal every Friday, had to stop, only a few days later a new volunteer called Nigel turned up and he offered to carry this on.

*"The generous will themselves be blessed, for they share their food with the poor."*
*Proverbs 22:9*

*"For I was hungry and you gave me food to eat, I was thirsty and you gave me something to drink, I was a stranger and you invited me in, I needed*

*clothes and you clothed me, I was ill and you
looked after me, I was in prison and you came to
visit me."*
*Matthew 25:35–36*

Some of the people who came to us were in such a desperate state that they wanted to go to rehab. Betel was a Christian rehab that displayed love and support and relied on the power of the Holy Spirit to set users free from their addictions. We'd contact them and arrangements would be made to take those in need to Nottingham, where Betel was based. Although the phone calls were made on one day, the person could be on the way to rehab within as few as two or three days, but they had to adhere to Betel's rules. Clothes would be replaced with new ones; they weren't allowed to smoke as this was also an addiction; and TV was monitored very closely and only allowed at certain times.

It was a chance in a lifetime to be able to go to this rehab without having to wait months for an appointment. But, as I'd seen over and over again, the people we took there couldn't cope with not being allowed to smoke. They knew there was something powerful going on there – they told us the Holy Spirit moved in people's lives and they felt an amazing presence. Yet they couldn't accept the no smoking rule, so they came home.

Rehab advised them to stay for a minimum of six months in order for their addictions to be broken and their lifestyle changed. If they were to leave, they were advised not to return to the neighbourhood and acquaintances they'd left behind, due to the temptations they'd be faced with again.

Sadly, the majority came back to Southport, looking and feeling great after being set free from their addictions, but they soon caught up with their old friends again and this led them back into their former habits.

One young lady who came to us was in such a bad state we were really concerned she'd try to take her own life there and then. She begged us to take her in and she couldn't stop crying.

I made the phone call to rehab and arrangements were put in place for her to go in the following day. Of course, we prayed for everyone we came into contact with, but this lady was in a worse state than anyone I'd seen. Would she come back the following day? Most people said they would but they never did.

However, she did come back and she was ready to go to rehab.

That was the last we saw of her. Until a few years later, when I was visiting one of the residents in hospital. She walked past me and looked really well. I said hello to her but she didn't seem to recognise me, which was good.

Another resident we looked after was a lovely Portuguese man. He hardly spoke any English and made a little garden at the back of the properties. He grew vegetables and salad there and fed most of the residents.

He came in to see me one day with one of his friends, Ollie, another tenant. He'd apparently been to hospital and been diagnosed with throat cancer.

I contacted the hospital and explained who I was, as he'd given permission for me to speak with the consultant. The consultant told me it was only a matter of time and he'd be lucky if he made the next few weeks.

I couldn't believe it, so Dave and I asked if we could pray for him. In his broken English, he agreed, and we laid hands on him.

After a while, he moved on from Derby Road to another quieter Green Pastures property just around the corner. I liaised with hospitals, district nurses and doctors all the time, and we continued to lay hands on him in prayer when we saw him. Eventually, he told us he was returning home to Portugal to be with his family.

It was over twelve months later when we saw him again and, incredibly, he was doing very well. I don't know if the cancer had gone but he looked much healthier, was stronger and had put weight back on. It was good to see.

*"If you spend yourselves in behalf of the hungry
and satisfy the needs of the oppressed, then your
light will rise in the darkness, and your night will
become like the noonday."*
*Isaiah 58:10*

# 30

# SOME OF THE MIRACLES

One day, I received a phone call from Mark, who was a friend of ours. He wanted to know what our church was doing to help the poor and needy in our town, apart from the work Dave and I were doing. He felt he needed to speak to our vicar and to shake up and wake up our church, as he felt churches needed to come together to support the work we were involved in.

Following this conversation, Dave and I were asked to speak at church about Green Pastures and what we did there. Dave, who had more confidence with public speaking than I did, talked about our work. He also asked for additional support to meet the ongoing demands and expressed his gratitude for what we'd already received.

As our volunteer Nigel had recently left us (he'd been helping out with preparing food for residents), it wasn't long before the church had put together a rota to make meals. This was fantastic. We weren't just able to feed our seventeen residents now, we also fed anyone off the street who came in hungry. It was amazing how there always seemed to be enough for everyone.

On one occasion, one of the wonderful volunteers brought in a large pan of chicken stew, but she hadn't had time to make enough for everyone.

"Oh, dear Lord," I prayed, "I need to feed at least seventeen people today."

Although it was a large pan, I knew there weren't enough pieces of chicken in it — certainly nowhere near seventeen. As the residents came down for their meals, they saw that the stew was running low. I prayed along the lines of: "Lord, thank You for this meal. Please bless it as we've nearly run out and we haven't fed everyone. I need You to perform a miracle like You did with the loaves of bread and fish, and I need enough for anyone who comes in off the street too. Please multiply this meal I ask, and thank You. In Jesus' name. Amen."

> *"Jesus [said], '...give them something to eat.' 'We*
> *have here only five loaves of bread and two fish,'*
> *they answered. 'Bring them here to me,' he said.*
> *And he told the people to sit down on the grass.*
> *Taking the five loaves and the two fish and looking*
> *up to heaven, he gave thanks and broke the loaves.*
> *Then he gave them to the disciples, and the*
> *disciples gave them to the people. They all ate and*
> *were satisfied, and the disciples picked up twelve*
> *basketfuls of broken pieces that were left over. The*
> *number of those who ate was about five thousand*
> *men, besides women and children."*
> *Matthew 14:16–21*

Dave asked, "Are you going to have enough?"

"We will now," I told him. "I've prayed and we're doing OK – look!"

Residents grinned when they saw that the supply of stew was endless. People off the streets came in too and there was plenty for everyone with some left over. We thanked God who supplies our every need and I told everyone about this miracle and how great our God is.

Over time, things were starting to improve. Although there was still an ongoing battle, there was a sense of calm. The additional security measures allowed the residents to feel safer and the atmosphere began to change. We knew God had orchestrated this.

Julie, a staff member, visited us regularly at Derby Road with food for the residents. She told me on one visit that she'd received a picture for me during her prayer time. She said she'd seen Dave and me walking together with a silver chain draped around our wrists and around the back of us. The links of the chain were bright, shiny stars and we both held a sword in our hands. She said we were solid and strong together. I was reminded of the armour of God.

Julie went on to tell me that, before we'd started to pray together, she'd seen me in a thick fog and she knew that I felt alone.

She was spot on with this as this was how I did feel at times. But it brought tears to my eyes as I knew my Lord Jesus was not going to abandon me. He was shaping, forming and preparing me for the next big thing.

It's strange how, no matter how many people are around you, you can still feel alone in the crowd. But Father God has promised us He will never leave us. This is our faith. We have to believe it despite our circumstances. God will never let us down.

Julie had another picture for Derby Road too. This one was of a big weed that needed pulling out, while the rest of the place blossomed with flowers.

I asked God to remove the problems that were in Derby Road after that; to move people away who wouldn't change. These were the ones who would zap every bit of energy that I had; the ones who would prey on and set snares and traps for the other vulnerable residents.

To share with each other as Julie had with me encourages us. It's important that we lift each other up when we receive a word or a picture from God. If I was ever uncertain about any word I received, then I'd always test it by asking Him to blow it away in the wind so I wouldn't remember it if it wasn't from Him.

I was amazed when I began to pray for God to get rid of the problems, as I started to see these people leave Derby Road, either by moving to another town for whatever reason, or they were put in prison, or, in some cases, they died. I never expected that but it did happen.

Many of the local people were glad they weren't around anymore to hurt them. It was very sad, but they were given every opportunity to turn their lives around and numerous chances, yet they preferred to bully and terrorise the weak and vulnerable.

Of course, there were still some very upsetting episodes to get through too.

Dave and I had been asked to speak about our work at Shoreline church one Sunday morning. We'd just finished speaking when Dan told me about our resident Chris: "He died last night, Pam."

I don't remember anything else he said. I don't even remember the rest of the service.

I kept thinking about the last time I'd seen Chris, which was the Friday two days before. I'd assisted him to have a bath. He was in a bit of a mess and he'd not long got out when he asked me if he could he have another one. I brought him new jeans as the ones he had on were badly soiled.

Later on, I saw him walking up the stairs with a can in his hand and I knew he'd an accident again.

"Chris," I said, "you've cut the beer down and you've done great. Don't start it again. I don't want to come in on Monday to find you not here."

How those words kept ringing in my ears – because that's exactly what I would have to do now.

Chris's funeral was a big one, held at St. Marie's. Chris always went there for his sandwiches and was well known by the priest and others. He told me he always lit candles and said a prayer so I knew he had some faith.

It was so sad to say goodbye to him. We'd spent many years helping him, listening to him and laughing with him. I thought back to the times when the hammer had fallen through his carrier bag; when he was arrested for stealing a push bike and taking it back; when he threw a chest of drawers at Dave and had given me a typewriter.

Then I remembered a more recent occasion when he told me how my son Joe had helped him one night by talking and listening to him when he felt very low. And when he first had a bath in the office. He'd forgotten how to bath himself so I went through it with him, explaining things.

He was in the bath when his friend Alan was in the office. He and Alan were always winding each other up. Chris asked me if I'd scrub his back and Alan heard this. He marched in with a large scrubbing brush and said, "Yeah, I'll scrub ya back for ya!"

"Get out!" Chris yelled at him. "This is against my human rights!"

They were so funny together. And Chris always saw the funny side of things in the end. He knew we loved him and were just joking about with him.

It was strange going back to work the following day, knowing that he would never be there again.


All this time, my walk with God was deepening and, during one prayer time in church, my Lord showed me a beautiful picture. There was a long table like a banqueting table. Jesus was at one end and I was sitting next to Him. He had either a box or a bag and was taking things out and giving them to me, as presents. I didn't know what the presents were but the Lord reminded me of a previous vision: He was preparing me for something but I wasn't quite ready for it at that time. As He gave me the presents now, I was opening them, but I still didn't know what they were. And I wanted to know. Jesus was watching and smiling at me.

This became an ongoing vision that I had for a couple of years and, one day, when I was talking out loud to the Lord, He told me: "Use them. They're yours."

Eventually it came to me that all I had to do was accept them. Jesus would show me how to use them.

In some of the visions, I saw lots of golden-coloured arms raised upwards. Jesus was sitting at the head of the table and I was on His left. He asked me if I was going to eat with Him and I said "Yes". He asked if Dave, who was standing on His right-hand side, was joining us and Dave said "Yes" too, but he hadn't yet sat down. Jesus and I were the only ones sitting.

There were empty bowls and used bowls on the table and there were other people around, but I didn't want to focus on anything or anyone else; just Jesus.

In another vision, I saw the same long banqueting table and I was there again. There were flames all around the table and Jesus was pouring hot coals out with His bare hands. But I wasn't burnt.

I had these same visions for a long time.

# 31

# ACTIVATING THE GIFTS

Since our marriage in 2007, Dave and I had continued to live in Ainsdale. However, over the months, things began to change for the worse in the neighbourhood. This came to a head for us with a particular first-hand experience.

Dave and I had gone to view a flat for Mick. We were sitting outside in our van when a gang of local men and women, who were clearly very drunk, surrounded us. They'd come out of the pub and were behaving in an intimidating and threatening way, accusing us of trying to break into the flat. Dave rang the police and two police riot vans and a number of police cars attended.

We told them what was happening. They informed us that we should be careful and should watch our property and vehicles, as these were the type of people who wouldn't let things go and would seek revenge. They also advised us to move out of the area as it was getting worse there. Then they watched us drive away and kept the gang back, as they were trying to stop us from leaving.

We arrived home quite upset. So I picked up my Bible as the words, "Move away from the area!" went round and round in my head.

*But where to? We couldn't just up and move – where would we go?*

I knew God had given me gifts. Was this His way of telling me to act on them? After all, what was the use being a Christian if I wasn't going to believe and rest in God's Word?

I knew I had to search for His promises as I opened my Bible. This is what I found…

*"He will cover you with his feathers, and under his wings you will find refuge; his faithfulness will be your shield and rampart. You will not fear the terror of night, nor the arrow that flies by day, nor the pestilence that stalks in the darkness, nor the plague that destroys at midday. A thousand may fall at your side, ten thousand at your right hand, but it will not come near you. You will only observe with your eyes and see the punishment of the wicked.*

*"If you say, 'The LORD is my refuge,' and you make the Most High your dwelling, no harm will overtake you, no disaster will come near your tent. For he will command his angels concerning you to guard you in all your ways; they will lift you up in their hands, so that you will not strike your foot against a stone. You will tread on the lion and the cobra; you will trample the great lion and the serpent.*

*"'Because he loves me,' says the LORD, 'I will rescue him; I will protect him, for he acknowledges my name. He will call on me, and I will answer him; I will be with him in trouble, I will deliver him and honour him."*

*Psalm 91:4–15*

At work the following week, I mentioned what had happened over the weekend, and I was approached by one of the directors who told me about a property that was available away from Ainsdale.

After a lot of work to renovate it, Dave and I moved in three months later.

Joe and Mick decided not to come with us, but to stay in Ainsdale. They had their own lives there and didn't want to leave them behind. They were still only young men but I had to listen to them.

Unfortunately, over the year, things got a bit too much for Joe, who lost his job when the company he worked for folded. He became depressed and turned to things which weren't good for him.

That's when he tried to take his own life.

I believed the visions I'd been getting were to show me God had given me gifts to use as I sat next to my son's bed in the hospital. God was wanting me to activate these gifts by stepping out in a new level of faith, but I never expected to be faced with this.

Joe had taken an overdose and I was told he wouldn't come through. I saw him coughing up blood. He was in and out of consciousness and delirious. All I knew was that Jesus was the answer as I asked the doctor to please help him.

Joe was admitted to a ward and kept in hospital for a week.

During this awful time, I turned inwards on myself. My heart was broken. But I remembered something I'd heard at a conference – that God loves mothers who are passionate in their hearts, who will fight in the supernatural for their children. Dave was the one asking the medical staff all the questions. I prayed silently all the while in tongues, as I was unable to express my prayers in my own language. I was numb. In shock. And I knew I couldn't do anything in my own strength. I could only pray.

The Lord reminded me of a past vision He'd given me of Joe. I saw him, strong and powerful. He was smiling and healthy and alive in Jesus. He was shining. I claimed this immediately as I laid my hands on his body again. And I spoke out loud something along these lines:

"No, Satan, get your filthy dirty hands off him. Joe belongs to Jesus. He is a son of God, the Most High. He may have backslidden but he's not yours and you can't have him. God gave him to me to bring up as a child of His. God's shown me a picture of Joe and he has work to do for Jesus who loves him. Jesus died and rose again for Joe and I command you, Satan, in Jesus' name to let go of him. I command the spirit of death off Joe now! And, Jesus, I pray You breathe life, new life, into Joe right now in Your precious name. I thank You, Jesus, for life and I believe You will not take Joe back to heaven as it's not his time to go yet. I believe You have a new life and job for Joe to bring people back to You, and I thank You for these things, in Jesus' name. I claim life and complete and absolute healing. Nothing less, in Jesus' name. Thank You, King Jesus."

I surrendered everything to Jesus. I felt hopeless sitting there next to Joe as, physically, I could do nothing. But spiritually, I had the gifts that Jesus had been showing me. Now was the time to unwrap them; to activate and use them.

I claimed Joe's complete healing and nothing less.

And I saw the miracle take place.

I'd not been to work for a couple days. I'd just sat at Joe's bedside. Pastor Pete gently reminded me that the residents also needed me as I was their family too.

I knew I had to trust God in this as I went back to Derby Road.

I didn't tell the residents why I was off, but Dave and I went straight to my son's bedside every night after work, and before work every morning.

And I remembered that God is faithful and good all the time, no matter what our circumstances are, and we must praise and worship Him.

*"Return to your rest, my soul, for the **LORD** has been good to you." Psalm 116:7*

After five days, Joe saw a psychiatrist who told him he had all his results back. They showed that there was no damage to his liver or to any part of his body. The psychiatrist said this was a miracle.

I cried and praised my God for His goodness and love.

His perfect love.

*"I will sing the **LORD**'s praise, for he has been good to me." Psalm 13:6*

Derby Road still had its ups and downs. Kaz, one of our female residents, came into the office one day with her hair all tangled up and sitting like a bush on top of her head. She used to have beautiful long hair but these days, somehow it just looked mangled and tatty as if it was permanently backcombed.

Most of the time, Kaz would get very drunk and she had the strength of an ox when she was like that. She was only small too and had lost a lot of weight due to her addiction. Rarely sober, she was courting one of the older residents. You would always know when they were having a row as everyone in the buildings would hear them.

Kaz's parents would often visit her and, on one occasion, her dad asked me if there was anything I could do with her hair as it was crawling with head lice.

Before her hair had got into such a complete mess, I would often put solutions on it to try to get rid of the lice. But she never let me follow up the treatment as she was usually too hung over, so the lice bred.

Her dad then asked if I could shave all her hair off. This really did seem like the only solution. Kaz was horrified at first. However, all the other residents were having to shave their hair off too as the lice were going round like wild fire.

Kaz's boyfriend, Paul asked Dave to shave his head. As Dave got on with it, the lice fell onto the carpet and crawled up his arms. Kaz saw this and, realising how bad the situation was, said, "Oh, OK. I suppose I'd better let you do mine too."

It was very sad. She had huge lumps filled with fluid in her head where the lice had been. Her hair didn't even look like hair as it was so matted.

When it eventually grew back, it was in beautiful condition.

Kaz was only forty when she was admitted to hospital. I went to see her regularly, as I did with all the residents. She was sober now and I spoke again to her about Jesus. I held her hand as I said the prayer for salvation, and I asked her to repeat it if she wanted Jesus in her life. She didn't speak it out loud but she smiled when I'd finished.

A few weeks later, she died.

Sometime afterwards, God placed Paul, her boyfriend, heavily on my heart before going into work one morning. I didn't know whether I'd been dreaming or if I'd had a vision of him. I just knew I had to tell him that Jesus was calling him, but I didn't know if this was a life-or-death situation, whether spiritually or physically. I knew this would be difficult too, as Paul always seemed to be high on something. But God had put on my heart to make Paul aware that, if he didn't listen and change his lifestyle, it would lead to his physical death.

I eventually found the right time to tell him this and said it was very important that he listened.

Sadly, three weeks later, Paul was rushed into hospital after being found on his back in his flat. He was yellow, rigid and couldn't speak. He'd told Kaz sometime before that he missed heroin and other drugs. Kaz had told us her money had been disappearing, and Paul had started to smoke heroin again, as well as taking pills and drinking alcohol.

It was due to the misuse of drugs and alcohol in his life that he died not long afterwards. He'd sadly returned to the old lifestyle that God was warning him against.

This was the story of most of the people we looked after. It was heart-breaking to watch them drink themselves to death.

David was a man who was constantly being bullied and beaten by the visitors. After discussing a care package to suit his needs, I asked David if he'd be happy for me to look into some protection for him.

"At least if you have someone to go out to the post office with you, then you won't have to worry anymore about people approaching you for money," I said. "Then you can go out on days out, can't you?"

David was happy for me to go ahead with this, so I contacted Home Instead Senior Care.

I loved this part of the job – assisting residents to get things sorted out, to look after themselves, to plan days out rather than spending all their money on alcohol or drugs.

I couldn't believe it when a lady called Irene came to do the assessment. I knew Irene through my brother as she used to work with him. She'd just opened her own business with a friend, which, as it turned out, was Home Instead. As she was leaving the office, she said that if I ever needed a full-time job, I should go and see her. She knew what we were doing in Derby Road and what hard work it was, and she also had a big heart for people.

David was glad to have a support worker from Home Instead to go with him to the shops and the post office, and also to the pub, as this was where David liked to go at times, without being hassled.

Many people came through the doors of our office. We got to know lots of them and it was always lovely to hear that some were moving forward.

Another man we housed had been living under a bridge for approximately twelve months. He'd lost everything. It was great to see that he'd got himself out of debt, off alcohol and had found a job at last. We supported him in every way we could by giving him a home, references and plenty of encouragement.

These were the successes of the job that only happened on occasions. But I knew that God wanted me there not just in the good times but in all of it.

Many people I spoke to assumed that people were homeless because they took drugs or abused alcohol. However, people came to us through all walks of life. One man had at one time been a millionaire with his own newspaper business. He used to call into the local pub on his way home from a hard day's work, then he began to drink at home. Before he knew it, he had an alcohol problem and, in time, he lost everything through it.

Another lady came to us who'd been abused by her father as a child. She'd had a child herself through him when she was only twelve years old. She'd turned to drugs and managed to come off them, but she was scarred mentally.

This reflected on her life with the partner she teamed up with, who also mistreated her by seeing other women behind her back and verbally abusing her. We supported them both and she became stronger mentally, which he didn't like at first, but they're still together to this day.

Then there was a man in his late sixties, an ex-Royal Navy officer. He was told he wasn't entitled to any benefits. He had no alcohol or drug issues, but he'd lost his home and had no family, so he lived on the streets where, one day, he'd taken a wrong turn and ended up in Southport.

Was it a wrong turn, though? He found us and we gave him a home. And he became one of our volunteers and drivers in the work we were doing.

The list of stories is endless. Homelessness is something that could happen to any one of us at any time. It's only through God's grace that we are saved.

Many of the people we knew were in debt and debt collectors were constantly at our office, chasing after them – even though the residents didn't have many possessions and the debt collectors knew this.

We put a lot of people in touch with C.A.P. (Christians Against Poverty). A man called Gaz was an advisor for them and he later became the centre manager. Gaz was based at Shoreline church and he ran a course that enabled people to get out of debt.

**If you're struggling with debt, do contact C.A.P. as they'll help you get back on your feet or point you in the direction of someone else who can. They have offices set up all over the UK.**

One day, a lady who worked alongside Jackie Pullinger (author of *Chasing The Dragon*) came to see us. She told us all about their work together.

Then she said, "You're more on the frontline than Jackie is. Jackie has security and you don't have anything like that here. Anyone can attack you if you're doing assessments or even if they just come into your office."

She was right. We were on the front line. For years I'd been told this.

I thought back to the man who'd just walked into the office and shoved me. What else would he have done if nobody had shouted to frighten him off? After all, he did say he'd been convicted of attempted murder.

I did tell people when they asked about security that I had my panic alarm, which was linked up to a monitoring station. We also had CCTV that recorded everything, and we had two-way radios and regular visits from the police.

But the one thing I knew that was above everything was that I had God. It was God who protected me from every harm. No one else. He was my guide, my light and my shield. My office was an open office. But God was my shelter and shield.

Every day, I prayed the whole armour of God over myself as soon as I woke up. I prayed at the end of each working day at Derby Road that God would sever and break off any unclean spirits that may have attached themselves to me, and wash me with Jesus' precious blood. These were my regular daily prayers.

As we saw changes in a lot of our residents, we wanted to do more for them. They weren't very adventurous and only seemed to want to hang around their own territory. We suggested a day out to the cinema and ten-pin bowling. We priced everything up and everyone was excited about it. And we emphasised that they wouldn't be allowed to go if they were drunk. We had some great fun doing this every few months, as it gave them time to save up for each trip. And there they'd all be, ready waiting for us when the time to go came, sober and excited.

One day I went into work to be met by Alan, one of the residents, who'd fallen down the stairs.

"I'm all right, Pamela," he said, "don't worry about me. It's nothing."

When he showed us his leg, I told him it was broken and that he needed to go to hospital.

Dave rang the ambulance and then we prayed. I put my hands on Alan's leg as we did so, and I began to feel a popping sensation under my palms.

Alan began to cry at this point and said, "Something's happening. My leg is really hot."

I thought he was crying because of the pain but that wasn't it. His tears were because he was touched by prayer and what God was doing.

The ambulance came to take him to hospital and he was kept in. Dave and I visited him and, again, I placed my hands on his leg and prayed. Once more, Alan felt his leg burning under my palms.

"Ow, Pamela, that's burning me!" he said, and he laughed as he knew that God was in this.

He was discharged the following day with a cast on his leg where it was broken in two places. I didn't know what God was doing but I did know that He'd touched Alan.


I realised that I'd begun to feel quite lost and tired. Todd Bentley was on TV during the Lakeland revival 2008, and a group of Christians in my church had been meeting on a regular basis after watching and hearing Todd. They'd been practising the gifts of the Spirit at church and the Holy Spirit was quite active amongst them.

I found a longing in my spirit to join them but, by the time I'd get home from work, I was too exhausted. Still, I was determined to meet up with them somehow.

One particular evening, I arrived home late from work and, despite being tired, I rushed around getting myself ready.

However, by the time I'd had my shower, it was too late to get there. When I realised, I burst into tears and became very agitated.

Dave was concerned as he knew how frustrated I was, so he prayed over me and told me to rest. He told me God knew my heart and would minister to me wherever I was.

As Dave prayed over me, I felt a wonderful peace. I turned over and went to sleep, and I knew God was ministering to me as I slept.

A couple of months previously, I'd received a picture of a volcano with smoke spewing from the top, but it hadn't yet erupted.

As I slept that night, I saw the volcano, only this time it was half the height of an adult. There were children around it. They were the children and youth from our church with a few of the adults too. I moved away from the volcano but the children were telling me to come back – the Holy Spirit was still ministering to me and hadn't finished.

As I moved away, I realised that I was the volcano. Even then, I still walked off as I felt I was too busy to stop!

This was me in real life. I was erupting. I was hungry for more of Jesus; more of the Holy Spirit. I'd begun to activate the gifts of the Holy Spirit and now I wanted to know how to activate other gifts. But I was always so busy with my ministry and my family that I didn't make enough time for Jesus. I needed to be still and just sit in his presence. I knew something was erupting in me and could feel the power of God in my heart.

It was time for the church weekend away to Blaithwaite. Someone had blessed Dave and me by paying for us to go as we couldn't afford it. We did desperately need this spiritual break.

Blaithwaite was a Christian retreat centre in Cumbria. Dave and I stayed in our van in the field with other campers, overlooking the beautiful mountains and another field full of cows.

It was wonderful to relax amongst our Christian family without having to worry about work. We had a fantastic time and some people had words from God for me. I was told that God had given me joy, laughter and wholeness, and I knew these words were from God as I'd been given them a few times previously in my walk.

The speaker talked of how Moses felt inadequate at times with, "What if?", "How?" and "Why me?" But God appoints faithful, godly people. Jesus chose messed up people first to work His miracles on.

We are told to pray, "Bring heaven on earth" and that we should pray this daily. We are ambassadors for Christ here, heavenly creations, born again, new creations on this earth, so we need to activate this. Jesus told the disciples to go and cleanse and heal. He told them they would do even greater things than He was doing (John 14:12–14).

The same Holy Spirit that raised Jesus from the dead lives in us to enable us to help others outside the church. So we need to go forward in the power of Christ.

The speaker also talked about Luke; about casting out demons and the healings that took place, and he told us to always give out our gifts. We shouldn't keep them to ourselves but pass them on and let the Holy Spirit top us up again. We should step out in a new faith and confidence – operate in the new things God may be calling us to and not let fear stop us.

We split into small groups to discuss our teaching and gifts, and what God may be calling us to.

I told my group about the pictures Jesus had shown me of the long banqueting table and the presents He was giving me. Someone said I was like a Swiss army knife – I had all the gifts appropriate for the time of need, especially in my ministry at Derby Road. I recalled how many times God had protected and used me in so many situations. I also recalled that every time I prayed for the broken in my ministry, I'd be heartbroken and cry for them.

The teaching and worship over the weekend were amazing as we got lost in praising our wonderful Father. The Holy Spirit was with us.

After the worship, Philip, one of the men in the group I'd been wanting to join in the evening at church, came to talk to Dave and me. I told him that I longed to be part of their evening meetings, and about the dream of the volcano. Philip asked me if he could get the youth from our church to come and pray with me. I was more than happy!

It was an odd sensation. As the youth of the church prayed, I found my legs went quite weak and I felt a weight pressing in on me, although no one was touching me. I ended up on the floor and I felt as light as a feather, and with a fresh state of mind.

I hadn't experienced this before. It was beautiful. The best feeling I could ever have imagined.

After they'd finished praying, I tried to speak, but my language changed to a different tongue. I was on such a high! My friends couldn't stop laughing. We were the last ones in the building and we couldn't get back to our rooms or van as we were so drunk in the Holy Spirit. My legs wouldn't even move. I wasn't frightened by this as I knew it was the Holy Spirit, and as my friends tried to lift me, they were caught up in it too.

The next day, as I went to give my friends a hug, I felt a surge of power hit us all and we started shaking again. This was the amazing Holy Spirit that had raised Jesus from the dead – no wonder I couldn't walk!

I thought back to a time at Ansdell Church when I'd seen a lady who'd been touched by the Holy Spirit. I didn't know much about it at the time and was horrified.

"Oh, I wouldn't like that to happen to me," I remember saying to myself. "That will never happen to me!"

I laughed at myself now. How wrong I was! I wanted to know more of my Father. I wanted more of Jesus in me. I wanted the Holy Spirit. I'd been chasing this so what was I to expect?

Some people don't understand it. But what I've learned is that not everyone has these experiences, and some people are afraid of them. But there's nothing to be afraid of.

I loved Jesus so much and I knew He'd shown me lots of different things in many different ways, but this was different again. What matters is that He loves each one of us exactly the same, but He reveals Himself to us in a variety of ways.

These manifestations of the Holy Spirit gave me boldness and confidence as I went deeper in my walk. I knew I'd never again say, "Oh, no! I don't want that to happen to me!"

I wanted all that Jesus had for me!

As I sought Him, the manifestations happened more and more. Not only had I received the gift of tongues, but I would be taken off my feet regularly by the Holy Spirit, experiencing a deeper understanding of and closeness to God. I'd often be brought out of church in a wheelchair as I couldn't walk, and I had many pictures and prophetic words for people during these times.

This was also a time when, as a church with the Holy Spirit using us, we went out in the streets, speaking to people and praying for healing for them.

I learned to use these gifts in my ministry too, where I felt this new confidence that Jesus had given me. I knew He was the restorer of my soul who'd given me a new life and I shouldn't keep quiet about Him. I was on fire.

All through this, my beloved husband always supported me. He was also growing in his faith. Many times he didn't understand what God was doing with me or where He was taking me, yet he was right with me and knew my heart was for Jesus. He was also touched many times by the Holy Spirit as we worshipped, but in a very different way. He seemed to be in another world, where he sat peacefully with his eyes closed, but still in God's holy presence. The heat that came from him was like a furnace as God gave him prophetic words for people.

# 32

# GOD'S PROTECTION

Even through the wonderful times, the enemy still constantly attacked us. Joe was going through difficulties and my health wasn't always good. I became run down and developed many chest and water infections, which seemed to really wipe me out.

Dave's ex-partner was always giving us a hard time too. She'd ring up and give Dave abuse about his daughter – what we did and what we didn't do, what she was wearing. She'd tell him she'd ensure he was wiped out financially and that we'd be left with nothing. The list was endless.

One evening, I returned home to find Dave looking very distressed but trying to stay calm. He told me not to worry, which I immediately did, as he said, "Mick's been in a car crash, love. He's OK but the car's written off…"

Mick wasn't badly injured, but as Dave told me the story of the events leading up to the accident, I felt physically sick.

He'd borrowed my car and had been out with his friend for the evening. He was on his way home after dropping him off in Ainsdale when he noticed he was being followed by a car full of large men. Mick didn't know who they were or what they were doing, but they started to chase him through the streets and try to run him off the road.

At one point, he thought he'd lost them, so he pulled over to calm himself down. Suddenly, the passenger door opened and a man jumped in.

He grabbed the steering wheel as Mick drove off, with the man shouting at him to pull over.

Mick was terrified and screamed at the man to get out.

"I'll kill you if you don't stop the car!" the man yelled back.

The car had veered into oncoming traffic, although the lights were red and the traffic was stationary.

Mick hit one of the standing vehicles.

Fortunately, the driver wasn't badly injured, but still had whiplash and shock. Things could have been a lot worse.

Mick jumped out of the car and ran and hid until the police came. He didn't know who his pursuers were. He was badly shaken and had minor injuries – and he was very worried about my car!

The police were baffled by the incident until they discovered who the men were. As it turned out, they were very well known to the police. The one who'd jumped into the car had a bad reputation and was a real bully, but the police advised us not to take things any further as there'd be repercussions. This man was known for it.

Neither Dave nor I could believe our ears when they said this. We couldn't understand why we were the victims and we couldn't do anything about it. Where was the justice?

The man apologised to the police and it turned out that he and the others thought my son was someone else. But it was still an evil thing to have done and added to the battles we were already going through. All we could do was draw on God's mighty protection for our family once again.

It was this promise, that I picked out of my little promise box, that God spoke to me during that time:

*"If you say, 'The* LORD *is my refuge,' and you make the Most High your dwelling, no harm will*

*overtake you, no disaster will come near your tent.*
*For he will command his angels concerning you to*
*guard you in all your ways"*
*Psalm 91:9–11*

This psalm seemed to pop up in nearly every situation in my life.

It was a couple of years later that we heard that the men who'd chased Mick attacked loan drivers for sport and entertainment. It was a game to them. They were known for picking on people at random and we were saddened to hear that one of the victims had suffered many injuries.

I always cried out to God when things were bad. He was the only one who could understand and help when life seemed out of our control.

Many times, Christian friends would say, "You're always going through something, aren't you? There never seems to be an end to your problems."

And, yes, there was always something big happening. We didn't seem to get much of a break in between. But we counted every blessing of God's goodness through it all: the miracle of how Joe came through his depression; the weekend away in Blaithwaite; the manifestations of the Holy Spirit in our lives; God's protection and guidance. These were all blessings and we needed to focus on them and be thankful.

As I sought more of Jesus' heart, I began to see things differently and prayers were being answered. God always wants the best for us. Even when we try to make things happen for ourselves, He gently guides us back as we seek Him first.

I discovered I was surrendering more and more of myself to Jesus and I loved it! I poured out my heart to Him so many times. And although I didn't understand everything that happened, I felt His presence and love.

Then again, there were times when I didn't feel anything at all. But feelings can deceive us so it's important not to rely on them, but to rely and trust what God's Word says instead. His Word prepares us for events that we may come up against like sickness, fear, death. So it's vital we read the Bible daily for it to take root into our lives, into our spirits. Then it will sustain us during difficult times.

It had been on my heart for a while to take the residents on a little holiday. It was something I'd spoken about to family and my work friends.

"That's a big mission, Pam," was the response. "I don't know if it's a good idea."

"Yes, but some of them have never had a holiday," I said with determination. "And I really want them to before anything happens to them."

My mind had been ticking over on this for a while and somehow I felt now was the right time to do something about it.

Derby Road was going well. My brother Sam and son Mick had been helping out with some of the residents in whatever ways they could. They were very protective towards the vulnerable and it was encouraging to see their hearts in the work we did. Joe had used his building skills too, to help out in other Green Pastures properties when he could.

I'd been looking for a holiday venue for the tenants and discussing the idea with them, and at last I found something in South Wales. It was a large, ten-bedroom property, with a big games room and a snooker table.

We were careful to explain to residents that, if they wanted to go, they wouldn't be allowed any alcohol. I knew those who were dependent on alcohol and those who just abused it. I knew that some could go without for a week or longer if they had to because they had no money to buy any more until they were next paid. There was one person who I was aware needed to have his cans and I would have to ensure we took them with us.

It was amazing how many tenants wanted to go, even when I told them the cost of the trip. Having to pay for it themselves was a big test to see if they did really want to go or not.

The total cost of the holiday worked out at one hundred pounds per person for four days. This included food, travel fare and days out. Everyone who wanted to go paid this off in instalments over the following months.

Our resident Alan was concerned as he'd broken his leg but didn't want to miss the holiday. I assured him he could still come. We'd just have to get a wheelchair for him.

There were thirteen of us altogether and we were worried about getting everyone in the minibus that Shoreline church had kindly loaned. At least another resident had been able to borrow a car, so could help with taking food, drinks and some of the extra luggage.

When we arrived at Derby Road on the day we were due to leave, we found the residents outside on the forecourt waiting for us. They were all sober. Some were quiet whilst others were very excited. One resident's support worker also came to look after him, as we thought this would help with the workload.

I thought we were in for a three-hour journey. To my shock, we didn't arrive until six and a half hours later! I didn't realise South Wales was so far away.

As soon as everyone started to get out of the minibus, one of the residents, David, collapsed. He hit the ground, split his head open and lay there unconscious on the gravel.

Dave rang an ambulance and David was admitted to hospital. There was nothing I could do except pray and hope he'd be back with us soon and wouldn't miss the holiday he'd been looking forward to so much.

The house and views were stunning. Michaela and her partner claimed the room with a small four-poster bed. It was a dream come true for her.

Everyone else found the rooms they wanted too and were very happy with them.

It was nearly ten o'clock when Dave and Brian arrived back from the hospital without David. David had been kept in with concussion.

Not a great start to the holiday, but Dave and I prayed with a couple of the other residents. Some of them had previously made a commitment. Others watched us but didn't want to join in. I felt a release of the Holy Spirit as we prayed and a sense of His beautiful presence, which made me laugh. Then the others started laughing too. They knew God was doing something and I told them not to be worried or afraid.

Every day of the holiday the weather was sunny and lovely. The residents seemed to be enjoying themselves, although some were strangely quiet, which we couldn't understand at first.

However, it wasn't long before they were wanting to go to a pub or buy alcohol, and they made it plain they'd make things unpleasant for some of the others if they couldn't buy what they wanted. One man wouldn't even look at me. He constantly moaned about me and complained about everything.

But we had to stick to the rules we'd put in place before we came away: no alcohol. It wasn't as if they had nothing to do, as there was the huge games room where they spent a lot of time after returning from days out.

I began to feel drained quickly in a way I'd never experienced before. I kept thinking I was just tired and I continued doing as much as I could so that everyone would enjoy themselves.

"It's only a few days away," I'd remind myself. "They'll settle down soon."

They loved playing the Wii games as they'd never done this before. It was very gratifying to see the appreciation of those who enjoyed them.

We had a rota system for cooking, washing up and so on. We were well organised and everyone made delicious meals. They told us they really enjoyed cooking them too. And we made sandwiches to take with us on the days out.

However, on one morning, Dave and I were upstairs getting ready when we heard everyone outside talking. They were complaining and saying very unkind things about us. We couldn't believe it and I felt very hurt and upset. But why was I so bothered that they were pulling us down here? It didn't get to me at Derby Road when they reacted badly to not being allowed their own way, so why should I feel like this now?

Something was happening that I didn't like. I felt as if Satan was in the midst of us, especially as one particular man just wanted to go home and get drunk. He wouldn't or couldn't look me in the eye when I spoke to him. He just grunted yes or no, then walked away.

What were we to do?

We approached them all about it and everyone changed their tune then and turned very sweet. We told them we'd heard them complaining and hadn't realised they weren't happy, but they insisted they were. It didn't make sense.

We continued to visit David every day in hospital but he'd become very nasty and vindictive towards us. This didn't make sense either. It just wasn't like him. We'd visited him many times in hospital before this incident and had seen him sober on lots of occasions, and he was never like this with us.

David was only small and had been bullied in the past, but he'd been looking forward to coming away. We thought maybe that was why he was being nasty – because he was supposed to be on holiday but was stuck in hospital. The other residents always stayed in the minibus as they didn't want to visit him, so we had to get the balance right to please them all.

When David was discharged from hospital, we all went to the beach. Most of the residents loved it. Apart from four of them. It was very strange as their language and behaviour towards us became quite bitter and threatening.

I felt I was in another world. We knew these people well. We more or less lived with them. I'd been working with them for five years. We'd come up against many bad things in Derby Road and had coped. Yet this was something different altogether.

I did wonder if it was because we weren't in the place where God had originally placed us. Were we now on Satan's territory with them all ganging up against the two of us? My mind began to wander, coming up with all sorts. But I was very tired so probably not thinking clearly. God was our protector and defender and Satan was not going to destroy us, I reminded myself.

It was our last day. We'd been to tin mines, waterfalls, tourist shops and different beaches. Although getting Alan onto the beach in a wheelchair was a problem, we'd still managed it.

And we'd saved the very best for the end.

Again, there were complaints when we told them where we were going. We were taking them to a birds of prey sanctuary where they could hold the birds and also have a go at archery.

The man who wouldn't look me in the eye on the holiday was adamant he wouldn't take part.

"Really?" others exclaimed in excitement. "You mean we can hold the birds of prey and do real archery? I've never done anything like that before!"

But the one man sneered, "I'm not paying ten pounds towards that!"

When we arrived, none of them could believe what an amazing place it was. And the one who was adamant he wouldn't take part reconsidered and joined in.

Alan was in tears as he held the birds of prey. "I've always wanted to do this, Pamela," he said. "This has been the best part of the holiday. I've had the best time of my life."

Lots of them said the same thing as they chatted excitedly on the way back to the house.

The holiday over, they all wanted one last trip to the beach. On the following morning, the weather was beautiful again, so we were able to make a final seaside visit before setting off on our six-hour journey back home.

Alan (who was dependent on his alcohol) had asked if he could call into the local shop for his beer, as the shop at home would be closed when we returned to Derby Road. I already knew he was running low. We agreed, but didn't expect him to start having sneaky drinks on the return journey. I wondered why he'd become aggressive and angry. Alan wasn't really an angry or aggressive man. He was generally the same so, again, it was strange to hear him speaking the way he did in the minibus. We noticed that other tenants became very quiet when he was abusive towards them.

All of a sudden, I'd had enough. Dave pulled the minibus into a small shop car park. I was in tears and I got out to ring my friend to pray with her, as I felt so drained.

After I'd briefly told her what had happened during the holiday, my friend said these were demonic attacks that had pushed me to snapping point. She prayed with me and said she would get others to pray too.

Dave seemed to deal with Alan's behaviour better than I did and told me not to let it get to me. But I couldn't help it. I was very sensitive by now. I even asked Brian if he'd take Alan back in the car with him but he refused.

Alan seemed to calm down after this, which was just as well. We'd told the others we'd take them to New Brighton on our way back as they'd never been there either. And we didn't want to let them down just because of Alan's behaviour.

We made sure to pull over into laybys to allow regular breaks for the smokers. It was while we were parked in one particular layby that only a single car passed us. As it went by, which seemed somehow to be in slow motion, Dave and I caught sight of the driver's face. It was long, white and thin – a scary face, something like a Halloween mask, with big, hollow, black eyes and an open mouth that appeared to be stuck onto the windscreen.

Both Dave and I looked at each other: "Did you see that? What was it?"

We both had an uneasy feeling as we asked the others if they'd seen it.

"Seen what?" they asked, and they looked at us as if we were weird. They'd seen the man driving the car, but not the scary, mask-like face.

As we continued our journey home, we saw another vehicle with a painting on the back of it. It was a dark figure wearing a long cloak with the hood up over the face and carrying something like a shepherd's crook. We thought the picture looked like the sign of death.

Over the next couple of days, we saw these types of figures regularly. It wasn't very nice and they seemed to be quite distinctive.

We eventually made it to New Brighton, where the residents enjoyed something to eat and a visit to the arcades. By this time, I was exhausted and really looking forward to getting home.

Everyone seemed to be happy, but I'd begun to wonder if they really were. Did I actually know these people at all? Was I being deceived myself and, if so, why didn't I see it? Why didn't God reveal all this to me? Was I just blind for some reason?

Question after question and I didn't have any answers.

One thing I did know was that I just wanted space to unwind.

Thankfully, it was now the weekend so I could relax a little. I knew we had to go to church as everyone was praying for us and looking forward to hearing how the few days away had gone.

Our vicar, Stu and a number of others told me I didn't look too good, even though I said we'd had a lovely time – which we had, apart from the incidents that had occurred.

"It's really taken it out of you, Pam," people said. "It was too much for you, you shouldn't have done it."

When I look back, I think perhaps they were right. But in my heart I just knew I wanted to give our residents something they'd remember for the rest of their days. In this line of work you see people come and go and you see people die, so it was important to me that they had a holiday.

Monday came round quickly and the days were taking a toll on me. I could feel myself sinking. I began to question if I was even in the right type of work.

I asked God to reveal if He wanted me to come out of my ministry; to reveal it clearly to me. I didn't have the strength mentally to think about what other type of work I could do. I just knew I was exhausted and needed time off.

Life slid further downhill when my dear sister-in-law and brother came to see us with some news. She'd been diagnosed with breast cancer. They poured out the story and my heart was broken for them.

In all of this, the only safe place I could run to was the arms of Jesus, who knew all these things. When trials hit, His arms are the only place to be. We may not know what to say but we can pray in our heavenly language, in words that we don't understand but are understood by our Father.

I cried with my sister-in-law and held her close. I prayed for her and Sam.

I put her on many prayer chains too, as she went through her treatment.

And we praised God when she was given the all clear and was on the road to recovery.

# 33

# PICTURES, DREAMS, VISIONS

Through the night-time was when my Lord would speak to me – a lot. I began to get pictures and have dreams of a crown of thorns. I didn't know what my Father was saying to me about this but I knew it was something.

During one of my prayer times, I had a vision of myself going into the Lord's presence. I was with a friend in the vision and the Lord filled her cup with something and she walked off smiling. As I was approaching God's presence, I noticed something huge to my left-hand side. But I was so engrossed in wanting to be with my Father that I ignored this thing and approached, holding my cupped hands to Him. It was as though I was holding up a small bowl. Then He gave me a tiny paintbrush.

As I walked away with my paintbrush in my hand, I turned and looked at the huge object that I'd previously ignored: it was an enormous blank, white canvas.

I knew God wanted me to paint. There was only one problem, though: I could draw and was creative but I couldn't paint!

I continued at Derby Road. Neither Dave nor I had any real time for ourselves as we were always on twenty-four-hour call, so it was nice to get away when we could. One of the places we visited was the *Catch the Fire* conferences in Lytham St. Anne's. It was here that I was given prophetic words.

The prophecy was that I'd been given gifts of art and creativity that I hadn't used for a while – and God was wanting me to start using them again. I was also told that there were gifts in my hands and one of these gifts was healing.

This prophecy was recorded at the time and when I listened to it at home, it all began to sink in.

The people who prophesied over me didn't know me and I knew without a shadow of doubt that my Lord was using them and speaking to me clearly through them.

But I didn't have space to do anything for myself whilst in my ministry, as it demanded every bit of time I had. So this was something I would have to address. When the Lord calls you to a ministry, yes, it's right to give one hundred per cent to it. But He doesn't want you to burn out or have no time with Him in the process. I'd allowed myself to be swamped in my ministry. I did make time for Jesus but nothing much else. I neglected myself to give more of myself to others.

During our church service on Sundays, I found that some of the marginalised people would come in to look for Dave and me to ask us something. Many times I'd be standing during worship with my eyes shut and hands raised, when I'd be tapped on the shoulder by someone asking if they could speak with me after the service. So we didn't really have time to listen and reflect even when church had finished.

But we did have great times on the streets of Southport, praying with people while the Sunday morning service was happening. A group of us would go out and pray for people, using the gifts God had given each of us.

These were precious times as we chatted and asked God for healing or anything else. So the prophecy that was spoken over me was being activated in this area, but the gift of art and creativity was still not being used.

I remember the picture I had many years earlier, with my hands raised, praising and worshipping God. The sky was full of flames and fire and there was a gold hoop through a gold heart. I never, ever raised my hands to praise God in my early years and I didn't think this was something I'd ever do. But here I am now, years on, doing just that.

"Why shouldn't I?" I asked myself one time in worship, when I hadn't realised my hands and arms were being raised as if it was the most natural thing to do.

"This is why we have the ability to raise our hands in praise," I found myself thinking, and I smiled as my hands were lifted. "People do it all the time when they worship their football teams and at concerts, so why shouldn't I lift my hands to praise someone I love?"

I continued to have the same picture of a crown of thorns every day for a few months, and each time it appeared in my mind, it became more prominent.

As I grew more and more weary, I prayed on many occasions for God to help me in all situations, including with the pictures I was receiving. I asked Him what He wanted me to do with them. He always gave me something encouraging or positive, either through His Word, family, friends or my daily UCB readings.

Sometimes I'd feel alone, even though I had my loving husband's support. But it's only God who can fully satisfy and give the soul the deep peace it needs.

This is one of the readings that spoke to me of the darkness God would soon bring me out of

*"God is on top of the situation. Be at peace; He will do whatever it takes to reach and rescue you. Your problem is just a platform to display His power*

*to act on your behalf. Night-time is when God does some of His best work. God dictates the time for our deliverance, He's never late."*

Passages from the Bible about rest also began to jump out at me. But there was one particular verse that was so overwhelming, I cried every time I read it, although it wasn't about rest:

*"The Spirit of the Sovereign LORD is on me, because the LORD has anointed me to proclaim good news to the poor. He has sent me to bind up the broken-hearted, to proclaim freedom for the captives and release from darkness for the prisoners"*
*Isaiah 61:1*

I told Dan as he was worried about me when I found myself breaking down in tears again.

So many Bible verses were coming my way yet I still carried on. I believed God wanted me there in my ministry at Derby Road. But there were other verses that seemed to suggest release for me from my work too. I did get confused in the midst of them all.

I remember speaking to close friends at the time, who felt God was wanting me to leave Derby Road. However, it was when I read the UCB *Word for Today* magazine one day that the truth stuck out like a sore thumb.

The piece I read was about moving out of a place where you've been for a long time. Now was the time to let go. The shining star you once were would lose its effectiveness if you didn't get out now.

Dave had always called me his shining star, from the very start of our relationship. He told me that, the first time he saw me, I stood out from the rest of the people like a shining star. So when I read the magazine, I did take the words on board:

1) *"She invested her life in something that had no future. John writes, 'This world is fading away along with everything it craves. But if you do the will of God you will live forever' (1 John 2:17). God tried to get Lot's wife out of Sodom but she couldn't get Sodom out of her. When she thought of what she was leaving she looked back and turned into a lifeless monument. When God says it's time to move, do not hesitate! Do not become like those who once walked with Him, witnessed on the job, stood out as shining lights in their communities, but now have turned cold and unresponsive. 2) Your decisions have consequences... Before you... tear up your life by refusing to break with your past, remember Lot's wife. She did not make it to safety but did make it into scripture long enough to warn us about three things: a) complacency b) involvement with the wrong things c) a divided heart!"*

This was a warning to me yet I still tested it out – even though I'd spoken to close, wise friends who'd prayed and all felt I should move on as they could see the toll my work was taking on me.

I was exhausted but I loved those people in my ministry. However, I didn't want to have an unresponsive, cold heart towards them. So, if that meant my leaving before that happened, then so be it.

Dave and I noticed that things had begun to change within Green Pastures. Tensions were rising, not only amongst the residents but amongst the staff too.

One colleague was brilliant with getting the flats ready for new tenants, but unintentionally had a way of making things difficult when visiting the Derby Road office. Many of the residents didn't like her and, as much as I would try to change this situation, she often made them feel isolated, telling them to leave my office upon her arrival. This didn't go down well at all, especially when I was in the middle of a conversation with one of them.

Many of the residents didn't have life skills and sometimes this lady could be defensive and abrupt. Life there was tough enough without additional unnecessary battles. This wasn't right and I became very uncomfortable about it. Over the months, I began to feel both mentally and physically drained by it all.

During this time, I leaned on Jesus and asked Him to reveal a way through the situation. I found, as I sought after His heart, that He spoke to me through various pieces of Christian literature that I read. Things jumped out at me and I knew it was God speaking directly to me.

Here are some of the passages that spoke into my life situations:

*"One of [William Carey's] more memorable quotes is: 'Expect great things from God; attempt great things for God.' But you can only say that with confidence when you know what God has called you to do. What He ordains, He sustains!... However, when you know God has given you a vision for your life, you trust Him, even when you can't see any way to bring it to pass."*

*"Instead of lifting them up, they're dragging you down... Be careful around those who are always trying to make you feel guilty for not 'being there'... There's a difference in helping somebody and carrying them. Your help may actually be a hindrance... Step back and let them walk on their own... Discern those who belonged in your past, from those who belong in your life now."*

I knew the residents were upset when I was off ill and would try to make me feel guilty by complaining to Green Pastures about my absence, even when they knew the reason for it. I did think maybe I was getting in the way of God and needed to step back and let them do things for themselves more often.

*"God will treat others according to how they treat us. God told Abraham, 'I will bless those who bless you...'(Genesis 12:3 NKJV) When we are in God's will, we don't have to promote or protect ourselves, God will do it for us... 'Do not touch my anointed ones' (1 Chronicles 16:22 NKJV)."*

*"Don't be controlled by mindless routine... Instead of ignoring your problems, resolve them. Act before they become chronic and start sapping your energy... If you're overloaded, don't take on more... When you burn the candle at both ends, you're the one who burns out."*

*"His intention is for you to discover His will for your life, unlock and develop the gifts He's given you, draw daily on His power, use your common sense, and don't live stressed out... You can't always control what happens to you, but you can decide how to respond to it... Tap into the power of God's Word... Feed your mind with scriptures, then meditate on them until they take root and grow in you."*

I knew I had to do something and, as I prayed, I asked God to keep me close and guide me in what to do. I felt it was time to give up and let go.

My brother Sam had been volunteering and helping me out with some of the residents. He had a real heart for the work that Dave and I did. I'd been praying for so long for someone to come on board who had a heart for the people and who'd continue the work if I left. All along it was staring me in the face who this person was but I didn't recognise it: my brother!

As I poured out my heart to Father God, He comforted me and drew me near to Him. I was low, exhausted, emptied out. I needed my Father's embrace and I sank into His arms.

Each night I had many dreams; some were spiritual, others weren't. But I seemed to know when my Father was speaking to me...

"Pam, listen to me. I will fulfil my promise through you in the work you have done. I am the Lord who keeps His promises forever. I will not tolerate violence or the instigation of evil. They will be safe if they obey me. Trust Me. You will see my promise fulfilled. Your faithfulness will protect and defend them."

These words were intermittent. God knew my heart better than I did. He knew I didn't want trouble in the ministry He had brought me to; that it was time for me to leave. He knew my heart for the lost and He provided in everything.

One night, I was woken up. There in front of me was the picture of a crown of thorns on canvas.

"All right, Lord," I said, in absolute awe, "tomorrow I'll go out and buy a canvas." I won't say I couldn't believe it as it was real, and I'd been asking God to show me what He wanted me to do with this picture He'd been revealing to me over the last few months.

The next day, I bought a boxed canvas. I'd never bought or done anything with canvas before so it was all new to me.

When I got it home, I could see plainly the picture in my mind but — "How do I get this on the canvas?" I asked God.

God showed me clearly what to do as I got string and long nails from my husband's toolbox in his van. And before and during the making of this sculpture on canvas, I prayed and listened to worship.

This was the beginning of the creation of many pictures, the largest being an eight-foot-high by six-foot-wide image of Jesus on a cross.

As soon as I finished one sculpture, the Lord would show me another He wanted me to get on with, and I never stopped until I'd completed them. I soon discovered I shouldn't leave the pictures for too long before getting to work.

This was something beautiful that God was revealing in me. He is the greatest artist who was using me as a vessel to produce these creations.

But, of course, at that time, I didn't know what else He had in store.

# 34

# DEPRESSION AND ART

I asked Green Pastures if I could stop going to the weekly meetings as it was here that I felt most vulnerable. However, my input was still considered necessary.

The meetings were run by another member who'd come on board, and I wasn't feeling very strong mentally. My time spent participating in them began to drain me. I'd feel numb and exhausted afterwards.

Inevitably, I reached a point where I couldn't take any more, and my final meeting at G.P. ended with a colleague slamming their hands on the table, leaning over, shouting and pointing their finger at me. At one time I could handle these situations but not now. Management later told me to take time out as I sat there shaking and crying. I didn't know what was going on in my body.

Both Dave and I went to see a friend who was a retired doctor and I told him what had been happening to me. As he prayed for me, he hugged me and commanded this thing to get off and leave me. He told me I wouldn't be going back to work for a long time. He was a beautiful man who had godly wisdom and discernment, but he also knew what was happening to me and told me to make an appointment with my own doctor.

When I sat at home the following day, Dave rang me. He was covering my job in Derby Road, as well as his own and one of the director's jobs, since we were all overloaded with work because the company was growing.

"What's up?" Dave asked, as it took me so long to answer the phone.

I couldn't get out of the chair. My body felt so heavy; my arms and legs wouldn't move; and when they did, I couldn't stop shaking and crying, and my speech was slurred.

Dave came home and made an emergency doctor's appointment for me.

My doctor sent me to have bloods taken as she didn't know if it was the start of Parkinson's disease.

I had lots of different tests done. In the end, I was told I had severe depression, stress and anxiety. This was a lot to take in but it seemed to make sense.

I'd worked alongside and supported many people who had suffered with depression, yet the way in which the illness affected me was totally different to my experience of it in others throughout my ministry. It's a traumatic illness for anyone and it strikes people in so many different ways.

I didn't realise what was happening to me and just started noticing small but significant changes. When I was driving, for instance, I'd look at road signs and the wording seemed to be elongated. I found the signs difficult to read and take in. I'd also noticed at work that, when I looked through paperwork, the words seemed to blur into a mass of ink on the pages. I couldn't retain information and I'd cry over anything. I had a lot of compassion for people, but I began to cry just when I saw them. So I knew something wasn't right, even though I was told by some that it was just the empathy that I had for them.

Not long before I was diagnosed, Dave and I had taken a couple of weeks off work. We took Dave's nine-year-old daughter on holiday with us and stayed in a little converted barn in Somerset that was run by Christians. It was a very beautiful, quiet place, just what we needed. I'd also put some of my artwork in the *New Wine* conference in Shepton Mallet.

This was a lovely time for us but I still had moments when I'd break down and cry for no reason at all.

I cried again when we flicked through photographs of our holiday on our return. It was when I saw myself. I was looking at someone who looked happy but I didn't seem to recognise that person was me.

My doctor told me that if I returned to the same type of work as I'd been doing at Green Pastures, it could knock me back worse than before. I had severe depression, stress and anxiety and I really had to listen to him. God had been trying to tell me this for some time but I'd carried on regardless.

I was put on medication and immediately began to feel different. I felt better but I was far from right.

Then one day, Dave, who continued to do his own job as well as mine, was sitting at the computer looking at a blank screen when he suddenly knew he couldn't do it anymore. He carried on for two months after I left and was then diagnosed with depression too. The stress of the job had caught up with us and eventually took us both out.

*"We now have this light shining in our hearts, but we ourselves are like fragile clay jars containing this great treasure. This makes it clear that our great power is from God, not from ourselves. We are pressed on every side by troubles, but we are not crushed. We are perplexed, but not driven to despair. We are hunted down, but never abandoned by God. We get knocked down, but we are not destroyed.*

*Through suffering, our bodies continue to share in the death of Jesus so that the life of Jesus may also be seen in our bodies."*
*2 Corinthians 4:7–10, NLT*

After I'd been off work for a few months, I began to think I was ready to return to Green Pastures, despite the warnings from my doctor. However, within two hours of being back, when I tried to read through a housing form I realised it was distorting again.

Everything was clear. It was God's timing for both Dave and me to leave for good. Besides, He already had plans for the person to take over from us: my brother!

We always felt that God would have to provide someone with a large heart and a gift for this type of work and people. My brother, through his volunteering, had shown these in all areas. God had it all worked out and had been preparing him for this time.

During the transition, one of the residents we looked after at Green Pastures was getting married and had asked me to be her maid of honour and for Dave to give her away. She was very happy and wanted me to help her with the arrangements. I loved weddings. In the midst of my depression, it was good to have something to focus on and I decorated the church and reception venue. Between our church and Shoreline church, lots of people helped out to make their day special, and it was. Their wedding was amazing.

It was very strange moving from a happy, joyous occasion to sadness and pain, which seemed to be a regular thing in our lives.

And things weren't just tough for Dave and me. My son, Joe, was struggling with his own battle against depression, which we were mentally carrying too.

"Don't give up on your children," I remember someone saying at a conference. "Continue to pray for them. Pray until something happens."

This was something I did every day as I prayed into the depression that hung over him.

> *"So be truly glad. There is wonderful joy ahead, even though you must endure many trials for a little while. These trials will show that your faith is genuine. It is being tested as fire tests and purifies gold – though your faith is far more precious than mere gold. So when your faith remains strong through many trials, it will bring you much praise and glory and honor on the day when Jesus Christ is revealed to the whole world. You love him even though you have never seen him. Though you do not see him now, you trust him; and you rejoice with a glorious, inexpressible joy. The reward for trusting him will be the salvation of your souls."*
> *1 Peter 1:6–9, NLT*

One evening, we had guests visiting. Joe came home and sat down next to me. He joined in with the conversation. Then, as he stood up to leave, he looked down at me and smiled.

Suddenly, it was as if God had switched a light on in me as I saw something beautiful in him. Amongst the tears and sadness of things going on in his life and all the prayers for him to come back to Jesus, I saw something wonderful and beautiful in him. His eyes shone a lovely luminous blue and the depth of love in his smile hit the core of my soul and spirit. Jesus was shining through him.

I thought back to the time when he was in my tummy; when I gave him to God. And I held that smile in my heart all through the night and cried tears of joy.

That depth of warmth and love was so tangible. I couldn't explain it but when I told Joe the following day, tears ran down his face too. I knew the Lord was showing me Joe would come back to Jesus.

I was still getting pictures regularly and putting them on canvas. After being out of work for a couple of months, the Lord gave me the name of an artist, Peter, in our church, who He wanted me to speak to. The church had a congregation of about three hundred people so, whilst I knew of this man vaguely, I didn't really know him to speak to. Anyway, what was I to say to him? I prayed and asked the Lord to give me the right time to talk to him.

I was so excited about what God had been doing with me and the visions and sculptures He'd given me to create that I told my vicar, Stu. I asked him if I could display them in church. However, I was told I could put them in the corner, which was pretty much out of sight. I put this down to Stu's lack of interest in art.

I was disappointed that they weren't on display as I was thrilled with what God had done through me. But it wasn't about me but about Jesus. So I kept trusting that God had given me this gift for a purpose.

I spoke to Peter in church the following week. I told him the Lord had put his name on my heart to speak to but I wasn't sure what it was about. He looked at my work and told me it was good and should be on display.

Peter told me he ran an art class on a Monday evening and he asked me to pray about whether I should join, as I'd done with my sculptures. He told me I could attend one of the classes to see if I liked it first. The classes ran for ten weeks and the next one was to begin in February, in just a few weeks' time.

I moaned to Dave, "But I can't paint. I just can't paint! Why did I even speak to Peter? I do sculptures on canvas – he's an artist. I don't do anything like him."

Dave told me to just give it a try and reminded me that God had put Peter on my heart for a reason and I shouldn't ignore it.

I began to panic at the thought of painting. Although I'd been to college in my teenage years, I'd never felt I was able to paint.

My birthday approached in February and I discovered that my dear Dave had bought me ten weeks of lessons on Peter's art course as a present. I didn't know whether to cry or run! Dave always encourages and supports me in so many ways and his complete faith in me really moved me.

At the first lesson, I made quite an entrance as I marched in with my large, twenty-four-by-eighteen-inch canvas, whilst all the other artists were working on A4-sized pieces or smaller.

I prayed quickly: "What am I thinking of, Lord? I've never painted on canvas before so please help me."

"Drift" was my first ever painting and I was so happy in this class. I met other Christians and got the opportunity to pray for them. God was really moving in me in a way that I never realised He would!

As the sculptures and now paintings were pouring out of me, I began to work on my biggest piece yet. And I knew I had to get "Priceless" finished by Easter.

"Priceless" is a sculpture on canvas and board representing Jesus on the cross. It's eight feet high by six feet wide.

When it was eventually finished, God placed on my heart to contact Liverpool Anglican Cathedral, who were eager to display it, along with other pieces of my work, in the Lady Chapel in the run up to Ascension.

"Priceless" was hung six feet from the ground and, as the sun shone down on it, it reminded me of the power of Jesus, the one who was crucified and who rose again.

My friend went to see my work there one day and was about to leave when the Lord told her to go back in. She returned and saw a lady crying. My friend asked her if she was all right and the lady told her that one particular piece of my work was speaking to her.

"Doubting Thomas" was a sculpture on canvas, showing hands with holes in them.

The lady told my friend that she felt really drawn to them; that she'd fallen away from faith but thought the Lord was calling her back, especially through this sculpture, "Doubting Thomas".

I knew that over the previous months God had been preparing me. It was during the visions of the volcano that I'd felt He was getting me ready for other things – things like painting, filling me with a new confidence and boldness to step out in the gifts He had given me: healing on the streets, prophetic words for people – these new gifts of creativity and more that I was beginning to discover.

One night, I had a dream about two skeletons. A lady I knew at church called Karen had to pick them up, rub the bones together and throw them away after she had spoken over them. I felt this meant there was something she had to do regarding her past. She needed to receive the prophecy and then she would soar. It was a bizarre dream but I felt I had to let her know.

It seemed to me that something new was happening in Karen's life. Changes were taking place, as if she'd lain dormant for far too long. She was a lovely lady who was quiet and stayed in the background. But shaking the dust from the old bones, rubbing them together and throwing them away was symbolic. Her life had been a certain way, but after she'd done this, she would soar.

A group of us from church had been to a prophetic and worship evening at another church and we all came back on fire for God. Karen had had an experience of electricity moving down her spine that evening and recalled my dream of the bones. A few weeks later, she got up in church and spoke about my dream and how she believed it was a prophetic word for her.

God was moving and encouraging us to persevere in our ministries and, once a month, we would all meet up and have an evening of testimony, praise and worship, and develop in the gifts God had given us.

I got up to give my testimony of how God had removed a lump from my thigh that I'd had for eighteen months. During that eighteen-month period, I was due to go to hospital three times to have it removed, but each time I received a letter to say the appointment had been cancelled. Thank God He removed it first without me having to have surgery.

As time passed, the Holy Spirit was doing powerful things while we stepped out in faith. The more we drew closer to Jesus and spoke of His love, the more His Holy Spirit guided us.

Many times the Holy Spirit would speak to us as we gathered together and drew strength from His Word. The following Bible verses were incredibly powerful in the movement of the Holy Spirit as people experienced Jesus' love. They helped them understand more about who the Holy Spirit is and how He can manifest Himself in many different ways.

*"The wind blows wherever it wants. Just as you can hear the wind but can't tell where it comes from or where it is going, so you can't explain how people are born of the Spirit."*
*John 3:8, NLT*

Jesus explains that we can't control the work of the Holy Spirit. He works in ways we can't predict or understand. Just as you can't control your physical birth, neither can you control your spiritual birth. It's a gift from God through the Holy Spirit.

*"And I will ask the Father, and he will give you
another Advocate, who will never leave you. He is
the Holy Spirit, who leads into all truth. The world
cannot receive Him, because it isn't looking for
Him and doesn't recognize Him. But you know
Him, because He lives with you now and later will
be in you. No, I will not abandon you as orphans –
I will come to you."*
*John 14:16–18, NLT*

The Holy Spirit is a powerful person, working on our side, working for us and with us. He will never leave us. Many people are unaware of the Holy Spirit's activities but to those who hear Christ's words and understand the Spirit's power, the Spirit gives a whole new way of looking at life.

*"...and he has identified us as his own by placing
the Holy Spirit in our hearts as the first instalment
that guarantees everything he has promised us."*
*2 Corinthians 1:22, NLT*

The Holy Spirit guarantees we belong to God and will receive all His benefits. The Holy Spirit guarantees salvation. It's ours now and we will receive so much more when Christ returns. Don't be ashamed to let others know that you are His.

Many people want something tangible, visible and real before they will believe. Jesus did healings and other miracles; God raised Him from the dead yet still people doubt.

Will visible signs convince anyone? The sign that really brings us to faith is the cry of the heart.

To the confused, God offers a mind enlightened by faith; to the depressed God offers a reason for joy; to the lonely, He offers eternal companionship. Don't look for a spectacular, visible sign. Instead, seek a cleansed and renewed life as evidence of His presence.

As responsible Christians, we must choose our battles, starting with prayers for wisdom, then prayers for courage. Once our battle is chosen, we need to act as faithful followers of the living God. We need to witness with strength, move mountains by faith and overcome in love.

I loved this new boldness and confidence Jesus had given me, and His word seemed to come alive in ways I'd never seen before.

I've discovered that when we are obedient and faithful, Jesus reveals His word in a new depth. This is why the Bible is known as the "Living Word" – it is *alive*!

I once heard someone say "pray all the time, have constant communication with Him. Heaven stops to listen each time we pray."

I found this amazing and there was more. I wanted to highlight everything that was speaking to me in a new light.

Some of the teaching I'd heard in my walk with Jesus was again being brought to my attention. Although I prayed morning and evening, I still spoke to Jesus throughout the day too. He's my friend and He's always there no matter what time of day or night. So you can imagine how amusing it was when the following spoke to me:

**Ask God to bless whoever you meet. When workmates act badly, "Lord, make me an instrument of grace and a light where it is dark."**

**Sitting still and listening is more important to what God wants to say to you.**

This certainly spoke to me as my new journey began in a fresh depth.

I'd been reading Judges chapter 15 about Samson.

*"Because [Samson] was very thirsty, he cried out
to the LORD, 'You have given your servant this great
victory. Must I now die of thirst and fall into the
hands of the uncircumcised?"*
Judges 15:18

As I glanced at the footnote of the *Life Application Study Bible*, this is also what it read:

*"Severe depression also follows great achievements so don't be surprised if you feel drained after a personal victory"*, NLT.

Alongside the prophetic words and outreach, my art and ministry, Father God had been trying to tell me to rest; to take a step back in my ministry of working with homeless people. But, as I'd failed to act upon this, I eventually had to leave work due to illness.

Amid the depression and unemployment, we struggled financially. And even though God had provided in many areas, through our family and church family, it was still an issue we would have to face.

The depression was so great that I knew this was not what God meant for me for the rest of my life, but I couldn't think or do anything.

The only book I could read was my Bible. Even so, it was only small passages that I could take in. I couldn't even read my mail or fill in forms as the ink continued to run into one big mess on the paper. The only thing I could do was rest in Jesus' presence and know that He had me in the palm of His hand. I wasn't going anywhere.

I looked at the depression as a visitor who had come in and tried to invade my life; who had tried to take me away from Jesus. All I could do was say over and over, "Jesus, I love You. Thank You that You are here in this with me."

It took a while before I could read again, and eventually I began to do more paintings, which the Lord used in many ways to reach others in their darkest times.

Times of illness can be very testing. We are surrounded by people who look at us in these times and by some who actually ask, "Where is your God in this?" But we may be the only "Bible" they read. We are accountable for our actions and responses at all times. People may not read the Bible but they will read Christians. If they don't like what they see in them, they're not going to want what they have.

We are human but the more we seek Jesus, the more He will transform us from the inside out. He loves us unconditionally no matter how many times we fail to get it right. He is there to pick us up and move us on, drawing us back to Himself.

I remember a young lady who had come to do her work experience with us at Derby Road not long before I became ill. Someone had upset her in the way she'd spoken to her. This really disheartened the young lady as she thought that was the way all Christians were. It emphasised to me how accountable we are to God and to each other in the ways we speak to and treat people. In whether we listen to or ignore them.

# 35

# VISIONS IN MY HEALING

During the darkness of the depression, I felt God's presence beside me as well as in visions.

In one vision, I saw myself standing on top of a mountain overlooking a beautiful lake. The Lord told me to keep my eyes fixed on Him through all of this. I was then standing at ground level, my eyes still fixed on Jesus. The Lord covered the buildings and the ground with what looked like a huge blanket of white, fluffy snow, glistening with gold.

He then showed me my recent painting, one I'd painted with my eyes closed, "Walk With Me". I'd painted this with my fingers when I was filled with the Holy Spirit. He put His arm round my shoulders as we walked. I was walking on air as my feet didn't touch the ground. And He told me I'd be blown away by what He was giving me.

I felt so at peace. No worries or fears, just an amazing calmness. It seemed so natural, as if it should always be like that. I felt as if I'd been in a different world: an altogether heavenly world. I was filled with the sense that there were to be many blessings for us.

I then saw rocks falling from the sky and someone standing on the mountain top, praising God with their arms in the air. And I saw an amazing, blinding light from heaven that covered the mountain and the earth. The Lord said, "Be prepared for what I will give you."

I was so thankful for being in His beautiful presence and He gave me Romans chapter eight to read about life in the Spirit. It really did blow my mind.

I've had many pictures and visions in my walk and some of them have been clearer than others. I write of them because, although I may not understand them all, God knows what He's doing and any one of them may be meant for you as you read this book. I'm just being faithful and writing of His great love for us, His children.

October was soon upon us and the Christmas light switch-on in Southport's town centre was getting close. My friend, Mary and I had volunteered to get involved and organise a church float for the big switch-on. And we certainly had some laughs doing it!

Obviously we'd prayed about it and God had provided everything we needed – a forty-five-foot-long articulated lorry and trailer, including the generator plus the driver. All we had to do was decorate it and have it ready on time.

My creative side came out as we planned what was going to be on the lorry. Over the past years, we'd noticed that the parade only featured Father Christmas, elves and fairies. There was nothing about Jesus, so we decided to bring the real reason for Christmas into it.

I met up with other people in the church and, between us, we made all the outfits that we needed. The children were dressed as sheep. Someone made royal gowns for the three kings, and Dave and I were Mary and Joseph. We decorated the truck with lots of lights and a Christmas tree. And I made a huge dove to go on the back of the trailer. We had shepherds, too, walking beside the trailer, giving out sweets.

I'd also suggested we have a real donkey. Dave couldn't believe what I was asking for and neither could Stewart, our vicar. They laughed when I told them and asked where on earth I'd get a donkey. Again, Mary and I prayed and the Lord provided!

It was hard work getting the trailer ready but Dave was so funny. He had to sit on the back to stop the Christmas tree falling off as the lorry raced through the town centre to get there on time.

The husband and wife who brought Pinky the donkey were lovely. They even dressed up as shepherds to play their part and walked behind the trailer.

There was one hilarious moment when Pinky decided he didn't want to walk any further and held up all the traffic. Stewart, who didn't like dressing up at the best of times, had agreed to take part as a shepherd, and he tried to push Pinky along. Everyone commented about the two of them being stubborn asses!

I was always thinking about and planning something creative to do for outreach and other events. During the depression, I organised and planned a wedding, I planned my husband's surprise 40th birthday party, and then had only three weeks to plan, organise and decorate the trailer for the Christmas light switch-on, as well as help make twenty-four costumes!

I knew the medication was helping me but, without Jesus, I'd never have been able to do any of that, as He gave me the strength. The Lord had given me the gifts of art and creativity, which I realised I had to put to use, and this was helping me out of the depression. Jesus was my rock once again when I hit rock bottom. It was upon Him that I stood, believing I would get through it all.

The following Easter, Dave and I were baptised together. I'd been going through a season of amazing touches from the Lord. When I was asleep, I dreamt many spiritual dreams. I'd wake the following morning feeling the Holy Spirit's power as He manifested Himself to me. I was being topped up regularly by Him.

When I woke up one morning, I remember I was still praising Jesus. I'd been doing so all through the night. Dave often told me I did this, as many times he could feel me shaking when the Holy Spirit was upon me.

One night, I dreamed about two beautiful gold creatures who had beaks like an eagle. They were larger than I was and were covered in gold and brass-like feathers. They told me to keep praising Jesus, keep focused on Him and not let go. I was floating and they were there around me and went everywhere I went.

It was as though I was in a spirit world but on earth. I could see other spirits, evil and angelic. These creatures told me they were always with me and around me and the angelic ones promised they'd never leave me.

Then I saw witches, some who were sleeping and others awake. They were trying to deceive my friend by putting their clothes on her as she was resting. I told her to throw them away quickly. I prayed and put my hand on the witch's head, praying with the authority Jesus gave us. As I did so, the witch shrivelled up.

I saw my son Mick and his partner at the time in a dream too. They were walking. I told Mick to quickly grab my hand, keep his eyes fixed on Jesus and not look back. It was as if there were earthquakes coming. His partner tried to keep him from running. I was floating and flying and when I thought earthly thoughts, I began to fall back down to earth. But I still insisted to Mick that he should grab my hand and run and stay focused on Jesus.

I then found myself on a beautiful mountain. I called it "Butterfly Mountain" because of its butterfly shape. There were beautiful colours all over it, like I'd never seen before. I went to take a picture of it as I was flying with the two gold creatures, but I realised I was starting to fall towards earthly ground again. It was only for a few seconds and I then re-focused on Jesus. And as I was soaring, I saw an evil face that had nails in its head. When I praised Jesus, it disappeared.

I woke up after that and felt the Holy Spirit very powerfully upon me, and I was like that for most of the day.

It had been a year of upheaval and change. I didn't know what type of work I'd end up doing, but I'd been out of work for nine months and I was ready to return to the workplace again. I just wasn't sure where.

It was my friend Mary who told me about her son and his book business. He had a warehouse and all that was needed if I worked there was for me to scan books and pack them.

This was a good start to get me back into the swing of things. There wasn't as much stress as in my previous job, even though we had to work at a certain pace. Mary also worked for her son, and we became close friends as we got on with the job together.

God was in the centre of everything, but where there are mountain-top experiences, there are also attacks, whether spiritual or physical, and sometimes both. With me, it always seemed to be both.

I soon discovered Joe had been taking drugs as well as drinking heavily. Once again, my heart was broken. When I saw him look into my tear-filled eyes, I knew I'd reached him somewhere in his soul.

I despised drugs with a vengeance. I'd seen the damaging effects of them too many times in my life with the people we looked after and with Joe's dad.

I'd given up alcohol in my early thirties and would just have the occasional glass of my father-in-law's fruit wine at Christmas time or on my birthday. But I even gave that up because I'd fall asleep after only half a glass.

Joe hadn't kept in touch with us and I knew something was wrong. I felt it in my spirit. Mums always seem to pick up on things when something isn't right with their kids. Joe worked hard but he'd been partying hard too.

Dave, my brother, Sam and sister-in-law were broken-hearted to hear about Joe too. Sam had always been close to Joe and Mick and, after a while, between us all we felt we were getting through to him.

Eventually, Joe came back home to live with us and Bob our Labrador. But along came Lola too.

Joe had rescued Lola. She was a German Shepherd puppy around seven months old. She was quite thin, timid and scrawny, and had a mite living under her skin that left her with bald patches. But she soon got better from this after a trip to the vet.

We didn't have a lot of space for another dog, but in my heart I couldn't let this beautiful animal be shipped off elsewhere, as she'd been mistreated before Joe rescued her and she was good for Joe.

We didn't know how Bob would take to another dog moving into his territory, but they got on really well. Lola knew Bob was boss when she pushed things too far.

She soon settled into her new home and family, but my patience began to run low when we discovered her habit of chewing things while we were out. We'd come home from work to find she'd chewed through the phone wire, the skirting board, the new stair carpet, and the outside tap and pipe lagging. She was very clever too, as she somehow managed to chew underneath the seat cushion on the couch and push the cushion back into place. We never discovered how she did it.

It got to the point where I was on the edge of re-homing her. Joe was very upset, of course, and pleaded with us to keep her.

It may sound crazy to do this to an animal, but I actually laid hands on her one night and I prayed that the destructive spirit would be gone from her and be replaced with peace, calm and happiness. After all, God created the heavens and the earth and everything in them. In God's Word it says:

*"...that at the name of Jesus every knee should*
*bow, in heaven and on earth and under the earth,*
*and every tongue acknowledge that Jesus Christ is*
*Lord, to the glory of God the Father."*
*Philippians 2:10–11*

Lola stopped destroying things after this prayer. I do believe Jesus intervened and the spirit of destruction was forced to leave her. She became a beautiful, affectionate companion.

In the midst of everything, I'd been crying out to God again for some confirmation that He would bring Joe back to Jesus, and I read this in UCB *Word For Today*:

*"Satan will attack when God is about to bring something to birth in your life. It may be a birth of a relationship, a career, a ministry, or even a child God will use. Your 'difficult child' may be a child of destiny; that's why they encounter more difficulties than your other children. They have an assignment the enemy has discerned. When the attack comes, stand on God's Word and say, 'Thanks be to God, who gives us the victory through our Lord Jesus Christ.' (1 Corinthians 15:57 NKJV)."*

It's hard watching your children damaging themselves, or seeing someone you love going through the refiner's fire, but it's the only way to get pure gold. Knowledge isn't the way to growth – pain is. We mustn't get in God's way by trying to rescue our children, as big or old as they are.

It hurt so much when, sometime after all this, due to a mixture of drugs and relationship breakdowns, Joe tried to take his own life again. We were all distraught.

Mick and Sam got the phone call and found him. It was devastating. Dave and I drove as fast as we could to find him on the floor in a real mess.

"My God, my God help him! Save him!" I cried, as I saw the paramedics putting him into the ambulance.

Mick and Sam's faces were ashen.

I tried to be as calm as I could but my heart was broken and aching so much I felt it was going to explode.

The mental health team were involved and Joe told us all about what he'd done, and about the use of drugs that had brought him to do what he'd done. He was told he was very lucky to be alive.

Lucky? It was God who saved him. There were many prayers going out for him and for us, and I felt God's presence through this difficult time.

Joe didn't seem to grasp the reality of what he'd done. He wanted to work and not deal with it all, but I was scared to let him out of my sight. I just had to trust that Jesus had Joe in His hands.

Eventually, after a couple of months, he began to settle down. He knew Jesus had plans for him. The drug-taking and the rejection he felt after the breakdown of his seven-year relationship nearly cost him his life. But he started to come back to church and to feel peace again. In fact, he met a young lady not long after and they began to attend church together.

# 36

# THE REAL NATIVITY AND CREATIVITY

During our house group prayer time, the Lord gave me a picture of a little stable on the lawns of our church. I prayed about this as more of this vision was revealed to me. Once more, God wanted us to do the "Real Nativity" for the Christmas lights switch-on.

The vision was to bring the churches together and to represent the nativity with real sheep, a donkey and a baby. The three kings were to be the leaders from the churches, giving out sweets and literature about the true meaning of Christmas to children and families. All the helpers would be dressed up as shepherds and would give out mince pies and refreshments to the public. Carol singers would perform whilst people came to look at the stable where the animals, baby Jesus and His parents would be. There would be a huge star fitted to the entrance of the church, which was in the centre of the town. This would be a beacon of light to those who felt alone at Christmas and a warm invitation for them to come in.

The "Real Nativity" was to be a very simple and beautiful way of evangelising about the true meaning of Christmas without speaking.

I spoke to my vicar about this and he gave me the go-ahead to organise it. He laughed when I told him we were talking about real animals and a real baby, as he thought my friend Mary and I had some crazy ideas at times.

"You watch," I said, "it'll happen. If God is in it, it'll come together."

Mick and I made a huge star with LED lights. It was nearly six feet tall. And I knew God had His hand on it all as we heard that a baby was expected to be born not long before the date of the Christmas light switch-on.

I laughed at God's sense of humour as Mary and I searched fields looking for a donkey. It was when we got word that Pinky the donkey was available again, along with two sheep, that things started to come together.

However, there were still some hurdles when the churches themselves didn't come together.

By the time our vicar had told the other ministers about this vision, it was too late as they were busy with their own church events.

However, the "Real Nativity" still went ahead. The city council loaned us some barriers that they used on the road sides whilst the parade was on, and we used these to pen in Pinky and the sheep. One of the sheep decided to make a break for it down the busy main road when the parade was on, but was rescued and penned in again.

It was a beautiful evening as Mary and Joseph sat on a hay bale, watching over the five-day-old baby who lay in the manger, the stable dimly lit with fairy lights. As the shepherds gave out mince pies and refreshments, with carol singers in the background, the atmosphere was electric. We handed out bags of "hope" too, which consisted of the nativity story and sweets.

There were thousands of people on the streets that night. They made their way to the stable and parents' eyes sparkled as they told their children the story of baby Jesus. God moved people's hearts and I'll never forget it!

When I looked back over the past year, I realised that God had been placing changes on my heart. I knew I'd be moving to another church although I didn't know where. Organising the "Real Nativity" was confirmation to me. I'd obeyed God by organising it, but I'd had a lot of negativity from some people, which troubled me.

I began to feel I couldn't fly, as if my wings had been clipped. I knew God had many plans for me but things were stopping me from fulfilling them and I had to do something about it. I discussed this with Dave and we talked about which church we might go to. I needed to stay faithful to God but I carried sadness in my heart over some people's responses to me in the way they began to speak to me.

I stayed on in the church but found myself feeling bored. I wanted more and I knew there was so much more because I'd experienced it many times. I wanted to feel alive again.

"What are You telling me, Lord?" I asked. "Where can I go? I know there's more and I know You're leading me to somewhere else. I've felt it for most of the year – but where?" I was hungry to find out.

One day, Stu asked if Mary and I would do an African-themed party in his garden.

Our ideas ran wild as we planned it, and Stu's face was a picture when we asked him if he had any swimming trunks!

We decorated his huge garden with big stuffed giraffes and lions, and we hid other cuddly animals in the trees. How we laughed when we planned the gorilla in the tree. Dear Dave – as usual we roped him in. But for this, we didn't tell him what we were up to until the last minute.

The local fancy dress shop was closing down and Mary had bought some of the costumes, one being a gorilla outfit. When I told Dave that we'd got it for him, he couldn't believe it. Dressed in the costume, he had to climb twenty feet up into a big tree and he was then stuck there for a couple of hours.

"But what am I going to eat when all of you are eating proper food down there?" he said, afraid he'd go hungry. "And it's too hot to be stuck in that gorilla suit for hours. It's scorching out!"

"No problem," I said, and I handed him a bag full of bananas. "You can have some of those to snack on."

Fortunately, Dave has a great sense of humour, which made the whole thing even funnier.

The children's faces were a picture as, dressed in the costume, he threw bananas down from the tree at them. At first, they couldn't work out where they were coming from. It was only when they eventually spotted him moving that they pulled at their parents' arms, telling them there was a real monkey in the tree. When their parents looked up at him, they thought he was a stuffed one like all the rest!

Poor Dave, he gave the children plenty of amusement – until they realised he wasn't a real gorilla. He sat in the tree for nearly two hours, boiling away in the scorching-hot sun.

We dressed Stewart up as an African king who had his two African wives with him (my friend and I dressed up in African costumes). We also decorated his garden shed so that people could have their photographs taken with him. There were crazy races and games, and people dressed to the African theme. Everyone enjoyed it.

Although I loved organising events like this, and God brought out the creative side in me bit by bit, I began to feel discouraged about my art. I even asked God if He wanted me to carry on painting, and to give me a sign as to whether or not my work was good enough and would sell.

Within a week, I'd received an email from a doctor in Berlin who was studying the subject of the "Heavenly" New Jerusalem in contemporary art. He was interested in a piece of my artwork that I'd sold. Then, a few months later, the Lord reminded me to keep up with my painting by revealing a promise from my promise box again:

*"Do not neglect your gift, which was given you through prophecy when the body of elders laid their hands on you."*
*1 Timothy 4:14*

After this confirmation, Dave set up nicksonarts.com, a website where I could display my work, although it didn't start to sell through the site.

God is so good. He keeps His promises to us. Even though we doubt ourselves, we need to look for these promises in His Word as His Word doesn't lie. It's the enemy who deceives us by making us feel inadequate.

I really had to hang on to who God says I am because, when I looked at other artists' work, I began to compare myself to them. I had to check myself and remember that I am unique – one of a kind. God has created me in His image.

Other people have their gifts and I have mine. And what God gives us is good. So, when we tell ourselves anything different to this, we're doubting what God has done.

# 37

# GROWING IN THE SUPERNATURAL

I discovered even more of what Jesus could do at a conference in Birmingham with friends from church.

Bill Johnson was among a number of brilliant speakers. There was so much to take in I couldn't digest everything, so I wrote down what I could.

It was an incredible time and the movement of the Holy Spirit was powerful as we went out onto the streets with the gifts God had given us, healing and telling people about Jesus' love for them. The atmosphere was electric.

It's amazing to see the Holy Spirit at work. He looks for people He can rest upon, who will host His presence. The resurrected Christ in us is released through us, so His glory is released and made manifest.

The manifestation of the Holy Spirit is our relationship with God. This manifestation is important, as it's God on us externally and not just internally.

We all have different personalities and the Holy Spirit will act differently upon each of us. Others shouldn't worry if God impacts some of us like this. We should all just keep our eyes fixed on God's message and on Jesus. Our relationship is more important than manifestation.

We need God's confidence and, when we seek it, God shows up. He empowers us to give out to others, so then His confidence will be in them too. They will hear words of prophecy and knowledge because God gives us insight into their lives. They will then know these are of God.

When the Holy Spirit is in us, no demonic force can block His fellowship with us. We are more likely to shift things in the Spirit when living in the heavenly realms. We live under an open heaven and one person in God is a majority, so anywhere we go we carry the presence of God; even in the darkest places, which I've discovered on many occasions.

I was learning so much but was still hungry. I learned that the Kingdom of God is within reach and at hand. When we speak, the Spirit of God is released into the atmosphere to bring about the very thing we decree – His presence is released through our obedience and miracles, and the more conscious we are of God, the more of Him we release. We learn how to host His presence as we are vessels who carry it.

We are great adventures waiting to happen as He has anointed us to change environments, our communities, nations and more, but only if we are obedient.

Over a period of time, this teaching was sinking deeper into my soul.

The Holy Spirit was moving powerfully amongst people and was so tangible at one conference that I could feel something happening all over me. I held out my hands and, in the Spirit, I could see angels weaving something gold in and out of my fingertips and all over my hands. I saw angels above me worshipping and moving back and forth across the hall. It was amazing. I didn't want to leave this beautiful presence.

The instruments had stopped playing as just thousands of our voices sang in tongues and worshipped together. The sound was so angelic – beautiful and something I'd never heard before. It seemed to travel from one end of the hall right across to the other.

The next day, we were told that angelic hosts had been with us that night. The music technician said they'd turned off the sound system so that only our voices could be heard. But something had happened, something wonderful as the music filled the room with a different sound: the sound of angels worshipping and praising God.

As I reflected one day on things from my past, I read this and realised we can do anything in Him who strengthens us:

> *"I know what it is to be in need, and I know what it is to have plenty. I have learned the secret of being content in any and every situation, whether well fed or hungry, whether living in plenty or in want. I can do all this through him who gives me strength."*
> *Philippians 4:12−13*

I also recalled a saying I'd heard somewhere, which was quite powerful:
*"If you live cautiously, you will be wise but you won't move mountains."*

Around this time, there was a night when I couldn't sleep. This was unusual for me as I didn't usually have any problems with sleeping.

It was then that I had a vision of lots of angels around me. They all seemed to be busy, but stopped doing what they were doing when I turned around to look at them.

Every time I turned my gaze away, out of the corner of my eye, I saw them being busy again. They were building something, passing things from one to the other.

I was in God's presence and I asked Him what they were doing.

It was as if He smiled over me and gave a gentle laugh, then said, "Sshh, my child, go to sleep now."

I asked Him about four times what the angels were doing but each time his reply was the same. I knew then that it was time to go to sleep, and I did.

When I woke up, I was aware of the vision from the night before. It was still there in my head.

About a week later, the same vision came to me again, only this time the angels were going up and down stairs, passing things to one another. I couldn't see their faces, but somehow I knew they were smiling and happy. I think I wanted to help them but Father God said to me, "Go to sleep, my child."

I started to drift off and, as I did so, I heard a female voice singing softly, repeating the same words over and over again: "Wake up, oh sleeper... Wake up, oh you sleepy soul..."

Then, as I drifted again, I heard Father God's voice saying to me, "Sleep, my child." I knew it was God as I did sleep.

A few weeks later, I had the same vision yet again, but this time I was wide awake in my bedroom. I'd just climbed into bed when it came, as clear as the other times. I could see the angels were building as I was speaking to God. They carried what looked like large boulders and set them down around me, but they held them as if they were very light. They walked up and down the stairs, passing things to each other, as well as opening things – large scrolls or plans of some kind. They also held objects that I knew were tools, but they didn't look like tools.

As before, every time I looked towards them, they would stop working, but while I was talking to God, they were busy building again. It was very strange but incredibly powerful.

I'd been praying for a while, asking God what He was trying to tell me. I felt it was to do with a move to another church and I knew there were going to be changes in Dave's and my life. I could feel it in my spirit. But I needed God to tell me what this recurring vision meant.

One of our friends was a retired Methodist preacher. I told him what I kept seeing and he felt God was showing me He was going to give me a new life. The scrolls were the plans He had for my new life and the boulders were the building of it. I prayed about this possible meaning and asked God to confirm it.

Reading this in the UCB *Word For Today* was some confirmation to me:

*"If you want to experience God's blessing in a new way, get ready to leave your comfort zone. When Jesus called His disciples they were on familiar turf, doing what they knew best: fishing. But they couldn't stay there and follow Him. Neither can you. The Bible records 'As Jesus walked beside the sea of Galilee, He saw Simon and His brother Andrew casting a net... for they were fishermen. "Come, follow me", Jesus said, "and I will make you fishers of men." At once they left their nets and followed Him. (Mark 1: 16-18 NIV). Notice, they had to leave the security of the familiar in order to fulfil their destiny. And in case you think you are too old to try something new, Abraham was seventy-five when he left the comforts of home to go out and establish a new nation. Your age isn't the issue, your faith is. Understand this: today you are just one step of obedience away from the next truth God wants you to learn about Him, so you can't afford to stay where you are. We all have a tendency to cling to the 'tried and true'. The trouble with that is, when you are no longer being stretched you shrink, you become complacent, you think you can handle things on your own, and you stop growing. That's a dangerous place to be. If you feel restless at heart today and believe that God has more for you than you've been settling for, then it's time to confront your fears, walk through them and launch out into a new experience with Him."*

Although I'd had many manifestations of the Holy Spirit, many visions, dreams and pictures and had felt His beautiful presence on lots of occasions, I believed God was building me up specifically. He was preparing me for the next battles, comforting me through the storms and furnaces I'd been through time after time. I believed then and believe now that He will never leave me, even in the darkest times, and I've been through many of them. I also believe He was pouring out His love on me at this time, just saying, "Be still and know that I am God."

Through all these things, God continues to be my solid rock, my beautiful saviour. I love my Jesus. He sustains me and gives me the strength to carry on. He is my counselor when I don't know where to turn. It's Jesus' arms I run to; it's His Word I pick up and read until I find out what He is saying. And I've learnt to realise that when times are difficult, we mustn't rely on our feelings as they can deceive us. It's believing on the Word of God that's the answer. That's where our comfort, peace, rest, strength and everything else come from.

# 38

# VISION FOR THE LONELY

We had some good friends and neighbours called Gemma and Al, who were also Christians. It was funny how we met them.

Dave and I had returned from visiting Joe in hospital one evening when he wasn't well, and Dave was reversing his van into the small residential car park where we then lived. At the same time, Gemma was backing into a tiny car space next to us and signing something to us with her hands.

Dave was upset about this as it made parking awkward. He was already not in a very good mood, and he said something in anger. I reminded him of the Christian sign we had displayed on our windscreen and told him it wouldn't be a good witness if he said anything nasty to the other driver.

As Gemma reversed into the space next to us, we saw the same Christian sign on her car.

I couldn't help but laugh as Dave realised what I'd said.

When Gemma and Al got out of the car, Gemma was able to explain that she was trying to indicate that she was reversing into the space next to us and hoping we wouldn't jump out of the van. She didn't want to knock us over or knock our door off.

We spoke to the two of them in the little car park and told them we were returning from the hospital. Al told us he was a retired Methodist preacher and that he had Alzheimer's. Then he said, "Come on, we'll pray for your son now," and we did so, huddled together between the two vehicles.

Gemma and Al lived in sheltered accommodation and we lived in the houses nearby, so we all became great friends. We spent a lot of time with them and I mentioned that I felt God was drawing me to another church.

As the months passed and Christmas was approaching again, I asked God what He wanted us to do for people this year – something we could bless them with. The Lord showed me clearly that He wanted me to invite people who were lonely to have their Christmas dinner with us.

Dave had walked past the sheltered accommodation many times. He'd seen people, sitting by their windows, staring out into space.

One evening he said to me, "I've been thinking, Pam. Maybe we should do something for the people in the sheltered accommodation on Christmas day. Maybe have a meal for them. Every time I walk past one elderly man's bungalow, he's just sitting there, gazing out."

I couldn't believe my ears when he said this and I told him what God had put on my heart.

Full of excitement, we ran over to Gemma and Al's. But before we could say a word, they told us *they* were wanting to do a meal on Christmas day for people who'd be on their own.

So that was it, and between the four of us we began to plan and organise everything.

As we didn't have enough room to fit many people into our small terraced home, Gemma suggested we use the little sheltered centre opposite. It was perfect!

We prayed before we began. Then Gemma made invitations for the residents of the thirty-three little bungalows and we gave them out to everyone personally. To our amazement, the majority of people declined and said they had other plans.

Even so, we continued to make Christmas a great day for those who accepted. My two sons offered their services for the day, along with my brother Sam and his wife Debbie, so we had plenty of helpers.

Gemma and I both enjoyed getting creative, and between us we made everything from place cards to table decorations.

I was very excited as I picked up little gifts for everyone. I chose things that matched each guest's personality. Gemma bought lots of little presents and people donated gifts too. We knew God was in this as people from different churches and farmers donated vegetables, turkey, money and gifts.

When God has His hand on something, He will fulfil it. And it was when I was at church one November Sunday morning that He began to speak to me again!

Stewart was talking about the diocese and what the churches in each part of the city were doing. He showed a DVD with snippets of each church's work. What leapt out at me as I watched was a lady vicar giving communion to a lady at home. Suddenly, tears began to run down my face. I wasn't crying. It was the Holy Spirit speaking to me.

During the worship, I closed my eyes and the Lord reminded me of the DVD we had just watched. I asked Him what He was saying to me, and a vision of a property began to unfold in my mind. I saw a beautiful building where lonely people lived under one roof. Each had their own flat or apartment. There was a large communal lounge where they could sit and chat. And there were other rooms: space to watch TV together, a prayer room, hairdressing room, laundry room, a large kitchen, and a little chapel with a Spirit-filled pastor for people who couldn't get out to church. It was a lively chapel, too, where the Holy Spirit was free.

As well as all this, events were laid on. There was always something for them to participate in if they wanted to – Bible study and other activities, such as arts and crafts, bingo, days out, events etc.

It didn't matter if residents had a lot of money or were on benefits as everyone helped each other. No one was treated better than anyone else. They could also bring their own furniture.

As I gazed into the vision, I knew it wasn't coming from me: it was Father God speaking to me – and clearly!

Father God made it very clear to me who this building was to be for. And it wasn't just individuals who were alone. Elderly couples who were lonely were to be included too. This was for people who wanted security and fellowship with others.

The Lord reminded me that the Church is one body and we should all be functioning together and supporting one another, with Christ as the head.

He showed me that churches would support this project and that, by working together, they would be building God's Kingdom here on the earth. He gave me the words: "Building my Kingdom on the earth." He also made me aware that time is precious and short-lived on this earth and I was coming up to my fiftieth birthday.

As this was a huge project, I was aware I needed to start to look into it straight away. And I knew I needed to act in God's strength not my own. I felt I shouldn't leave it too long but I still continued to ask Him to lead me as I didn't want to jump ahead of Him.

I asked the Lord where the resources would come from – how the project would be financed as it may cost millions. God told me not to worry as everything would come. He would provide through churches as they supported it and through other places too.

This would be the first of such projects opening up across the UK and possibly other nations as well, but the Lord showed me that only people with the same heart and vision should be involved.

I also saw it as an opportunity for the younger generation of Christians who were looking for employment – a place to offer them jobs, to build them up.

This vision was so clear that I somehow felt I couldn't speak about it to my husband.

But the Lord continued to unfold more of it to me, and it was two days later when I felt I could finally tell Dave. I discovered I had to guard the vision and not just tell everyone about it. God would unfold things to me as time went on.

Dave told me it was a huge project and vision and asked me to ask God to confirm it. He was as stunned as I was about all this. Neither of us had the finances to put into it as we were struggling ourselves, so I knew God had to reveal more of Himself in it if He wanted me to carry it through. I continually asked Him to confirm it.

By the end of November, the Lord had given me my first confirmation as I read the book of Ecclesiastes. He told me to read it three times. I didn't know why three times but if I hadn't done so, I would have missed it:

*"Though one may be overpowered, two can defend themselves. A cord of three strands is not quickly broken."*
*Ecclesiastes 4:12*

I went on to read the footnotes in my study bible which really confirmed things to me:

*"...life is designed for companionship not isolation, for intimacy not loneliness... We are not here on earth to serve ourselves however but to serve God and others. Don't isolate yourself and try to go it alone. Seek companions, be a team member." NLT*

Little did I know God would begin to fulfil this vision in 2018.

Christmas Eve was on us. We were wrapping gifts and making final arrangements for the Christmas Day meal for the people in the sheltered housing.

Dave hadn't been feeling too well. He had very bad back pain and swelling behind his knee. He got an emergency doctor's appointment and was sent directly to hospital with a suspected blood clot travelling up to his lungs.

The enemy really was having a go. As we arrived at hospital, the place was full and we were told we'd be there for hours. We prayed as we knew we had turkey to cook and other food to prepare for Christmas Day, and time was getting on.

Praise God, Dave was seen immediately and sent home with clear results. We were there three hours in total.

Fortunately, I had a real peace about everything. I knew the enemy was just trying to distract us and break that peace.

Back at home, we were able to finalise things for Christmas Day and get the centre ready for those who would otherwise be on their own.

The following day, Christmas morning, the sun shone brightly. We didn't make it to church due to the preparations. Gemma and I had cooked the food in our own homes as the centre's kitchen was too tiny and didn't have a cooker that worked, and all the helpers carried it over.

There were only fourteen of us altogether but it was a beautiful day as we witnessed to the guests. Those who had lost their faith in hard times told us how the meal and everything that went with it had now changed their views. Jesus, the reason behind all of this, gave us our strength as we served people and waited on them.

At the end of the day, we were exhausted. The rest of the week was then just as busy with family visiting, and both Dave and I began to feel run down.

Shortly afterwards, my friend contacted me and asked if I'd been to the church not far from where I lived. I thought she meant the little chapel near our house. I told her this was too quiet for me, but she said she didn't mean the chapel and there was a very lively church near us attached to a school.

It turned out it was only a couple of minutes' drive from where we lived, so we decided to visit.

As soon as we walked in, we just knew we belonged there. I knew this was what God had intended as I listened to the sermon about what seemed to be my life – the recent vision God had given me, our community and involvement.

Both Dave and I felt at home there and it was on our doorstep. It made sense to join this church family as we knew God was drawing us to our community and here, we'd be more involved in it.

We went there for the following four weeks and spoke to Stewart about it. He was pleased for us and gave us his blessings. He felt it was right for us to be in a church in our local community.

God had given me a clear vision about moving churches and I still pondered over it. I asked Him if there was something else I had to do and to guide me to the right kind of job, as I certainly wasn't in the right place to move forward where I was. After two years of repetitive work, scanning and packing books, I was feeling restless. I knew I had more to offer and I felt I was becoming stagnant. I worked part-time, three days a week, and I was very grateful for my job as it was my first step back into the workplace after being out of work for nine months. But I was on a basic income and financially things were becoming more and more difficult to manage. Dave's job took him away from home on occasions but, due to the nature of his work and the increased pressure of everything, he became ill with depression again and had to stop working.

It was now January and a job was advertised in our local newspaper for Home Instead Senior Care. They were looking for a community development officer. I wasn't sure what was entailed but Dave told me to give them a call.

Whilst asking for God's guidance for the vision, I read this in UCB *Word For Today*:

*"We walk by faith and not by sight" (2 Corinthians 5:7 NAS). Walking requires that you get up and start moving. You can't just sit around aimlessly, waiting for the rapture. Walking involves: Motivation – you're moved by a purpose. Direction – you've chosen a destination, a goal to reach. Motion – you're committed to mobilising your energy and resources in the pursuit of your God-given destination and purpose. To walk by faith you must be engaged in consistent, forward movement intended to bring you into God's destiny for your life."*

I asked God for me to get an interview with Home Instead if I was heading in the right direction, so I don't know why I was shocked when I got one. I was very calm as the day approached, although it was my first job interview in many years. When the time came, it felt quite surreal. I had an overwhelming peace and calm about me that I knew was the Holy Spirit.

The interview was held over two days. I was there for nearly two hours while Dave waited outside in the car park for me.

When I came out, I told him I didn't feel it was the right job for me, but he said, "Pam, they won't let you go. They know you'll be valuable to them. I bet you'll hear back from them soon with a job for you. I just know it."

As we travelled home, I asked the Lord, "Why go this far and it not be right for me?"

When my mobile phone rang shortly afterwards, it was the lady who'd interviewed me.

"Pam," she said, "I know you applied for the post advertised but we feel you will be perfectly suited to another position in the care management team. Can you come in next week to meet the manager? If you're happy after that, then the job's yours."

After meeting the manager, I felt this was just where I was meant to be, and I thanked God for His guidance in my new role.

There was a lot to learn and understand because it was a very busy office. Any kind of care work is extremely demanding. It never ends, and I know how hard people work behind the scenes to try to make sure everything runs smoothly.

This was a new beginning for me, and I started my role with the care management team just before my birthday.

The staff were lovely and I got on well with all of them. As the months passed, God continued to confirm things to me about the vision too.

Here are just a few of the confirmations from some of the UCB *Word For Today* readings I found and conferences I have attended:

- *"Business person, God doesn't want you settling for temporal success; His purpose in blessing you is so you can help to extend His Kingdom. There's no shortage of resources; God just needs people He can entrust them to."*

- *"You are going to succeed because God has already determined your destiny. Before God establishes the procedure, He decides the purpose."*

- *"God is building a solid foundation under you so that you'll be able to handle the pressures that accompany His blessing, and go through the storms of life without being moved or shaken. Anything that's made well is made slowly. Anything that's worth having is worth fighting for."*

- *"When you have received Jesus you are transferred to another kingdom where you operate as an ambassador on God's behalf. God's representative with His authority to bring heaven to earth."*

- *"For the kingdom of God is not a matter of talk but of power. You are qualified, empowered and now it's time to be activated."*
- *"What did you do with the gifts I gave you? Did you fulfil your assignment on earth?' In that moment, nothing will be more important than how you answer that question."*

# 39

# FASTING AND BATTLING THROUGH BANKRUPTCY AND OPPRESSION

There have always been many ups and downs in my life and, after going through a very tough and dark time financially, I'd asked God for a breakthrough in all areas of our family life. Although His peace remained in me throughout everything, the battle had been hard for too long and I was becoming tired.

I found hope as I fasted and prayed once a week. "Now is the time for our sorrow to end," I cried. "Turn our mourning into joy. Bring life and breathe on us once again, Lord."

Enough was enough. I'd seen mountains moved. I refused to let the enemy deceive my family anymore with the lies he was feeding us.

Having gone through all the trauma with Joe and watching him sink so low, we at last began to see hope. Joe was starting to build himself back up again with help from medication and support from Christian friends.

And in the midst of pain came joy when our beautiful first grandchild was born. Hope! She was gorgeous and her dad, Mick was over the moon with her. It was lovely to see my baby, now all grown up, become the proud, loving father of a little daughter.

My emotions were up and down as I battled with everything that was happening, and poor Dave didn't know which way to turn himself, but the joy of our new granddaughter gave us hope.

After praying for some time about our financial situation, I spoke with Dave about C.A.P. (Christians Against Poverty). I told him God had put on my heart to speak with Gaz from the organisation. We'd tried to get out of debt ourselves but with no joy. We didn't go out; we didn't drink or smoke. We couldn't understand where we were going wrong.

Gaz came out to see us and he was very supportive. C.A.P. set up a new financial plan for us that worked really well, even though we were on a very tight budget. We just about managed and within two years we were debt free. This was a big weight off us as we continued to battle through everything else.

It was around this time that I'd entered some of my artwork into a painting competition in an artists' magazine. Arriving home from a stressful day at work, I played a message on the answerphone. I'd won an award as Artist of the Year in the beginners' category – the June Bretherton Award, which included an engraved crystal goblet and one hundred pounds to spend on artist materials in the magazine.

I enjoyed painting as this was a gift that my Father God had given me, but I didn't know what to do with all my paintings. Hearing this news built up my confidence again. And it couldn't have come at a better time, so I continued to enter my work into competitions and local art exhibitions. As I won more awards and sold my work, I was encouraged further.

But there was bad news around the corner. My brother Sam's wife had been diagnosed with secondary breast cancer. She'd gone five years and had had the all clear, but she'd begun having pain in her hips and legs and it was then they discovered the cancer had returned, this time in her bones.

This was a massive blow to us all. Sam was devastated. I prayed and fasted for his wife, asking for healing, and I waited for a miracle.

She was so strong. She asked the doctor, "Is it worth me buying Christmas presents?" He just shrugged as he didn't know. She had nurses visiting her regularly but things took a heavy toll on Sam as he tried to handle everything. He only really had me to talk to. Mick visited them often too, even though he was going through tough times with his partner.

As I fasted and prayed, this is what the Lord gave me:

> *"For my people will live as long as trees, and my chosen ones will have time to enjoy their hard-won gains. They will not work in vain, and their children will not be doomed to misfortune. For they are people blessed by the* LORD*, and their children, too, will be blessed. I will answer them before they even call to me. While they are still talking about their needs, I will go ahead and answer their prayers!"*
> *Isaiah 65:22–24, NLT*

I claimed this promise for my family and I believed it. Dave struggled in his Christian walk as he couldn't understand why bad things were happening to us and around us on such a regular basis.

But it was in my darkest times that I found God's comforting love surrounding me.

There are treasures in dark times.

*"When you pass through the waters, I will be with you; and when you pass through the rivers, they will not sweep over you. When you walk through fire, you will not be burned; the flames will not set you ablaze."*

*Isaiah 43:2*

# 40

# LOCAL OUTREACH

In 2010, Dave and I were invited to the local residents' meeting at the small, sheltered community centre where we lived. This centre was supposed to be used for the sheltered scheme tenants and their relatives. Some of the older people who lived in the non-sheltered houses within the community also used it occasionally.

At Christmas, the sheltered scheme would have their annual Christmas party mid-December, and local people who had lived on the close for a long time were also able to attend.

We were asked to join the local committee and we both became members, with Dave voted in as chairman. The centre had never really been used much. We'd heard that many people in the past had tried to make a go of it but no one seemed interested.

There were ten of us on the committee, five who lived in the houses and five who lived in the sheltered scheme.

During Easter, we invited all the local residents to an open day and, through local support, were able to provide hot cross buns, chocolate eggs and daffodils. We were disappointed as few people came, but we carried on regardless and knocked on doors to give out the flowers and chocolate eggs. Most people didn't answer, so we left the gifts tied to their door handles. Those who did answer were very cautious.

As things were starting up, the Lord gave me a picture of a still, calm lake. The water was like glass and surrounded by beautiful mountains. There was a rocky, narrow path up the side of the mountain. Then the Lord said to me, "I'm preparing you for the next big mountain-top experience and you won't want to come down."

I then saw a pair of lace-up shoes, like walking shoes. God told me to put on my shoes and I heard myself say, "Shoes ready to announce the good news of peace." And I remembered the whole armour of God.

"I will lead you to the dry parched land there you will bear much fruit."

I didn't really understand this as whenever I spoke to people, they seemed to have hardened their hearts and weren't at all interested in the message of Jesus.

In the picture, Jesus reached down to me and took my left arm. "Do not worry or be afraid as I will be with you," He said. "You will have many mountain-top experiences and not want to come down."

It was as though I'd be living in these experiences regularly, but I wanted Dave in them with me!

The Lord knew what I was thinking and I heard Him say, "He will be, but later. He'll have his own. For now, don't worry."

God then told me, "My child, I love you."

As I said, "I love You too, my Father," the tears rolled down my cheeks and I felt a warmth in my body.

Jesus told me He would be holding my hand through the mountain experiences – "Because I have chosen you."

It was very moving and powerful, as I did have the mountain-top experiences as well as the mountains in my life.

A lady from church encouraged me to contact a canon from the Blackburn diocese re my vision and, after a lot of prayer and research, I eventually found him.

He told me God would bring the lonely to me and that I was already on the right track through my involvement with the community and the local residents.

We organised many events at the centre: hot pot nights, fish 'n' chip nights, fireworks and food, outreach days, fundraising events, table-top sales, Macmillan fundraising day, craft fair, support and advice for the community when we invited C.A.P., health care and mobility aid providers, chiropodist etc.

We also held weekly art and craft days and regular coffee mornings, but they weren't a great success. No one was very interested, and only those who supported the centre really came along.

The other members of the committee were retired, while Dave and I had jobs. I was working part-time three days a week and sometimes didn't get home until late in the evening. Eventually, I began to struggle again with tiredness. All our spare time was spent planning events and, over time, cracks in the committee started appearing. Two members fell out and one resigned and threatened to dig up dirt on everyone who was involved. He even began to threaten the other members and some were very worried and afraid.

It soon became apparent that this man had complained to local residents and to the council about those of us who lived in the houses, saying we shouldn't be allowed in the centre. Dave and I were shocked as this was one of the men who'd invited us on to the committee in the first place.

It was very sad as we had planned an outreach day that would benefit the local community, especially those in the sheltered scheme.

The local chemist, chiropodist, C.A.P. advisor, mobility shop displaying their mobility aids and a home care provider had all agreed to give up their time to put on this free event and offer support and advice.

However, in organising it, I had nothing but complaints, plus phone calls whilst I was at work from the local council, who believed we were selling motorised scooters and other large items, and deceiving vulnerable adults. They told me they'd put a stop to this event happening and they didn't want any of the public attending.

I did try to reassure the woman from the council about what the day was for, but she'd already spoken to the committee member who had resigned. He'd told her we were out to deceive.

It was very hard constantly coming up against negative responses and opposition. Even though we had the support of the mayor, the council still weren't happy.

In the end, the outreach day did go ahead but on conditions from the local council: we weren't allowed to sell any of the products and we had to put a sign up saying the event was nothing to do with the council. They even sent in a spy to try to catch us out and see if we did sell anything. Another member of the council came too to check we weren't doing anything wrong, but she was more than happy and could see it had all been well planned. And the mayor himself visited us and supported what we were doing.

As the months passed, it became clear we were not welcome to use the centre, even though we'd put so much time and energy into it, as well as finances through the support of our family, church and friends.

We held our last fundraising event there not long before Christmas – a craft fair. God had always blessed what we'd done financially for the benefit of the local sheltered residents, and the committee had agreed to give a small percentage of the money raised to the local children's hospice. Dave and I were stunned to hear nasty comments and complaints from the local residents about this.

These escalated until I was informed by the council that donating money to the children's hospice wasn't allowed. Any money raised could only be used for the benefit of the sheltered housing residents. It seemed unbelievable that we were constantly in such a huge battle and it was draining me.

Christmas was approaching and, once again, we organised a meal for people who would be on their own on Christmas day, to be held in the centre. The meal would be free of charge but, again, this turned out to be a stressful time. Constant obstacles were thrown in our way by the local council and residents.

Dave and I were in Birmingham visiting friends when we got a phone call. It was from a committee member who told us that both Gemma and Al had pulled out of helping us with the meal. They were upset because of all the backbiting that was going on and the complaints about it being held in the centre. Gemma also seemed to be upset as she felt I'd left her out of things. She'd done a lot but felt she could have done more.

"What is happening?" I asked God. "Why all the unrest and nastiness?"

I felt as though the Lord was speaking to me. From out of nowhere, Sodom and Gomorrah came to my mind.

It was then that I looked back to the Christmas party held only the week before.

The Lord showed me that He loved the people but that their hearts were far from Him. They were hardened and wouldn't be changed; they were bitter and angry but didn't want to be anything different. The people were happy to help themselves but not others. They had no shame or morals and didn't care who they hurt. They wanted to keep "outsiders" out.

"Do I want to help people who are only interested in helping themselves?" I asked myself. Not only that, what about the poorly children in the hospice?

The questions came into my mind so many times that I realised I didn't want to give my heart to people who thought only about themselves; who didn't care about those sick, dying children; who complained to the council that we shouldn't be donating any funding to them. I struggled with these emotions and I felt guilty because I didn't want to judge these people. And I knew Jesus loved them. But I could see they didn't want any help or anyone else in their lives.

Then the Lord spoke to me again: "Do not depend on man but on me alone. Trust me."

I knew in my heart that the Christmas day meal should continue but I was under so much pressure constantly from the council and local residents to stop what we were doing. And I didn't feel I could go anywhere unless the Lord wanted me to.

Dave and I resigned from the committee. Most of them had said nasty, hurtful words. Only two of the committee members stood strong. They resigned because Dave and I had, and they were also attacked verbally.

A few days previously, Dave and I had approached our pastor about holding the meal at our church. God's hand was certainly on it as we were able to change the venue. However, Dave and I were concerned that we were down on funds to buy gifts for the guests.

It was when I cried out to God, "What are we going to do, Lord, about the funds?" that He reminded me, "Trust me, I am your provider."

I began to understand when God showed me it was like Sodom and Gomorrah. It all made sense. And things began to go smoothly once we knew we weren't holding the meal at the centre. I felt such a release, as if a huge weight had dropped off me.

Beautiful Father God – He supplied our every need and every penny that was required to cover costs. I received phone calls from members of the public, a local brass band and people in our church who all donated their time, gifts and financial support, and we had a fantastic day. Our family helped us out on the day too, and we were up until 3.15 on Christmas morning, preparing vegetables, making amendments and wrapping personalised gifts for eighteen people.

Many of the guests said it was the best Christmas day they'd ever had, while others said they would have been on their own with a bowl of soup if they hadn't come.

God is so amazing. Even when we can sometimes feel He isn't there, He is. He knows and has our best interests at heart as long as we are obedient.

I'd faced up to things about the committee and the outreach work we were doing at the centre. If people didn't want us around, that was one thing. But it would be God's decision as to whether or not we left. I wasn't going to be pushed out by man.

However, God had shown me that people's hearts were hard and they didn't want to change. He also showed me it was time for me to step back. He knew my heart was broken regarding my friendship with Gemma because I cared deeply for her. But he revealed how much stress I was under and this was not His plan.

It took me a long time to bounce back after everything that had happened over the past six or seven months. But although I'd been badly hurt, I had to choose to forgive.

I'm sure many people have been hurt by Christian friends but I know Jesus doesn't want division in His church. He wants unity. The only way you can heal and recover from pain is by facing it. Anything else is up to God Himself as He is judge. Forgiving is the one and only way to help yourself, as well as releasing the other person.

I visited Gemma and Al a couple of times after the Christmas period and felt no anger towards them. I loved them. They were God's children too, but that didn't mean I had to be a doormat and get walked over again. Still, I'd be there for them if they ever needed me.

Dave reminded me of these verses in the Bible:

*"If any household or town refuses to welcome you or listen to your message, shake its dust from your feet as you leave. I tell you the truth, the wicked cities of Sodom and Gomorrah will be better off than such a town on the judgment day."*
*Matthew 10:14–15, NLT*

*"Don't waste what is holy on people who are unholy. Don't throw your pearls to pigs! They will trample the pearls, then turn and attack you."*
*Matthew 7:6, NLT*

These were very harsh words and I certainly saw the meaning in it all. We later heard that one committee member had told people we were "bringing religion into things". At Christmas time, cards and posters were taken down from the centre, anything that pertained to Jesus or the Christian faith. They didn't want Christ in Christmas – they wanted Him out!

But how can you have Christmas without Jesus? He's not just for the season, He's the reason.

We later heard that the rest of the committee had folded. It was sad really as there was so much opportunity there. But people's hearts were hard and God had other plans!

As the Christmas meal was such a blessing to so many people, we knew that couldn't just be it for another twelve months. So we prayed about it and asked the people if they'd like to meet up every two months. Everyone agreed.

We were aware that some of them had no transport and needed to be picked up, so this was what Dave and I did. We'd then all get together somewhere for a meal and spend a few hours in each other's company.

The group began to grow too as different people brought friends along who were also on their own.

Dave and I didn't want to keep calling the friends we'd made "people from the Christmas day meal" so we prayed again, this time for a name for the group.

We called it "Cherish" – as we cherished each other's company.

# 41

# THE RETREAT

My fiftieth birthday was approaching and I wanted Jesus to be in this celebration. After praying, I felt very strongly that Jesus wanted me to spend time in His presence in a place where I could focus on Him.

For a long time, I'd had a longing in my heart and spirit to go on a retreat. But we couldn't afford it so I felt this was the Holy Spirit's prompting, even if it meant I didn't have anything else for my birthday. Financially, we were just about managing and I asked God to confirm this to me.

That Sunday at church, I found myself sitting next to a lady called Jill. Out of the blue, she spoke to me about a wonderful retreat she'd just been on in the Lake District at Elterwater Country Park Guest House near Ambleside.

"Thank You, God, for that confirmation," I said, absolutely stunned, as Jill didn't know me well and she certainly didn't know this was part of God's plan for my birthday.

When we got home from church, I told Dave what had happened and that I believed it was meant for me to go there.

Dave had already been planning surprises for me with the family and church friends and I had a lovely birthday. He'd booked the two of us into the Premier Inn in another town for the evening and then we went "birthday shopping" the following day. On the way home, we dropped into my lovely sister-in-law who, with Dave, had planned a small surprise party for me at her house with all my family there. It was beautiful!

And my birthday still wasn't over. A week later, I was off on my retreat. Dave had booked for me to go and he came with me. While I spent my time with God, he went out to take photographs of the beauty that surrounded us.

The day we arrived, I was asked to go out and enjoy the scenery to relax and prepare for the following day.

Then, the next morning, I wandered off into the little garden to look at the views from higher up. My intention was to walk back down to the lake, but instead, I sat on the small wooden swing bench at the very bottom of the garden away from the house.

It was a frosty morning and the fields were white but the sun was shining and the birds were singing. I sat down and spoke to God and asked Him to come to me. I felt Him say, "I will come."

I waited and waited with His beauty all around me, looking at the snow-capped mountains. It was a stunning sight. I drifted off a few times but each time I woke, I had even more of an awareness of His presence; His love and beautiful creation around me.

There was a bare bush in front of me and I heard the Lord say, "What do you see?"

Every time I looked at it, it seemed to be full of tiny new buds. Then my Father reminded me of Moses and the burning bush.

I didn't want to move and my Lord had told me, "Be still, physically and emotionally." So I stayed put.

Without being aware of time passing, I found I'd been on the bench for three hours. I was sitting on my hands as my bum was cold and numb, when suddenly a very soft whisper came to me: "My child, you are precious to me and I love you."

Tears streamed down my face as my Father said this to me and I couldn't stop smiling. I was so filled with an awe and love for my Lord, for my Jesus. His Spirit had touched my soul and spirit once again.

"I love You too, my Lord," I smiled.

It was now twelve noon and I was supposed to meet up with Lesley, the lady who was running the retreat, so off I went to see her.

All through my time there, I had the feeling I should take off my shoes in the house as I was standing on Holy ground. So I did this. I told Lesley how God had told me I was precious, but every time I said the word "precious", the tears seemed to take over.

Precious was in every part of my conversation and Lesley told me to read Isaiah 43:1–7. She told me to ask God when I prayed: "Lord, how are you looking at me?"

The Lord had given me these verses a few times before now, so I knew they were meant for me.

"Do not be afraid... I have called you by name; you are mine. When you go through deep waters, I will be with you. When you go through rivers of difficulty, you will not drown. When you walk through the fire of oppression, you will not be burned up; the flames will not consume you. For I am the LORD, your God, the Holy One of Israel, your Saviour... because you are precious to me. You are honoured, and I love you. Don't be afraid, for I am with you. I will gather you and your children from east and west... Bring all who claim me as their God, for I have made them for my glory. It was I who created them."
Isaiah 43:1–7, NLT

I felt the Lord was renewing something as well as doing a new thing in me. Every time I spoke to Lesley of my encounter with Jesus, I could see in my mind something that looked like a long chute from the top of my head to the centre of my being. There seemed to be things being poured into it and coming out of it all at the same time.

During this time as I spoke to my Father, my thoughts tumbled out:

"I am who He says I am. His! His child, precious, adored, cherished, loved, receptive, hearing, wanted." Then, "How are you looking at me, God?" I asked.

Again, I could feel the depth of His love; the warmth of His beautiful embrace. It was as if He was smiling at me as I felt Him say, "Precious child, I love you. You are mine and I love you with an everlasting love. Do not despair for you are mine. I have chosen you. I have called you by name. I have appointed you."

> *"You didn't choose me. I chose you. I appointed you to go and produce lasting fruit, so that the Father will give you whatever you ask for, using my name."*
> *John 15:16, NLT*

The tears were now pouring down my face. I was overjoyed and the amazing sense of the Holy Spirit was so powerful that I felt incredibly humble.

Lesley asked me to spend some time trying to draw or paint what "precious" looked like to me. All I could see was a huge rock of multi-coloured gem stones, with facets reflecting multi-coloured lights in every direction. They were colours that I could never have imagined as they shone so brightly, and they were priceless.

I felt very tired after this, although I hadn't been anywhere, just resting in my beautiful Saviour's arms of love in His garden.

I tried to draw what God had given me, but every time I even attempted to write the word "precious" I felt completely overwhelmed, humble and thankful. I sensed that Father God wanted me to stop and sleep, so off to the bedroom I went and, as I was lying down, I had a picture of myself lying on my left-hand side on Jesus' knee. He was stroking my hair. This was exactly the way I'd fallen asleep and I woke up in the same position. I'd slept for two and a half hours but I couldn't believe how tired I still felt.

There was something that had stuck in my mind before I arrived at the retreat and also while I was there: *God had invited me to come and meet with Him.* He had invited me on this retreat and I knew it. I didn't just "decide" to go along. This was a very special appointment with my Father. It had come about through His Holy Spirit's prompting and I would never, ever have wanted to miss it.

As I pondered and asked God to give me the meaning of "precious", these are the words that came flooding into my mind: fragranced, chosen, diamond, loved, sweet, lovely, beautiful, priceless, cherished, adored, whole, full, protected, calm, forgiven, defended, treasured, fresh, vital, beloved, no secrets hidden.

They made me think of heaven. There will be a day when we will no longer be here on this earth as it is now. I can only say the fears and troubles we go through today will end when we meet our beautiful Saviour.

My time at the retreat took me into another level of trust.

# 42

# PRAISING GOD IN MOUNTAIN-TOP EXPERIENCES AND IN THE DARKNESS

Two weeks after my fiftieth birthday, there was an Aglow outreach meeting that was held in the local pub.

I'd been to these meetings a few times and the testimonies I'd heard were powerful. I always found God seemed to be speaking to me through them, so I'd come home feeling blessed, encouraged and with my spirit lifted.

Twice a year, the meetings were extended out to our husbands and this particular meeting happened to be on our wedding anniversary. I told Dave that I really wanted to go and make it part of our anniversary celebration. I was still full of joy from the Holy Spirit through my retreat and was eager for more of Jesus. I wanted as much as I could get so that I could give it back out.

As it turned out, Dave had other ideas. He wanted us to be on our own and go out for a meal together, but eventually he agreed to come.

We arrived at the event and met up with some of our friends. Dave seemed to feel a bit uncomfortable as he didn't know many people, but he soon began to settle in – until, that is, the speaker got up to speak. He spoke of the power of Jesus in us but I could see Dave's walls closing in on him.

As the evening came to an end, I asked Dave if he'd come up for prayer with me.

"What for?" he asked. "You don't need prayer."

"I want us to both to go up for prayer!" I exclaimed, but his walls were right up by this time.

I couldn't understand why he was being like this and I began to hesitate myself about going for prayer. But I certainly didn't want to miss out on anything that God had for me. I didn't even really know what to ask for, apart from that I wanted to be used by Him to bring people to Jesus. I wanted more of Him. I wanted to speak life into hardened hearts and heal the sick and broken-hearted. But above all this, I loved Jesus so I went up on my own.

The speaker prayed with many people standing on either side of me. Then a little voice whispered inside my head, "Why are you still standing here? The speaker's gone past you and prayed with everyone else. Go and sit back down, you don't need prayer. Don't you feel stupid with everyone looking at you?"

I chose to ignore the voice and stayed put. I wasn't going anywhere until I'd had prayer.

It seemed a long time before Alex, the speaker, finally came and talked to me. He asked what my heart's desire was and prayed with me. Then he anointed me with oil.

Soon after this, the Holy Spirit manifested on me again. I was full of joy and couldn't stand. I could only speak in tongues, God's power and love washing over me as well as others.

Dave couldn't wait to get me out of there, bless him. He'd never been like this before and I knew something wasn't right.

When we got home, I was still in the Spirit and Dave was very quiet, very defensive. He began to look for anything online to disprove the speaker, but there was nothing. I prayed God would give him a shake and wake him up spiritually.

That evening, I had the most beautiful sleep I'd had in a long time. Dave, who seemed far away from God just then, didn't sleep for three nights without having nightmares. This really shook him up.

Suddenly, it was as though a light had been switched on inside him, as he began to read his Bible again and grew closer to God than he'd been in a long time. He was really hungry for God's Word. The Lord spoke to him in many ways as he continued to read His Word. It came alive to him – so alive that he began to text me, our friends and our pastor throughout the day about how God was speaking to him.

I soon discovered how God was answering my prayers. Mick, my son, had been asking questions about Jesus on and off throughout his life, but suddenly, there was a torrent of questions flooding from his mouth, one after the other.

Mick had broken up with his girlfriend and had been watching Christian events on his computer. And they spoke directly to his spirit. He knew Jesus was speaking to him and soon went up for prayer in church to ask Jesus back into his life.

Over the weeks and months, I could see and feel the Holy Spirit upon Mick. There were times when he'd be shaking and I could feel the heat from him during the church service. He was in a new walk with his Saviour and I knew he was growing when he joined a home Bible study group. This was breakthrough!

Things were still tough with Joe, however. His relationship with his partner was up and down. Even so, we became grandparents again, this time to a beautiful grandson. Joe was so proud of his boy and he settled down for a short period of time. But sadly, his relationship with his partner continued to deteriorate and the effects of it all began to take a toll on me. Even as our children grow into adults, it's hard to let go. We still just want the best for them.

Due to the stresses that were once again piling up, Dave and I booked a weekend away in the Lake District. The weather was lovely so we went on some stunning walks that reminded me of my retreat.

Just before I nodded off to sleep on one of our nights away, I heard a soft whisper telling me: "Go up the mountain again and I will speak to you there."

I told Dave this as he was still awake and I asked the Lord to confirm if this was Him speaking to me the following morning, as I might not remember it.

The next day I got up and I instantly remembered what God had said to me the previous evening. I asked Dave if he remembered it too. He said yes and went on to repeat what I'd told him.

I was so excited and I prayed for good weather to climb the small mountain, which could be very slippery if it rained.

As we climbed, we could see God's country spread out before us: lakes, mountains and more mountains. It was stunning.

At the top, it was very windy and we couldn't hear ourselves speak. I managed to keep my notepad open and write down a few things that I felt the Lord was saying to me. Dave went for a wander as he knew I wanted to be alone with my thoughts and listen to my Father. And it wasn't long after that when I heard my Father speak: "Look at the beauty that surrounds you everywhere. How much more can I give you? My hand will guide you."

I was then reminded of the words of a song be Gene MacLellan:

*"Put your hand in the hand of the one who stills the waters.*

*Put your hand in the hand of the one who calms the sea.*

*Take a look at yourself and you will look at others differently*

*By putting your hand in the hand of the one who calms the sea."*

The Lord continued to speak to me: "I am your Father. I will lead you, I will guide you. Trust me in all that you do. Lean on me. I will protect and defend you. Listen! Don't run away when you come into opposition. I will be there to help you through it. I hear your heart's cry and I will deliver you."

I knew that my Father God was telling me something more, but time was getting on and the weather was changing. I was writing as fast as I could so I'd remember everything.

At that point, I couldn't understand what all this meant. It was only in the following days and months that things began to unfold.

The Lord my God reminded me about the "burning bush" I'd seen on my retreat, and taking off my shoes as I was standing on holy ground. I was then led to read Exodus 3:2, about Moses leading the people out of Egypt. But it was verse 12 that jumped out of the page at me:

> *"God answered, 'I will be with you. And this is your sign that I am the one who has sent you: When you have brought the people out of Egypt, you will worship God at this very mountain."*
> *Exodus 3:12, NLT*

I carried on reading into chapter four:

> *"But Moses protested again, 'What if they won't believe me or listen to me? What if they say, "The LORD never appeared to you?"'... But Moses pleaded with the LORD, 'O Lord, I'm not very good with words. I never have been, and I'm not now, even though you have spoken to me. I get tongue-tied, and my words get tangled.' Then the LORD asked Moses, 'Who makes a person's mouth? Who*

*decides whether people speak or do not speak, hear or do not hear, see or do not see? Is it not I, the* LORD*? Now go! I will be with you as you speak, and I will instruct you in what to say... Talk to him, and put the words in his mouth. I will be with both of you as you speak, and I will instruct you both in what to do."*

*NLT*

I knew my Father was showing me something as I'd been given this passage before by Christian friends. But I was called to read further, and other passages too in Jeremiah chapter 1:

*"I knew you before I formed you in your mother's womb. Before you were born I set you apart and appointed you...' 'O Sovereign* LORD*,' I said, 'I can't speak for you! I'm too young!' The* LORD *replied, 'Don't say, "I'm too young," for you must go wherever I send you and say whatever I tell you. And don't be afraid of the people, for I will be with you and will protect you. I, the* LORD*, have spoken!' Then the* LORD *reached out and touched my mouth and said, 'Look, I have put my words in your mouth! Today I appoint you to stand up against nations and kingdoms. Some you must uproot and tear down, destroy and overthrow. Others you must build up and plant.' Then the* LORD *said to me, 'Look, Jeremiah! What do you see?' And I replied, 'I see a branch from an almond tree.' And the* LORD *said, 'That's right, and it means that I am*

*watching, and I will certainly carry out all my*
*plans.'... 'Get up and prepare for action. Go out and*
*tell them everything I tell you to say. Do not be*
*afraid of them, or I will make you look foolish in*
*front of them. For see, today I have made you*
*strong like a fortified city that cannot be captured,*
*like an iron pillar or a bronze wall. You will stand*
*against the whole land – the kings, officials,*
*priests, and people of Judah. They will fight you,*
*but they will fail. For I am with you, and I will take*
*care of you. I, the LORD, have spoken!"*
*NLT*

This was powerful, very powerful, and I knew God was speaking to me. It was what He'd told me up the mountain but I still didn't get it. I still wasn't sure what I was supposed to do.

God knew my heart. He knew how afraid I was to speak out in public meetings. I could speak to small groups of people but was very nervous in larger groups. I was exactly like Moses.

I knew that one day I would speak out, maybe giving my testimony. But which one as He had rescued me so many times? Little did I know what was in store for me.

Back in the workplace, I was very committed to my work and was asked if I wanted to go full-time. Financially this would be a big help, but I knew how my health was. I had a lot going on with family and I needed to get the right balance for myself.

My manager told me to have a think and get back to her. I prayed about it and, as I only originally worked three days a week, I committed to a fourth day as it was time for the annual audit.

Quite quickly, I began to feel the pressure of working the extra day. I was also on call one evening per week and I'd struggled immensely with this for eighteen months.

Being on call was a juggling act and a lot like a puzzle, and somehow I found it very difficult. I did wonder how other staff managed but I knew some of them struggled too.

"It's part of my job," I told myself every week when it was my turn. The phone would ring constantly, alerts going off, so I'd have to chase the girls up as some had forgotten to log in.

Dave told me he could see me shutting down when I was on call. I wouldn't speak to him or to anyone. I couldn't eat my tea without the phone going off. This had a big impact on me.

During my appraisal, I told them how it affected me.

My appraisal was supposed to be two hours long with my manager and one of the owners. They weren't Christians but were lovely people. They knew I was a Christian and that Jesus was my life, so it was only natural for me to talk about Him at times during the appraisal.

The person due in after me called in ill, so I ended up talking to them for four hours and Jesus was a major part of the conversation.

At the end of the time, they asked me to pray for them that God would give them a direct sign that they wanted. I don't know if they got the sign but I continued to pray for them for a long time.

Very soon after the audit, I realised that working three days a week was enough for me, so I had to decline the offer of working full-time.


I continued to go to the monthly Aglow meetings and I enjoyed helping out. After a while, I began to make the table decorations, which brought more of the creative side out of me.

One thing I noticed was that every time I was looking forward to the meeting, I would suddenly get a panic come over me. It was as if I shouldn't go, or something would happen to prevent me from going. I learned pretty quickly that the enemy didn't want me to attend as there was always a word from God for me at these meetings.

I met some beautiful people there too, warm, welcoming and Holy-Spirit-filled women on fire for God. They were gentle but full of God's holy power, ready to use the gifts He had given each of them.

I felt I had a connection with these ladies. They didn't push themselves on me or force me to take part in anything, but God put on their hearts things I could be involved with.

Due to the artistic gift of painting God had given me, I felt He'd put on my heart to write a book where I could show my paintings and the story behind them. I'd never written a book in my life but I knew I had to be faithful and write it, so *Words Behind The Pictures* was created. It took me around sixteen months to complete.

My husband was wonderful as he put my book together. I had the ideas in my head and I knew where I wanted the pictures to go. I could see the front cover of the lion, "I'm coming", which represented Jesus' return, so I knew how I wanted the book to look. But it was Dave who managed to pull it all together for me by using an online publisher.

I was very pleased with my book when it was published too. It was exactly how I'd imagined it to be because I knew that my Father God was in it all.

It was towards the end of writing it that my Father also put on my heart to write a second book – this time about my life.

The one thing about self-publishing *Words Behind The Pictures* was that I had to sell it myself. I contacted shops, churches, cathedrals but found that it sold mainly through family, friends and their friends. Copies even sold as far away as America and Australia.

My book was meant to encourage the reader with the gifts God had given them. God wants us to use our talents and not to hide them; not to let them lie dormant. I prayed before I sent each book out that it would penetrate the heart of the reader; that God would speak to each reader personally.

There are lots of Christians with gifts that aren't being used in churches because people feel they can't use them, or they don't feel they're good enough. But the Lord wants you to know you can and you are! With Christ in the centre, you can do all things.

*"Therefore I tell you, whatever you ask for in prayer, believe that you have received it, and it will be yours."*
*Mark 11:24*

Most of my books began to sell at the Aglow meetings that I attended every month. At one of these meetings, a lady from Liverpool named Pauline, who was the guest speaker, had a very powerful message about how she used not to have the confidence to speak out publicly in large groups.

Here it was again, the same message of when God called Moses to go out and speak to Pharaoh. It was a message that kept coming back to me again and again wherever I went.

During Pauline's talk, one of the statements she made was this: "God's looking for faithful, obedient people who will do as He asks. If He's giving you a vision – do it. There will be people who'll think your mad, crazy and won't believe you. But when God says it, let it happen. Be faithful. Be obedient."

Despite the setbacks and hardships, years later I'd be sharing my testimony at Aglow meetings in different locations, and would also have the chance to pray for women who were going through similar circumstances to the ones I'd been through.

# 43

# SPIRITUAL ATTACK

In the Christian walk, there are many highs and many lows, and although I seem to have had more than my fair share of the lows, I have found comfort in Jesus time after time.

My sister-in-law Kaz had booked a holiday in Crovie in Scotland and she invited Dave and me to spend a week there. It was a beautiful place and we were really looking forward to it, although I knew the journey would be a long one. Dave said we could break it up and stay overnight somewhere, which is what we did. We stayed in a Premier Inn in Dundee and were so glad to have a rest from the travelling.

Driving up to Dundee was wonderful as we listened to worship songs, and the power of the Holy Spirit's presence was so tangible.

During this time, I felt as if I had to pray against a spirit of death. I didn't have anything more specific but just felt strongly that I needed to sever this spirit from my family and whoever came to my mind.

I prayed until the urge ceased, but then my niece kept coming into my head. So I severed this spirit of death from her too, although I didn't know why I felt I had to pray that way. I hadn't seen my niece in many, many months and she was popping into my head quite a bit. So I knew that I had to pray for her as the Holy Spirit guided.

"Ring her when you get back, love," Dave said when I told him.

We arrived at the Premier Inn, tired and hungry. We dropped our luggage into our room and went downstairs for something to eat before heading to bed.

During the night while I was asleep, a sense of unease must have come over me. I woke up around 1am, terrified.

Above the door, I saw something like a thick, black strip where the light would normally come in. I opened and closed my eyes a few times to make sure I wasn't imagining it but it didn't go away.

I turned over to try to get back to sleep but I couldn't. I was wide awake and I kept glancing from one side of the bed to the other. The room was dark but there seemed to be a thicker, blacker darkness there and I sensed it.

I looked down to the floor. Somehow, I found myself expecting to see dead bodies because I thought I was walking through hell. Then, suddenly, a huge black shape in the form of a human figure appeared at my bedside. It was so big, it appeared to rise beyond the ceiling, which seemed to have disappeared.

As the figure approached me, it became even larger as it lifted up its arms and, with what looked like an enormous baton, struck me on my right-hand side as I lay in bed. When it hit me, it began to shrink to less than half its original size. Then it disappeared.

I was frozen. Terrified. I thought I was in a horror film. I thought perhaps I was dead and no one was around to help or hear.

Suddenly, I heard Dave speak. When he did, I didn't know where I was or what was happening. I felt different; completely disorientated. I touched Dave's back but it felt slimy, like a jellyfish.

He shouted out in fear, "What's up? What is it? What is it, love?"

I didn't realise, but we were both in this horror film together. The two of us were terrified and started to scream but nobody came.

I fumbled for the light switch next to me and knocked my glass of water over and everything else that was on the shelf.

Both Dave and I knew evil spirits were there as I was frozen. I couldn't pray, speak or even think of the name "Jesus". But as the darkness of this figure hit me, I knew the light of Jesus in me dispelled it. Jesus was looking after us.

I hadn't known fear like that for as long as I could remember. Neither had Dave.

We prayed together, switched off the light as we knew Jesus was with us, and we slept well.

What had happened really knocked me up over the next few days, especially at bedtime as I felt it was still there, watching, waiting to attack me again. But I had to put my trust in Jesus.

We rang a couple of our Christian friends the following morning to ask them to pray for us, as we knew there'd be no phone signal where we were going.

Despite that terrifying night, we had a lovely holiday. The weather was beautiful, sunny every day. But, still, the uneasy feeling that something wasn't right wouldn't leave me. I didn't know if it was because of what had happened in the Premier Inn or whether something wasn't right at home. I just knew I was very shaken and I didn't feel the same in myself. I was drained and tired and the fear kept returning. I had to remind myself that God had not given me a spirit of fear or timidity but one of power, love and sound mind, and it was this verse (2 Timothy 1:7) that kept me strong.

The time away passed by quickly. It was very relaxing and I thought I'd have more energy when we got home, but I was still drained.

We'd just got into bed when Dave checked Facebook and found that my niece had tried to contact me. I rarely looked at Facebook and asked Dave to give her my phone number but to ask for her number too.

This must have been a God incident as she hadn't tried to contact me before. She told me it had been on her mind for a while to get in touch with me.

I rang Rose and she sounded really low. She told me she'd recently come out of the mental health unit after trying to take her own life and that she had a history of self-harming. She also said she wasn't doing too well mentally again.

Dave and I got dressed and went to pick her up.

Rosie and I sat up talking until the early hours of the morning while Dave left us to it. She told me nobody could help her and I told her Jesus could.

She stayed with us for a week as she loved the peace and could feel a lovely presence in our home. I prayed every night with her until she settled down to sleep.

In my mind, I saw black wings enfolded around her head, wrapping themselves tighter about her as I prayed, as if they were struggling to hold on to her.

We had many good, long talks about Jesus, the one who could rescue and heal her, and she even came to church and gave her life to Jesus. She shed many tears and I knew she'd been touched by Him through the sermon and prayers.

However, as soon as she returned to her friends, she was back to self-harming and overdosing again.

It was so sad to see her going through all of this and my heart was torn. She was my niece and I loved her. I didn't know who to talk to about it and she didn't want her parents knowing anything anymore as she told me they did know but couldn't do anything.

Rosie was affected deeply when her parents split up and her mum said herself that she wasn't really maternal and just lived life the way she wanted to. Lots had happened in the family and my niece struggled to come to terms with it. Even though she forgave her parents, she still had ongoing issues with her mental health.

She was rushed to hospital one teatime after we'd been out for a walk with the dogs. Her jaw had begun to lock and she was in a lot of pain. We arrived at the hospital and I stayed with her until Dave finished work and joined us.

After a few hours in the hospital, I then got a phone call to say that Joe wasn't doing too well either. He'd broken up with his partner again and was very low. My heart sank. I was tired and worn down. I couldn't take any more mentally. Mick and my brother Sam had gone to Joe's aid but they rang and asked me to visit him.

Dave was angry with Joe because of the situation I was in with my niece and we didn't really speak to each other. I just asked him to bring Rosie home with him when the doctor had been to see her. She was feeling better when I left to go to see Joe, who had by then settled down.

On leaving Joe's, I met up with Mick and Sam at the petrol station but, as I tried to speak, my voice had gone completely through the stress of everything. Big tears began to roll down my cheeks as I tried to prevent my brother and son from seeing me break down.

I headed home and, within minutes of arriving, Dave rang to say Rosie had been discharged and they were on their way back from hospital. She'd apparently been out with friends the previous evening and had taken an overdose of tablets, causing the lockjaw. She didn't want me to contact her parents as she insisted they couldn't help her. Her mum had once given her tablets to try to help but Rosie had abused her trust and taken them all at once.

However, although Rosie was an adult, I told her I would call her parents and she eventually agreed to it.

I rang both her mum and dad numerous times and left voice messages to contact me urgently. A few hours later, her mother turned up at my door. I hadn't had any contact with her in over eight years since the breakdown of her marriage to my brother Jason. She listened to what I had to say, then got in touch with him. Jason, Rosie's dad, was naturally upset. Sadly, he then fell out with me because I hadn't rung him when it happened. But my priority had been to get her to hospital.

I continued to pray through this darkness, asking constantly for breakthrough.

There is nothing greater than to have God's peace in your life. People seek money and material things but absolutely nothing can satisfy the desires of our hearts – only God. God gives complete peace and rest to your heart, soul, spirit and mind.

I'd been through and seen brokenness many times: my dear sister-in-law with cancer; my own son's tormented mind; my niece and many other things that had gone on.

My son was so tormented in his relationship and when he turned to drink, it was then that the demons would manifest, playing tricks with his mind. Mick and Sam were worried sick about him. We all were. My heart's cry to the Lord was for my family; for them to seek after Jesus' heart. I knew that once they did this, the rest would fall into place in their lives.

Amid all of this, I didn't know whether the Lord was calling me to change jobs. I felt like I wasn't going to stay at Home Instead for the rest of my life, even though I loved it there and my work colleagues too.

It wasn't long before I came out of work again, ill with stress. I knew I was unable to carry on the way I'd been doing, so I took a few days' leave.

"Exhaustion and stress," my doctor told me and signed me off for a few weeks. I needed this time just for me, to regain some strength.

Although I was still there for Rosie, she knew I wasn't well enough to do anything, so she spent some time back at her mum's home.

As the days and weeks passed, I prayed that the Lord would speak to me. I asked Him to speak to me in my dreams. One particular night, I dreamt that I was speaking to a man who had once before prophesied over me in Lytham St. Anne's church. He'd previously told me that I'd be a good leader; that I highlighted things in God's Word and must stay close to Him as He would guide me.

In my dream, this man told me God had put a twinkle in my eye. He said my eyes glistened for Him, that God loved me very much, and that I had such potential and God would use that. There would be plenty of things ahead for me and people would see through the glistening of my eyes that I loved my Father. He said my eyes sparkled for the Lord and His eyes were on me.

The man also told me that my husband loved and adored me. He cherished me. But my Father cherished me even more. I was the apple of His eye. My Father wanted to take me to even greater levels, greater heights than I'd ever been to, and He promised me all good things because I was His daughter who He loved endlessly.

There was so much more that the man was telling me that I couldn't take it all in.

When I woke the following morning and prayed, this is what I felt the Lord say to me:

"I am your God. Your shield and rampart. Whoever trusts in me will not be harmed. I will deliver them if they put their trust in me. I, who speaks from the heavenly realms, knows everything about you. Do not be afraid. Put your trust in me."

Then I felt Him say, "Pick up your bed or mat and go where I lead you."

I knew I had to trust my Father as He was the core of my whole being, so this was how I lived and continued to live.

Very soon after receiving this, I had to have our beautiful dog Bob put down. He had prostate cancer and it was time to take him back to the vet, who'd done everything they could for him over the past months. Bob was nearly thirteen years old and had given us years of fun and laughter. He had his own unique personality. He was so funny at Christmas time – he knew we always bought him a present. I remember coming home one day from work to find him walking round me, teasing me and wagging his tail, with this squeaky toy in his mouth. I didn't take too much notice at first until I found the Christmas wrapping paper on the floor. Bob had got behind the Christmas tree, sniffed his toy out and opened it, without disturbing any of the other presents!

His last Christmas with us literally went with a bang. Holly, Dave's daughter, was opening her Christmas presents, and Bob couldn't resist helping her pull the wrapping off with his teeth.

Suddenly, there was an enormous bang. Bob had bitten into a canister of perfumed body spray as he was helping her unwrap it! Dave felt his contact lenses burning his eyes, the smell of the 'Impulse' body spray filled the house, and Bob was the nicest-smelling dog we'd ever known for weeks!

After the explosion, he wandered around the house, sneezing and sliding his head along the floor. We couldn't stop laughing at the whole scenario. He looked so puzzled but still wanted to help unwrap Holly's gifts.

We read only a week later that another dog had done the same thing as Bob, but the explosion had blown the windows out of the house! We were really lucky that didn't happen to us!

Bob certainly brought a smile to many faces. He was so faithful and loving and it was heart-breaking having to see him put to sleep. Dave, Mick, his partner and myself were with him as he lay, staring at me while he breathed his last breath. He wasn't suffering now. He'd had a great life and it seemed he knew his time had come.

# 44

# COMING TO A HEAD

The monthly Aglow meeting had soon come round again and this time, it was for both men and women, a mixed meeting that we have twice a year.

A few people prayed over me, one being my friend, Elaine: "Rise up, you mighty, valiant woman of God. Put on the armour of God. 'Stand firm, stand strong and lean on me,' says the Lord."

Another lady spoke over me: "I can see that the Holy Spirit is all over you right now. Don't fight it. Keep tight hold of Him. Don't let go of Him and tell Him to never let you go," she said.

She told me she had times like these too. "Treasure them," she said. "I have them all the time now but keep hold of Him. Ask Him to keep you like this all the time and never let you go but keep tight hold of you," she emphasised.

The speaker spoke over me as she prayed: "God has given you a great ministry. You are a blessing to so many people with your creativity. He wants to reach out to other people through your ministry."

Here I was, once again drunk in the Holy Spirit, so many encouraging and uplifting words spoken over my life. The Holy Spirit was so tangible I felt as if I was high up in the sky. And then the heavenly language came. My native English language disappeared and I didn't want to be anywhere else but where I was, right there. Right then. I felt free. It was beautiful being in that place with my Father once again.

"She's being topped up because she's given out so much," I heard a male member of Aglow say.

I loved soaking in those special times of the Holy Spirit's beautiful, glorious presence. I felt so at home there and I never wanted to come back down. I absorbed and remained in the Spirit even when I got home, and when I went to bed I could still feel Him.

The following morning, the Holy Spirit was still upon me. He wanted me to continue to rest in Him and I did.

Christmas was approaching and, once again, we were planning the Christmas day meal for those who would otherwise be on their own.

This is a busy time of year for everyone and, for me, it was like doing two Christmases. I loved getting things together, shopping for gifts, getting in touch with the local newspapers to reach out to those who would be alone, making contact with and visiting people so that they wouldn't feel uncomfortable on the day. I loved it all.

People who wanted to help donated their time, money and gifts to support this event. Many were so kind that they gave up their own Christmas day to provide entertainment, pick up guests and take them home afterwards. It was an amazing time for all involved.

I was still tired, though, and felt the pressure of managing ongoing family problems and difficulties and working part-time.

I gave more of myself to get my work finished in my job. Sometimes, I'd spend up to ten hours a day to get on top of it, but care work never ends. I rarely took a lunch hour as I ate my lunch whilst working, or I'd even skip it altogether. There were times when I did go out of the office for lunch and would pull into a car park and soon be asleep! Then I'd wake suddenly as the hour came to an end. But I knew something wasn't right as I shouldn't be falling asleep during the day.

And I so looked forward to bedtime. One evening as I sat in bed praying, I found myself praying in a different, strong, authoritative tongue. I felt as if I was smashing through atmospheres.

I saw a black rock with jagged edges, very sharp, but some of them were sparkly.

I then saw myself in a silver-blue and grey suit of armour. I was sitting on a big boulder with my head down, leaning on my hands over my sword. I was surrounded with fire and darkness but there was a bright light shining down on me even through the flames.

Suddenly, as I was praying, my tongue began to move very fast and I broke down crying from deep within the core of my soul, the very centre of my whole being. Then my tongue began to slow down, even though I was still praying in tongues, but this time it was very soft and quiet.

Next, I saw a huge figure in armour and I thought it was me. But when I looked down, I saw myself in my own little suit of armour on my knees at the feet of this giant. Its sword was enormous, pointing at me and over me. The figure must have been about eighteen feet tall or even more. I was bent over on my knees, only as high as its foot.

Suddenly, I saw myself in Jesus' hand in exactly the same huddled-over position. He was stroking my back and head as if I were a little kitten. I was so tiny.

The figure was still standing in front of Jesus and it was so very clear.

Jesus then spoke and said, "Leave her alone now. She's battle worn. She's had enough. She's worn out and tired. Leave her alone now. Let her rest, that's enough. I have her now. Let her rest in me, she's worn and torn."

I was still in the palm of Jesus' beautiful hand when I became aware that there was something touching the centre of my back. I believe it was my Father's touch; Jesus' touch.

I felt that my spiritual battle was over. I believed it and I thanked God for that vision and felt the love of His embrace in the picture He'd given me.

> *"A final word: Be strong in the Lord and in his*
> *mighty power. Put on all of God's armor so that*
> *you will be able to stand firm against all strategies*
> *of the devil. For we are not fighting against flesh-*
> *and-blood enemies, but against evil rulers and*
> *authorities of the unseen world, against mighty*
> *powers in this dark world, and against evil spirits*
> *in the heavenly places. Therefore, put on every*
> *piece of God's armor so you will be able to resist*
> *the enemy in the time of evil. Then after the battle*
> *you will still be standing firm. Stand your ground,*
> *putting on the belt of truth and the body armor of*
> *God's righteousness. For shoes, put on the peace*
> *that comes from the Good News so that you will be*
> *fully prepared. In addition to all of these, hold up*
> *the shield of faith to stop the fiery arrows of the*
> *devil. Put on salvation as your helmet, and take the*
> *sword of the Spirit, which is the word of God. Pray*
> *in the Spirit at all times and on every occasion.*
> *Stay alert and be persistent in your prayers for all*
> *believers everywhere."*
> *Ephesians 6:10–18, NLT*

I was still feeling quite low. I'd prayed in tears for my son Joe to come back to Jesus. He was going through dark times himself but it was very draining on all the family.

"He is not yet ready," I heard the Lord say. "It will be too much for him just yet, what I have for him. But don't worry as I am watching over him in everything."

I was learning to trust my Father God in a new way. I knew He was speaking to me so I believed Him no matter what was happening. But you can imagine my surprise when Joe responded to a leaflet that I had for a healing ministry that was taking place later that day.

The previous week, Joe had been very low. This was an ongoing thing with him. He rang me up one evening, very drunk. He was insecure and thought God wasn't real in his life.

I had leaflets about the next healing mission that was due to take place at a church in Southport. I wasn't sure if I'd be going and I put them in the small bin next to my bed. But I felt the Lord wanted me to ask Joe and his partner to go. I didn't think they would but I told them about it and I gave them a leaflet. I then asked God if He was going to do something, as I'd done my part.

I went along to the meeting. Dave sat in the church and did some Bible study and I went in with Joe, his partner and my grandson. I asked God to keep me from interfering in His plan for my son and not to get in His way. This is what happened:

Ifeoma, the speaker at the meeting, called people up for healing. She believed there was someone who had been suffering with stomach problems and ulcers. Joe went forward as he'd been suffering like this. She asked Joe if he knew Jesus as Lord and Saviour or if he wasn't sure. Joe replied, "I'm not sure."

She then led him through the prayer of commitment to give his life back to Jesus and, with Joe's hands raised, the Holy Spirit came in mighty power as she cast off Satan's hold on him, and the influences on him through his involvement with the wrong crowds. He was told to leave them behind as she continued praying over him, breaking off the drug and alcohol addictions. Ifeoma prayed for fullness of healing – complete healing for Joe to be set free.

Joe was shaking. He couldn't stand properly as he was buckling under the power of the Holy Spirit and the sweat poured off him.

My hand was outstretched as Ifeoma continued to pray for him. The lady in front of us had a hand outstretched too. She said she'd never sensed the power of God to be so strong. I could feel an immense heat as Joe fell back onto the chairs behind him.

Ifeoma then asked Joe how he felt. He replied that he didn't feel rage or anger anymore, but quite different and very peaceful. When she asked if he knew why he was shaking, he said, no, he didn't.

We all laughed as we knew it was the Holy Spirit.

She then went on to anoint Joe's head with oil, as a sign that he'd be set free and set apart. She prophesied over him, that he would evangelise; that God had given him a gift in his hands to heal people. She told him he would heal the sick. She also prayed for him to speak in tongues and told him this was his life now and he wasn't to go back to the old crowd or old ways, but move forward as God had lots in store for him.

Wow! I knew God would never let him go but it was now up to Joe to make the changes and activate the gifts God had given him.

Even in the midst of fiery trials, we must never doubt God; never doubt His promise that He will never leave us.

Sometimes, when we feel prayers aren't answered, we need to continue to pray and trust that God will have His way in the storms, even though it may not be in our lifetime. We must just continue to trust Him.

# 45

# ANSWERS TO PRAYERS, LIVING
# OUT PROPHESIES

Out of the blue, I received a phone call from a lady I knew from my old church in Bootle. I hadn't heard from her in years.

She rang to tell me the new St. John and St. James Church had been built and Dave and I were invited to go to the "opening service".

St. John and St. James had been my home church before I moved to Southport. The original building had been knocked down a few years before and a new one built in another part of the area.

I recalled the times when God had put on my heart to seek Him first and knock down the old church. So it was wonderful to attend and see what He had done.

There were many new faces but also some of the same who had guided me in my walk – Sue, Al, Jan and Anne. It was lovely chatting to them and Anne (the lady with the big glasses) said she wanted to speak to me before I left. She told me it was wonderful to see how God had kept me in the palm of His hand; how she remembered me being a little girl in Brownies and Girl Guides, growing in my faith to where I was now and still growing. With tears in her eyes she told me she hadn't seen this with many people, and she hugged me before I left.

This moved me in my spirit as I thought back to my childhood and growing up. I told Anne I'd come back to Jesus in my late twenties or early thirties and hadn't looked back.

The monthly Aglow outreach meeting was also approaching and I'd been blessed and encouraged every time I'd gone by people's powerful, real-life testimonies: things you don't hear in the church – how women had been touched and transformed by our amazing, wonderful, loving God. They shared how Jesus had changed their lives and rescued them from the depths of despair.

I was a member of Aglow International and was asked if I would come on board as part of the leadership team. I knew God had been drawing me to the Aglow meetings for a very long time and wanted me to become more involved, and the leadership team had already prayed about it and felt I should join them. I was overjoyed as this was a great ministry to belong to and I wanted to bless others in any way I could. Despite lots of family and health issues, I knew this was where I was meant to be and so, after praying, I accepted the position of recording secretary.

It was then that the prophecy spoken over me at Lytham St. Anne's by the young man from the Toronto church came to my mind. The young man had told me God was calling me to leadership. I praised and thanked God for this once again as I committed my future to Him as a board member for His Kingdom's cause. I wanted my life to be pleasing to Jesus in every area. I wanted Jesus and the Holy Spirit to rest and live in me; for His glory to be released and manifested in me.

Jesus had done so much for me and saved me time and time again. But it wasn't just when I looked back at those times that I realised this. It had become evident that He was in everything at all times.

God is good ALL THE TIME. He promises good to us.

*"Mercy, peace and love be yours in abundance."*
*Jude 1:2*

During one Aglow meeting, a young girl who was only about sixteen turned up. A few of us had been asked to give our testimonies. I was supposed to be the second one up to give mine but, for some reason, I was asked first. As I gave my testimony, I could see this young lady crying and I knew God had touched her heart. However, as soon as I'd finished speaking, she left. I wanted her to stay so that I could pray for her.

The following day, the lady who'd brought her phoned me and thanked me for my testimony. She told me the young girl had been moved by it and understood what I was saying, as she was going through similar things in her life and didn't feel alone in them after hearing me speak.

Following this, the girl rang me herself and kept in touch from time to time. I told her about Jesus and what it meant to give her life to Him. She wrote it all down and I don't know if she fully accepted Jesus, but I heard there had been changes in her life. I also sent encouraging scriptures for her to read and reflect on of God's promises, and I prayed regularly for her and for her needs to be met.

A few months later, I discovered she'd been fostered by a Christian family. God had done wonderful things in her life and, although she was still wild at heart, He had her in the palm of His hand.

This reminded me again that, although I wanted her to stay that night so that I could pray for her, we can be assured that God listens to our prayers and answers them. It may not be in ways we want or expect, but He can move the mountains and His ways are better than ours.

Aglow meetings have always encouraged me and I sold most of my books and other crafts I'd made there. I gave twenty-five per cent of the profits towards the vision my Lord had given me, and ten per cent back to Aglow.

I was delighted to see how the vision fund was growing. I still had a long, long way to go, but I knew that God would provide as He'd promised.

As I read through my spiritual diary of events that had occurred during my lifetime, I could see how many spiritual attacks and rollercoasters I'd experienced, but also how my wonderful, dear Father God had loved me, blessed and protected me on the way, and kept me safe throughout them all. He had never left me. His blessings are my beautiful family and friends, despite the setbacks and hardships.

God also blessed us with our third grandchild, who brought with her lots of joy. Mick certainly had his hands full with these two precious little girls.

And, of course, God had given me my beautiful husband, who is the most wonderful man I've ever met, inside and out. He is faithful, loving, kind, honest, supportive, protective, patient and a good listener. God gave us to one another to cherish each other, but we're not supposed to keep this to ourselves. Father God wants us to bless, encourage and reach out to others too.

One of the ways my Father wants me to reach out to others is through writing this book. He wants you, the reader, to be encouraged and blessed and know you are not alone in the storms you go through in life. You will not drown.

God sees the centre of our hearts. He enlightens them with wisdom, knowledge and discernment. He knows those who are hungry and searching for more; those who want to go deeper. We can't get to the Lord through riches or finery. We need to put Jesus first, walk humbly and follow Him. There's no point putting our trust in material things or in man, only in Jesus. And in Jesus we must humble ourselves.

As my walk with Jesus grew in depth, the tough times or attacks always came too. There did seem to be more of the tough than the joyful times in my life where we never seemed to get a break, and many Christians repeatedly told us this. There was always something going on.

They were right, too. But I'm also aware that when we are doing things for Christ Jesus and walking the Christian walk, the enemy will do anything he can to stop us, or he'll go for our Achilles heel. He's certainly done that with me, but God is stronger. He's won the battle already and my part is to believe His word, be faithful and obedient and trust Him.

It's easy to focus on what's wrong in life but we mustn't. We mustn't look back and feel self-pity. We must continue to march forward, remembering the armour of God and praising Him at all times.

# 46

# CROSSROADS

Things were still hard as my own health seemed to be taking a hammering. I was having ongoing issues with my heart. It seemed to beat faster than normal, then it was as if it wasn't beating at all. Dave said my pulse was erratic when he found it and he could see my heart pounding through my clothes.

I began to feel weak and lethargic. My heart felt as if it might come out of my mouth. My speech began to slur and I just wanted to sleep. Then, after I'd slept, I'd wake with a banging headache and sometimes feeling sick.

Dave noticed this was happening a lot more regularly and was very concerned. Each time, he wanted to ring the ambulance but I managed to convince him I'd feel better after a sleep.

I was at an Aglow outreach meeting when I began to feel quite unwell. I didn't think too much of it as I began to help clear away and do the washing up. "It's probably just me panicking about getting here on time," I thought to myself. I'd really been looking forward to hearing the speaker and it was important to me to get the tables decorated before the guests arrived.

As I helped tidy up, I began to feel very breathless. I returned to my seat and I could feel my heart had been thudding deep inside my chest and I was hot. I tried to shake it off but felt very unwell.

Dave looked at me as we stood up to worship and asked if I was OK. I nodded and tried to focus on Jesus. I really struggled as I didn't know what was happening to me and so I prayed.

As the night ended, I couldn't remember everything the speaker had said, which was unlike me. Dave told me the colour had drained from my face during the meeting and he was concerned something was wrong. I told him I felt better but I was extremely tired. I couldn't put into words what had happened to me.

A few weeks later, it was the same thing again. This time, I was at home, moving something from under the stairs. I stood up but my heart was racing. I kept still, waiting for it to regulate, but it didn't. Then, I had a funny sensation race up from my neck into my jaw and head.

Dave tried to find my pulse and when he did, he said it was erratic and very faint. He could see my heart fluttering through my blouse. My speech was slurred and I just wanted to go to sleep. But I wouldn't let him ring the ambulance. I told him I'd be all right after a rest. I lay on the couch and slept for twenty minutes and woke up with a banging headache. I felt better but absolutely drained.

Dave made a G.P. appointment for me online as he knew I probably wouldn't ring my doctor myself the next day.

It was March 2015 when these attacks began to happen more often and last longer. There were times when they'd go on for about half an hour. There were times, too, when they'd last for hours and I needed to get to hospital.

My doctor told me I should ring 999 when they happened as I might be having mini strokes (TIAs) or it could be my heart. He referred me to a stroke specialist who later ruled out strokes after my appointment with him.

I was put on many different types of medication whilst waiting to see a cardiologist. This was a very frustrating and worrying time for us as the medication didn't seem to make any improvement. I was very weak, tired and didn't feel right and, on top of this, my appointments to see the cardiologist kept getting postponed. This resulted in many emergency trips to A&E.

I was eventually diagnosed with Paroxysmal Atrial Fibrillation (AF). This occurs when the atria (upper chambers of the heart) lose their normal rhythm and beat chaotically.

The symptoms are chest pain, light-headedness, weakness, pounding heart, breathlessness, and further complications can also occur. When this happens, blood isn't flowing through the heart and body efficiently. This inefficient flow can cause blood to pool inside the atria, increasing the risk of blood clots.

Paroxysmal A Fib is an episode of uncoordinated movement of the atria that occurs occasionally and then stops. Episodes can last from minutes to days, before stopping and returning to normal "sinus" rhythm.

Stroke and embolism are the most serious complications. Blood pooling inside the heart can coagulate and form clots. Those clots can travel to the brain, causing a stroke. They can also lodge in the lungs, the gut and other sensitive areas, blocking blood flow and starving tissue.

It was at another Aglow evening, when I'd arrived at the pub early to put out the table decorations, that I began to feel very unwell again. I was slumped over the table, unable to speak, when the ambulance arrived.

"Are you sure it's Atrial Fibrillation and nothing else?" one of the ambulance ladies commented to Dave, rather cockily.

"It is," he replied, trying to hold it together.

I'm sure she must have thought I was just some drunken woman as my speech was slurred, and the ambulance crew began to talk to me about alcohol and its damaging effects.

By the time I arrived at the hospital, my heart had gone back into rhythm and my speech was normal. The hospital kept me in overnight and I was discharged the following afternoon, "only because I had a cardiologist appointment" I was told.

As I walked out of one hospital to go to my appointment, I received a phone call to say it had been cancelled. The cardiologist had apparently had to cancel his afternoon clinic appointments to go to an emergency in the hospital I'd just been discharged from.

Going in and out of hospital had become a regular thing for me and I began to feel I was a nuisance every time I was admitted.

Due to the two cancellations of my appointments, I didn't get my results and was put on some medication that helped a lot of people but didn't agree with me, even though I hadn't yet seen a cardiologist. It was very clear it didn't suit me as I felt ill with it and was having increased AF attacks every day. I told the hospital doctor this when I arrived again by ambulance, but he increased the dose and I was told I'd feel better after a week or two.

Dave was really upset when he told them they didn't see the effects it had on me. He said I wasn't getting any better and nobody was taking it seriously.

I came home absolutely drained and in tears. "I'm never going back to that hospital ever again," I sobbed. "I feel like I'm a nuisance."

"I'm sorry, love," Dave said, "but you will be going back if you're ill again like you have been. They *will* get you right," he comforted me. "You wouldn't be there if you were a nuisance."

I was taken back into hospital the following evening after waiting over an hour for an ambulance. The rapid response came first and stayed with me, but he wouldn't let Dave take me to hospital as he said I needed to go by ambulance to be monitored and I had to be on a stretcher.

My heart was jumping up to two hundred and eighty beats per minute then down to twenty-four beats and everything in between. A normal heart rate is supposed to be sixty to eighty bpm.

Back on the same ward again, this time I was put on a monitor throughout the night to monitor my heart. Dave rang me on my mobile the following morning to see how I was.

After finishing my breakfast, I got up to go to the bathroom when a patient who saw me stand up noticed I wasn't well and called the nurse.

"Get back on the bed, Pam," the nurse said. "Your heart rate's shooting up and is quite high. Stay where you are and I'll get the doctor."

"Give her another 100mg of flecainide," the doctor said.

"NO!" I cried. "That makes me worse. I've just had 100mg and it's started another attack. It doesn't work for me." I slurred as my speech began to get worse. The maximum dose you could take of this drug was 200mg a day.

But I was told to take the second dose of 100mg as it would settle my heart down, even after I'd told them it didn't work.

As I knew would happen, it didn't work and my condition worsened. I just wanted my Dave. "Please call my husband," I tried to say, but my speech was so slurred I didn't think anyone could understand me.

There were so many people around me. I could hear them all talking.

Someone said, "She's going!"

My eyes were opening and closing and everyone seemed to be moving fast. A mask was pressed over my face as my oxygen levels were very low, and I later found out that I was given an injection of adrenalin.

The next thing I knew, I had the crash team around me: doctors, nurses, the anaesthetist.

With the mask over my face, I was told not to be afraid when I woke up as I'd be on a big heart-monitoring machine. They were going to stop my heart and restart it again.

"Lord Jesus, intervene in all of this," I said silently as I saw the anaesthetist about to inject me. "Be with me. I know you have plans for my life and you've given me a vision."

"STOP! STOP!" I heard someone shout. "She's going back into rhythm."

"But it keeps doing this. It keeps jumping in and out all the time," someone else said.

"No. Look it's staying in rhythm. It's steady," the other person replied.

I suddenly began to feel better. As soon as I opened my eyes, everyone looked shocked. I could see panic on some of their faces.

"I told you, that medication doesn't work for me," I slurred.

I was then taken to the critical care unit where I was monitored 24 hours a day. I wasn't allowed to get out of bed as any movement could kick off the AF. The nurses eventually allowed me to use a commode, providing my heart stayed in a steady rhythm.

I was taken off the medication that made the AF worse and was to be introduced to a new drug the following day. I wondered how so many people with AF managed as they were brought onto the ward for a day to have their hearts stopped and restarted.

"Why am I so unwell with it?" I asked myself.

Some of my friends had it, and one of them couldn't work as it was debilitating for her. Another said she'd had it for ten years but was managing and doing OK, which made me quiz myself even more. It was the cardiologist who told me I was one of the five per cent of people who suffered to the extreme that I did. He'd only come across one or two people like myself.

"Well, I'm unique, aren't I?" And I laughed as I told him. He said I wouldn't be allowed home from hospital until I was feeling better and more confident.

Poor Dave was so upset when he arrived to visit me. I could see the anguish and pain in his face as he kissed me on my head and wouldn't let me go. Amidst the pain, I could see anger too, as this is what he'd been afraid would happen.

It was then that Dave shouted at the doctors and told them about the past five times I'd been fobbed off from the hospital and how they'd cancelled my appointments at the last minute.

"We only found out she has a heart aneurism when she was about to be discharged from the A&E," he said. "It was the doctor there who told her she needed to see a cardiologist and referred her to a ward, only to be discharged the following day. She's been having these attacks regularly," he finished angrily. "We've been told she's at high risk of having a stroke. How did it get to this?"

The medical staff were lovely with us. They could see Dave's frustration and assured him they were going to do everything they could. They said the aneurism wasn't a problem or cause of the AF.

This reassured us but it emphasised the failure of the system in my appointments being cancelled. I was getting bits of information about my results only when I was admitted to A&E. But I had confidence in the critical care unit where I now was, as I was constantly monitored.

The next morning, I woke early to hear pigeons cooing on the roof below. I smiled as I thanked God for them and for another new day.

"Thank You, Lord, for these little birds," I said. "It'd be lovely, Lord, if You were to send one of them to me. It'd be great if one came near or into the room as a way of You showing me Your presence, even though it's a pigeon and not a dove…"

Suddenly, I heard a pattering on the metal window sill.

"Coo-coo," I heard as I was still talking to Jesus.

"Thank You, Lord."

I smiled, looking back over my shoulder at the little pigeon as it shuffled its way along the inside window sill nearer to me.

"Coo-coo," and it shuffled as close as it could get, fluffing its little wings as if it was about to fly in.

"Good morning, Pam, how are you feeling?" The nurse's voice broke the moment.

"I've got a visitor." I smiled and glanced back over my pillows towards the pigeon, knowing this was an absolute confirmation that my Jesus was not leaving my side. He was carrying me through this. This was a sign He was right here with me.

"Oh, no!" the nurse said as she spotted the bird. "I can't let him in. I have enough work to do without trying to catch a pigeon flapping around in here. Shoo, shoo – go on, out." She then tried to scare it away and out of the window without it flying around the critical care unit.

I laughed as it wasn't going to be scared off no matter how close she went.

"Coo-coo," it went, flapping its wings and moving its head towards me.

I smiled, still thanking Jesus for this sign, knowing He'd sent this little bird to me to make me laugh again, but also as something to be used for His glory; for me to tell others about.

One last time, the pigeon cooed at me and hopped along the window sill before flying out. It then perched on a large pipe or chimney that was just outside my window and sat there, looking in for a couple of minutes, before taking off.

My stay in the critical care unit was a bit of a blur but I had an immense sense of peace that I know was from Jesus. And I knew there were many prayers being said for me. My reassurance was that I knew God had given me a vision – a very big vision – and I kept sight of that when I was unwell.

I was referred to another cardiologist, this time from Broadgreen Hospital (Liverpool Heart and Chest Hospital), who had asked for further tests and investigations whilst I was in critical care, and one of these was supposed to be quite horrible. One of the doctors told me she'd had it and one of the nurses looking after me had too. They both told me it was very painful and not nice.

The time for the procedure came and, as Dave left my side, I felt as though Jesus had come and sat down in his place, holding my hand. I smiled and was reassured by His beautiful presence.

I had to have an injection that was something to do with pathways and electrical impulses round the heart. It would slow my heart right down and it may stop – only for seconds but there would be a very unpleasant feeling. One doctor described it as something squeezing her heart very tight and the pain was really bad. The nurse said she'd seen people quite ill after it.

I had to have two doses of this, the first a lower dose, the second a higher one.

Although it was very uncomfortable, the nurse and doctor told me I sailed through it and I dealt with it better than they had done. I didn't know it was over as they looked on astonished.

"Tell Dave prayer was answered," I said to the male nurse who came in to see if I was all right, as Dave had been worrying.

One morning as I was praying, I asked Jesus to speak to me, and for Scripture to confirm things would be all right and answer a lot of the thoughts I'd been carrying in my heart. He'd given me a big vision that I had to be well enough to see through, but here I was, weak, tired and weary. For now, it seemed He wanted me to rest in Him as He is my strength.

Suddenly, I had lots of thoughts coming to my mind all at once. I tried to write them down. These are just some of them:

*You are my favoured child. I love you.*

*You are the apple of my eye. (Psalm 17:8, Deuteronomy 32:10, Proverbs 7:2)*

*Do not be afraid of the trials that you will go through, for I am your loving Father who keeps His promises. (Isaiah 41:9–10, 1 Peter 4:12–13)*

*I am with you always and will never leave you (Genesis 28:15), for you are my treasured possession. (Deuteronomy 7:6, Deuteronomy 26:18)*

*No harm will come to you for I have got you in the palm of my hand. No evil will come to you.*

*Don't be afraid of the pestilences or dangers that are around you. They will not touch you for I am your shield and protector, your defender. My promises are your protection. (Psalm 91)*

As the days passed by, I received cards and texts from friends. I was amazed by the Scripture verses. They were the same as those Jesus had spoken to me only days before. He was confirming things to me again.

# 47

# TRUSTING GOD IN THE
# RECOVERY

It was wonderful to be home, but it was when Dave had returned to work that I noticed something wasn't right with me. I went to the fridge to make myself a sandwich and stood there not knowing what to do. I took all the cheeses out, holding them in my hand. I just stared at them.

I told Dave when he phoned to check on me and to ask if I'd taken my medication. I'd forgotten that too.

I soon discovered I was forgetting all sorts of things: forgetting where I'd put things even after leaving myself reminder notes; forgetting where I'd left them; forgetting why the reminder alarm was going off on my phone. Things came to a head when I left the iron on a couple of times when I went out shopping with Dave. My son came home after having a feeling he should check everything was all right and discovered it.

I struggled making a meal too. I found it extremely difficult to put things together and remember what I was doing. I put the bacon on in the grill and forgot all about it, even when the smoke alarms were going off and the room was full of smoke. I opened all the doors and windows but still didn't think to take out the bacon or turn the grill off. Dave came to my rescue as he knew what I'd done.

Things were very difficult for me. I discovered that when I was speaking, I'd miss the main word out that connected the sentence. My memory was a lot slower functioning than it used to be. I couldn't add up simple shopping bills and I struggled with change from shopping. I couldn't multi-task.

There were lots of other things that Dave noticed about me that I wasn't aware of. I seemed to get upset more easily and agitated, which wasn't like me. My emotions were all over the place and I felt tearful for no reason. When I used public toilets, I'd forget how to wash my hands or how to turn the tap on.

The little things that we take for granted I was made fully aware I had to concentrate on, but a lot of the time I didn't know what to do.

Dave was very concerned and made an appointment for me to see my G.P. My doctor fully understood what was happening and told me I'd been through a bad time. He nodded when I asked him if I'd nearly died when the crash team came. He said my heart condition was something else and he felt what I was experiencing was the effects of the stroke I'd had. He told me to mention it to my consultant when I next saw him, but he also felt that it could be to do with depression and stress relating to everything my body had been through.

The stroke consultant listened to everything I told him, but didn't want to start me on any medication as I was on high doses of strong chemicals already. He told me it could take up to twelve months for me to heal perhaps eighty if not one hundred per cent, as I was quite young to have had a stroke. He also said he'd refer me to an O.T.

Most of the time, I felt as if I was floating and mentally not here; as if I was on the bottom of a pile and couldn't get up. Emotionally I'd been drained, drained of everything; of any bit of energy or life I'd had. When troubles came and stresses, which were ongoing in my life, I found it was just another one making the pile higher as I didn't have any energy to fight anymore.

Soon after I came out of hospital, Joe moved back in with us due to the breakdown of his relationship. It was the right thing to do but consequences came with it.

As with many relationships that break down, Joe's ex-partner stopped us all from seeing our grandson. I was broken-hearted as he needed his dad as much as his dad needed him. Things became very difficult and messy and I struggled to keep strong. I found it hard to forgive Joe's ex-partner and remember that Jesus loved her as much as He loved me, and I missed my little grandson very much.

I believed and trusted God that I would see him again but I didn't know when. My O.T. suggested I get a memory box and put all his cards, money gifts etc. in it and keep them until he grew up, and I did.

Life went on but I didn't go out on my own. I'd noticed when I was out with Dave that my heart would pound away, I'd be breathless and I'd have to stop. I also walked into things and couldn't walk in a straight line.

All of this really had an effect on me. I still wasn't allowed to drive due to not being able to multi-task and my reactions being a lot slower now. I only really went out with Dave to our home group, who were very supportive. But I found it difficult to concentrate there and got agitated if too many people spoke at the same time. My emotions were all over the place. There were times when I just wanted to leave but I stayed. I'd be very tired before the end of the meeting and drained, and the following day I wouldn't be able to do anything.

Life was tough but I took it one day at a time. And I never understood why I was so exhausted during the day. Even trying to concentrate on something would make me fall asleep.

The occupational therapist visited me weekly and discovered that my multi-tasking skills were not good. I couldn't manage to do two things together. I had lots of small assessments, which she did each week, and she left me homework to do. But I always felt exhausted and would fall asleep after she'd gone.

Although my life seemed to consist mainly of medical appointments, I still tried to do some craftwork, like making small flower arrangements. This relaxed me and I could put it down when I wanted to without feeling too stressed by it.

A few months later, I received a letter telling me to go to the Liverpool Heart and Chest Hospital for heart ablation. This was a four-and-a-half-hour procedure in which I was given a general anaesthetic and kept in overnight. The procedure went well but I was told I may need to have another one in the future for it to work properly.

I knew I was on a slow road to recovery and there would be many medical appointments. My treatment is still ongoing. I've had two heart ablations and I haven't yet returned to work. I feel as though God is opening up another doorway for me. I believe with all my heart He has allowed me to have this time to rest and make a full recovery, but I also feel as if I've come to a crossroads. I know my job is still open to me and I've loved it, even in the stressful times, which is most of the time, but I'm fully aware that I may have to take a different direction depending on my recovery.

Father God still has me in the palm of His hand and, even though He's given me a vision that will require my full ability to manage it, I'm still recovering and I wait on His guidance as I trust Him.


Over the past three years, Dave and I had prepared a Christmas meal for those who would be on their own, and it was coming up to our fourth year. I didn't have the energy this time to organise it on the larger scale we'd done before. Dave was concerned about my health, but we prayed and felt we should hold it in our home, which is only a small terraced house.

Dave did the cooking and Joe helped us, and we managed to squeeze eight people in. They all had a lovely Christmas. Local businesses, individuals and church helped support it financially, as well as picking guests up and taking them home afterwards. Everyone was blessed abundantly.

Sam, who was still looking after the homeless in Derby Road, told me that Ken, one of the residents, was quite poorly and deteriorating. Ken had been a resident there from the very beginning when I started to work for Green Pastures in 2006. He was a real character who loved to do *The Times* crossword. He was very knowledgeable but had fallen on hard times. He couldn't walk properly and occasionally went out in his wheelchair so, when God placed it on my heart to visit him and pray with him a few days before Christmas, I knew I had to go. This was a divine appointment.

I rarely went to Derby Road these days but heard all about what was happening there through Sam. Most of the residents Dave and I had cared for had passed away and Ken was one of the remaining few still there.

I only had half an hour to visit some of the residents, but I knew this was a crucial, God-divine appointment with Ken as I told him about Jesus, how He loved him, and I then led him through the prayer of commitment.

After this he said, "Does this mean I'm a disciple now?"

I told him there was a party going on in heaven right now because he'd accepted Jesus as his Lord and Saviour. Then Ken told me some stories of when he knew God was with him when he lived on the streets.

I could feel the love of Jesus in Ken's small flat where he was surrounded with his few belongings, and I knew this was the last time I'd see him. The alcohol had finally taken hold of his body and his life, but Jesus had bought him back.

I had to leave as my friend had been waiting for me outside to take me home, but I broke down crying in the car with joy and sadness as I said, "I'm never going to see him again, Dan. God wanted him to give his heart back to Him and he has. He'll be going home soon to Jesus."

A couple of days later, Ken had a massive stroke. He was taken to hospital where he died peacefully a few days later.

It's so important we act immediately when God puts something on our hearts. It doesn't matter if we get it wrong as God knows our hearts. He just wants us to be obedient.

# 48

## "IT'S A GIFT"

Over the last few months, I'd been asking God for some breakthrough as I'd been out of work due to health reasons so didn't have the financial resources to be able to get my book published. I asked Father God if this was something He really wanted me to do. If He did, He would have to finance it in some way as I simply couldn't see how we could afford it.

God had always provided so I didn't really worry. I just left it in His hands, knowing He'd always allowed me to go to the very last hour or even minute. But I was coming to the end of writing my book and there was no sign of our finances improving.

Just as I was finishing the writing, a beautiful Christian lady I'd known for a while asked if we were all right financially. She knew I was still unable to work. I told her we were managing and she asked how my book was coming along. I said I'd nearly finished writing it. That's when she told me to let her know how much I needed to get it published.

I couldn't believe it. God had assured me not to worry as He would provide.

When I told her I didn't know when I'd be able to pay her back, she said, "No, Pam, it's a gift. It's for God's ministry and I don't want it back. After all, everything is His anyway." She told me that God had put it on her heart to support me in this so that my book could be used for His glory.

I was shocked and couldn't find the words to thank her enough. I asked her to pray about it and I told her I would too, to see if this was what God really wanted.

When I prayed, I had an amazing peace, as if it were already set in place. And when I saw her again, she asked me if I'd found out the cost yet. I told her I was still in the process of doing that and I was praying.

"Oh, are you?" she said. "I prayed the once and have a peace about it as the Lord said to give it to you."

I was so humbled by her kindness and her relationship with Jesus. It really touched my heart.

Although I was coming to the end of writing it, I still didn't have a title for my book. I'd prayed about what to call it and I felt the Lord my God would tell me when I listened to my worship music.

Taking the Christmas decorations down the following day and listening to music I said, "Lord, I still don't know the name of my book," and I carried on doing what I was doing. I was trying to think of titles but nothing stood out.

A short while later, I burst into tears as I listened to the words of one particular worship song: "I am Hephzibah".

I sat there, tears rolling down my face. My Lord Jesus had journeyed with me as I'd revisited my past. He'd shown me how He'd guided and protected me throughout my life.

"That's it! Thank You, Lord!" I cried. And I knew with absolute certainty that this was the title for my book.

When I researched what Hephzibah meant, my Father showed me more. I knew it meant "my delight is in her", but in the Bible it also means "one who is guarded, a protected one".

Jesus has guarded and protected me throughout my life. Words from the song flooded my mind as I related them to my own relationship with Him:

*"I am Hephzibah*
*I am Your delight*
*I am Hephzibah*
*the one that You love*
*for I am Yours and You are mine*
*and we'll be together far beyond the boundaries of time*
*for Your desire is for me and mine*
*mine is for You, mine is for You*
*I'm clean free washed*
*washed in the blood of the Lamb*
*I'm clean free washed*
*washed in the blood of Jesus*
*it's my name, this is who I am*
*it's my name, it's my name Hephzibah."*
Julie Meyer

# MAKING A COMMITMENT

During my time writing this book, I've believed with all my heart that God wants to speak to you, the reader. He knows your every need and everything about you. He gave us Jesus to bring us life in fullness, not in part. If you've been affected by anything in this book, believe that Jesus loves you. Turn to Him. Let Him heal and restore your heart and life. He alone can give you everything you need. He will set you free.

This book was written to encourage and bless others in the midst of their storms of life. Hang on in there. Don't let go of your Father's hand – He is your lifeline. It's never too late to turn back to Him. His loving arms are waiting to embrace you, dear child. You are not alone in the midst of your fears and worries and, as Jesus has promised, He will never leave you even when you don't see the final result.

Everything is in God's timing and not ours. We are to be faithful, obedient servants of the one and only living God, who gave His only son for us so that we may have eternal life.

If you haven't yet made a commitment to Jesus or, for whatever reason, have turned away, you can say this simple but powerful prayer of salvation. If you mean this prayer, Jesus will come into your heart and live in you as He's promised. He will NEVER leave you.

**Dear Father God, thank You for loving me and sending Your one and only son Jesus Christ, to die on the cross and rise again so that I would be set free. Forgive me when I have hurt You and others, physically, spiritually or mentally. I am sorry. Come into my life, wash me clean with the precious blood of Jesus and fill me with Your Holy Spirit. Mould and shape me to be the person You want me to be. I love You, Lord, and thank You, Jesus. In Your holy name. Amen.**

If you've prayed this prayer and meant it, be assured that your sins are forgiven and there's a party going on in heaven right now for you, as you now belong to Jesus. Tell someone you know what you've done and, as soon as possible, find a church in your area to go to or look online for a Christian church.

Don't be afraid now as you walk with the living King Jesus:

> *"Now if we are children, then we are heirs – heirs of God and co-heirs with Christ, if indeed we share in his sufferings in order that we may also share in his glory."*
> *Romans 8:17*

> *"So you are no longer a slave, but God's child; and since you are his child, God has made you also an heir".*
> *Galatians 4:7*

We are sons and daughters of God.

Go – be blessed, be ready for the great things He has in store for you. Receive His forgiveness, His blessings, His love, the fullness of His promises. Don't let anyone tell you differently as God's Word is light, life and the truth. Read His Word daily and discover the fullness of His love as He nurtures you into a beautiful relationship with Him. He takes great delight in you.

So who am I?
**Hephzibah.**

# SCRIPTURE AND COMMENTS

During my many trials in life, the following scriptures, study notes and comments have spoken directly to my heart. There are too many to record here, so these are just a few. But you will find all you need in God's Word.

I have been convicted again and again by these words, but it was in those times that God was transforming me. I hope they help you in your walk with God and in your life.

Sin is deceptively attractive. The NLT study notes for 2 Chronicles 7:17–22 say: "Turning away from God brings suffering, punishment and ultimately destruction. Choose to obey God no matter what happens, knowing He will eventually bless your efforts. Following God brings benefits and rewards, not necessarily material."

Jesus tells us, "I am the way and the truth and the life. No one comes to the Father except through me" (John 14:6). As the way, Jesus is our path to the Father. As the truth, He is the reality of all God's promises. As the life, He joins His divine life to ours both now and in eternity. Jesus is, in truth, the only living way to the Father.

"For God so loved the world that he gave His one and only Son, that whoever believes in him shall not perish but have eternal life" (John 3:16).

When we allow any desire to rival God's proper place, we have taken the first steps to moral and spiritual decay.

Doing right is more important than doing well.

"'For I know the plans I have for you,' declares the LORD, 'plans to prosper you and not to harm you, plans to give you hope and a future'" (Jeremiah 29:11).

When the enemy brings something to your door that's contrary to God's will, you have the authority to rise up and say, "If it's not done and approved in heaven it has no place in my life here on earth." When it comes to disobedience, refuse to accept the package and sign the receipt. The one thing Satan hopes you will never discover is that you have the God-given authority to restrict his movements in your life.

"Don't you realize that all of you together are the temple of God and that the Spirit of God lives in you? God will destroy anyone who destroys this temple. For God's temple is holy, and you are that temple" (1 Corinthians 3:16–17, NLT).

"The blessing of the LORD makes a person rich, and he adds no sorrow with it" (Proverbs 10:22, NLT).

"Therefore, there is now no condemnation for those who are in Christ Jesus" (Romans 8:1).

"No, in all these things we are more than conquerors through him who loved us" (Romans 8:37).

"But seek first his kingdom and his righteousness, and all these things will be given to you as well" (Matthew 6:33).

Words are powerful but God's Word is full of creative power.

"The LORD directs the steps of the godly. He delights in every detail of their lives. Though they stumble, they will never fall, for the LORD holds them by the hand" (Psalm 37:23–24, NLT).

"God causes everything to work together for the good of those who love God and are called according to His purpose for them" (Romans 8:28).

What you speak in your life are words of life or death. Only speak as Jesus says or do as Jesus does. Speak words of life not death, blessings not curses. "I choose to hear and obey Your Word. I submit myself to You, God, and I will resist the devil." (See James 4:7.)

We are anointed to do miracles as Jesus did.

Anointing is to bring good news to the poor, to the broken-hearted, to any form of captivity i.e. addictions, afflictions, blindness and sickness. If God is with you, who can be against you?

Go to people no one else cares about to carry out your ministry.

You are more important to God than to be used for someone's sexual pleasure.

As our Father reaches out to us, in return He wants us to reach out to others.

"My child, don't lose sight of common sense and discernment. Hang on to them, for they will refresh your soul. They are like jewels on a necklace. They keep you safe on your way, and your feet will not stumble" (Proverbs 3:21–23, NLT).

# USEFUL CONTACTS

If you or anyone you know has been affected by any of the things in this book, you can contact the relevant organisations below who will be able to help you or point you in the direction of someone who can.

Please feel free to contact me by email if needed:
pamelanickson64@gmail.com

Domestic Violence Freephone helpline
0808 2000 247 (24 hours)

Rape and Sexual Abuse Support Centre
0808 802 9999 (daily 12.00pm – 2.30pm & 7.00pm – 9.30pm)
www.rapecrisis.org.uk

MIND info line – (Mental Health)
0300 123 3393 (Monday – Friday 9.00am – 6.00pm)
Text service 86463
www.mind.org.uk/information-support/helplines

Samaritans – Listening Ear
116123 (Freephone)
www.samaritans.org/

Mercy Ministries for young women aged 18 to 28 (eating disorders, self-harm, depression, abuse in all its forms)

01535 642 042

www.mercyuk.org

info@mercyministries.co.uk


Premier Lifeline and Crossline (National Christian helpline for prayer and listening ear)

0300 1110101 (daily 9.00 am – midnight)

www.premier.org.uk


Young Minds (for parents or carers looking after people up to the age of 25 years old)

www.youngminds.org.uk/for_parents/parent_helpline


Bipolar UK – support line for family/friends and people suffering with bipolar or similar symptoms

0333 323 3880 (Monday – Friday 9.00am – 5.00pm)

www.bipolaruk.org


C.A.P. Christians Against Poverty – Debt Counselling Charity

www.capuk.org (find out where your nearest office is)


National Debtline – free advice and support

0808 808 4000 (Monday – Friday 9.00am – 8.00pm)

www.nationaldebtline.org


A.A. – Alcoholics Anonymous (advice and support)

0800 917 7650

www.alcoholics-anonymous.org.uk

Narcotics Anonymous – advice and support
0300 999 1212 (daily 9.00am – midnight)
www.ukna.org

Betel UK Christian Rehab – not-for-profit Christian community. Free admissions – restoring homeless and substance-dependent people. Age 17 years and over (17-year-olds need parents' permission first)
Phone 01564 822 356 (typically replies within one hour) (9.00am – 12.30pm & 1.30pm – 5.00pm)
People can be received within one to five days after phone interview.
www.betel.uk

Alzheimer's Society Dementia helpline
0300 222 1122 (Monday – Friday 8.30am – 6.30pm)
www.alzheimers.org.uk

Shelter – The Housing and Homelessness Charity – National Helpline
0808 800 4444 (Monday – Friday 8.00am – 8.00pm & weekends 9.00am – 5.00pm)
www.shelter.org.uk

42972861R00219

Printed in Poland
by Amazon Fulfillment
Poland Sp. z o.o., Wrocław